D1420436

Yeats as Precursor

Yeats as Precursor

Readings in Irish, British and American Poetry

Steven Matthews

First published in Great Britain 2000 by
MACMILLAN PRESS LTD
Houndmills, Basingstoke, Hampshire RG21 6XS and London
Companies and representatives throughout the world

A catalogue record for this book is available from the British Library.

ISBN 0–333–71147–5

 First published in the United States of America 2000 by
ST. MARTIN'S PRESS, INC.,
Scholarly and Reference Division,
175 Fifth Avenue, New York, N.Y. 10010

ISBN 0–312–22930–5

Library of Congress Cataloging-in-Publication Data
Matthews, Steven, 1961–
Yeats as precursor : readings in Irish, British, and American poetry / Steven
Matthews.
p.   cm.
Includes bibliographical references and index.
ISBN 0–312–22930–5
1. English poetry—Irish authors—History and criticism.   2. Yeats, W. B.
(William Butler), 1865–1939—Influence.   3. American poetry—20th century—
History and criticism.   4. English poetry—20th century—History and criticism.
5. Ireland—Intellectual life—20th century.   6. Influence (Literature, artistic, etc.)
7. American poetry—Irish influences.   8. English poetry—Irish influences.
I. Title.

PR8771.M38   1999
821'.8 21—dc21
                                                                            99–043510

This book is printed on paper suitable for recycling and made from fully managed and sustained
forest sources.

10   9   8   7   6   5   4   3   2   1
09   08   07   06   05   04   03   02   01   00

Printed and bound in Great Britain by
Antony Rowe Ltd, Chippenham, Wiltshire

Contents

Acknowledgements

My greatest debt is to Elleke Boehmer, for her constant wonderful support, her enlightening reading, and, most, for all the time she has given me. Time in which this book, and much else, could happen.

I would also like to thank my mum, dad and sister; Vicki Bertram, Terence Cave, Ian Fairley, Hugh Haughton, Charmian Hearne, David Mehnert, Nigel Messenger, John Perkins, Ashley Taggart and John Whale. I have especially enjoyed, and benefited from, my conversations with John Campbell about various aspects of the argument.

Completion of the book was made possible by an award made by the Humanities Research Board of the British Academy, under the Research Leave Scheme. I am grateful to the Academy for their support.

The book is dedicated to the memory of Violet Tuckwell, and for Thomas.

List of Abbreviations

Books by Yeats

A   *Autobiographies* (London: Macmillan, 1980 Edition)

AV   *A Vision* (London: Macmillan, 1981 Edition)

CP   *The Collected Poems of W.B. Yeats* A New Edition, edited by Richard J. Finneran (London: Macmillan, 1991, Second Edition)

E   *Explorations*, selected by Mrs. W.B. Yeats (London: Macmillan, 1962)

E&I *Essays and Introductions* (London: Macmillan, 1989 Edition)

M   *Mythologies* (London: Macmillan, 1989 Edition)

1
Yeats: Influence, Tradition and the Problematics of Reading

W.B. Yeats has proved to be one of the most influential writers of the twentieth century, even perhaps more so than his modernist heirs Ezra Pound and T.S. Eliot. Conflicting perceptions of him as poetic revolutionary and as traditionalist, as belated mediator of romanticism and as promoter of emergent modernity, have offered a rich and divergent range of possibility for writers coming after him. His work shadows, and is mourned within, much major poetry written immediately after his death and subsequently.

This book sets out to think through the implications of Yeats's position as originating presence within both twentieth-century poetry and also within the century's major movements of poetry criticism, from formalism and New Criticism to (more latterly) the textual deconstruction of the Yale-based theorists Harold Bloom and Paul de Man in their negotiations with the work of Jacques Derrida. Ideas of formal integrity and completion; tropes of presence and absence; ideas of the text as the site of family quarrel; aporia and undecidability; poetry as the place of both haunting and mourning: each of these conceptions in both areas of writing has something to say about reading Yeats himself and about the nature of work written consciously or unconsciously in his shadow. These conceptions also trouble convenient literary-critical labellings of the twentieth century as essentially modernist, then postmodernist. The haunting echoes of Yeats in subsequent poetries locates modern reading – both theoretically and practically – within essentially Romantic indeterminacies and their aftermath, indeterminacies which call into question the whole process of labelling and categorization itself.[1]

Yeats's own notion of influence as 'magical' transference and visionary reanimation, implicated as it is with his ideas of cultural and

1

national founding, and itself animated by his sense that personality and style are formed in the face of death – all have had a radical impact upon ideas of poetic rhetoric, reading, and their relation to historical event across the century. His position 'in-between' in relation to so many of the essential discourses and problematics within and surrounding poetry has led to a variety of responses which, in its turn, says much about the nature and function of poetry across this time, and across a breadth of cultural spaces. In this opening chapter, I will consider the bases of these qualities within Yeats's own work, and their relation to key ideas which will be considered in later chapters.

I

> – I asked if Blake had influenced him & he says no, he knew nothing of him, but that minds act on each other – 'If you shut yourself up in this room and think with sufficient vigour, you will impress your thought on others' –

Lady Gregory's Diary record of an after-dinner conversation with W.B. Yeats on 5th March 1899 shows the poet making a striking elision between his continuing mystical preoccupations and a surprisingly physical, dynamic definition of literary influence.[2] Yeats's Peter-like denial of Blake is astonishing, given the appearance of his co-edition with Edwin Ellis of *Blake's Writings, Poetic, Symbolic and Critical* of 1893. But the rapid movement in his mind from the issue of literary influence into that of the magical transference of energetic thought is character-istic, and remains a potent one within many of his later descriptions of the action of that transference.

In his 1901 essay, 'Magic', for example, Yeats outlines three doctrines of belief, the first of which is that the 'borders of our mind are ever shifting, and that many minds can flow into one another'. (*E&I*, p. 28) Flow into, or influence; Yeats's 'magical' belief itself seems to open him to the whole notion of the possibility of the living 'impressing' their thought upon their contemporaries, but also that the dead might impress their thought upon the living. Yeats's assertion to Lady Gregory ('you will impress your thought on others') is itself freighted with multiple potential when glossed by his later writings on the subject. This potential might include the kinetic (as in the description of the mystical experiment in 'Magic', where 'my imagination began to move of itself and to bring before me vivid images') to the Franken-steinian:

images that...had yet a motion of their own, a life I could not
change or shape, ...my acquaintance... said...'When I was a child
I was always thinking out contrivances for galvanising a corpse into
life.'   (*E&I*, pp. 29, 33)

The impress, the marks of influence are irrevocable. The dead come alive
to the visionary when 'minds act on each other', and take on a life that
the living cannot 'change or shape'. 'Being dead', as the later poem 'The
Tower' has it, 'we rise', and might relate all that is 'discovered in the
grave'. (*CP*, pp. 199, 198) Such 'impress' might be taken, therefore, as
both implicated with, and as overcoming, the human work of missing
and mourning the dead as well as the poetic work of elegy. In a pre-
figuration of Yeats's doctrine of the mask, imagination and the energies
transmitted through influence in these cases take the self out of itself,
and create 'vivid' images which usurp the power of the personal, shaping imagination. As a result of such theoretical beliefs, of course, Yeats's
poetry is continually haunted by having 'mummy truths to tell /
Whereat the living mock', as 'All Soul's Night', the poem which serves
as epilogue to *A Vision*, has it. (*CP*, p. 228) Or, as 'The New Faces' sees it,
'the living are more shadowy than they'. (p. 211)

In the 1913 essay 'Art and Ideas', written on the threshold of the
more direct poetic style which was to emerge the next year with the
publication of *Responsibilities*, Yeats's review of the way in which his own
attitude to the nature of art had changed across the years shows
him modifying and clarifying the linked notions of 'impress' and influence. He is also now, however, resisting certain implications of his
earlier definition of those qualities. When he began to write, Yeats
recalls, he had been under the sway of Arthur Hallam's essay on Tennyson, which had compared the manner of Tennyson's work to that of
Keats and Shelley, a manner untinged by 'the general thought' but
written instead 'out of the impression made by the world upon
their delicate senses'. Hallam's influence, Yeats recounts in this essay,
had led his own and others' writing of the day towards an excessive
preoccupation with detail which stimulated the senses at the cost of
meaning.

The milieu in which his younger self moved, then, is very much one
which Yeats sees as lacking in 'ideas'. He even attributes his early
researches into the forgotten beliefs of Ireland, his seeking 'some symbolic language' there, to a need to escape from the loneliness of living all
the time amid the 'obscure impressions' of his senses. His whole uneasi-
ness with that milieu, he now realizes, had rested in his yearning for a

world pre-dating Renaissance individualism, a world when, as he had put it in an 1897 review 'The Tribes of Danu', the poet was not a 'solitary', and the 'world and poetry' had not 'forgotten' one another. His whole Celtic Twilight project had pivoted upon the sense that 'the people of a Celtic habit of thought' might 'best begin' reviving that Homeric lost unity and 'happiness'.[3]

Later in this 1913 essay, however, Yeats's notion of 'ideas' in art expands even further, and seeks to challenge another error involved with the emphases of his past writing and thought:

> Yet works of art are always begotten by previous works of art, and every masterpiece becomes the Abraham of a chosen people. When we delight in a spring day there mixes, perhaps, with our personal emotion an emotion Chaucer found in Guillaume de Lorris, who had it from the poetry of Provence; we celebrate our draughty May with an enthusiasm made ripe by more meridian suns; and all our art has its image in the Mass that would lack authority were it not descended from savage ceremonies taught amid what perils and by what spirits to naked savages.   (*E&I*, p. 352)

In this remarkable passage, Yeats manages to claim for art not only an ability to modify our responses to the world but also an association with pagan religious power.[4] The emerging Arnoldian force of the self-critical vocabulary in this essay (Yeats later writes of contemporary poetry that it displays 'an absorption in fragmentary sensuous beauty or detachable ideas') is countered by an imaginative primitivism. Rousseau's naked savage becomes the first inspired artist, and could we but, 'by reintegrating the mind', rediscover 'our more profound Pre-Raphaelitism, the old abounding, nonchalant reverie', modern solipsism and abstraction could be overcome. (pp. 353–5) Further, there is a curious sense in this passage about spring days, that the past as inscribed in traditional texts resonates within the present, and has its only actuality there – each act of writing becomes a projection of futurity.[5]

'Ideas', here in the form of literary tradition, therefore save the poet, in Yeats's view, from the Paterian loneliness of our obscure sensory impressions and also from a correlatively fragmented and 'detached' style. Western culture, 'like the gods Heine tells of', amounts to 'old emotions' and 'old images' waiting to be 'awakened again to overwhelming life... by the belief and passion of some new soul'. (p. 352) 'Belief', reawakening or revivification, 'impress', all are – through his attention to literary history – reborn in Yeats's reading of his own career trajectory from the realm of 'magic' into that of 'ideas', 'ideas' which in their turn retain the numinousness of their origin.

Further, this vision of the role of tradition ideally places little value upon the original contribution of the particular artist. In spite of the self's ability to 'impress' its thought upon others, 'tradition' in Yeats's reading of it would seem to *efface* the self, render it indeterminate. In an earlier (1909) re-rendering of the sense of 'aestheticism' as an 'Anarchic revolt' of individualism Yeats had both reasserted the tradition, and predicted the tenor of his argument in 'Art and Ideas':

> Supreme art is a traditional statement of certain heroic and religious truths, passed on from age to age, modified by individual genius, but never abandoned. ... Anarchic revolt is coming to an end, and the arts are about to restate the traditional morality.   (A, p. 490)[6]

Art becomes the place in which personality interacts with history and tradition, a tradition that resonates with its pagan religious origins. In the process, the artist is saved from solipsism or egotism by the 'morality' that they can 'modify', but never change. Yeats does not agree with what he would perceive as Wordsworthian complacency in the 'received', but neither does he suggest that it is possible to escape history as it is figured in past texts. Indeed, such texts resonate behind and within our most fulfilling (and most aesthetic) moments in the present.[7]

It is this conflictual sense of the interaction, but also and at the same time of the irreconcilability, of these two possibilities, the personal and the artistic, which characterizes Yeats's work early and late, making 'The Choice' one of his key poems, and, as this book will demonstrate, one of his most influential. As I will discuss it further below, his troubled retention of the notion of 'personality' or 'individual genius' within this interaction continues to set his work apart from that of modernist conceptions of tradition and influence. It of course counters Eliot's classic statement made only ten years after this essay, that 'The existing monuments [of tradition] form an ideal order amongst themselves, which is modified by the introduction of the new (the really new) work of art...'. Tradition here forms an autonomous order in which the individual poet is reduced to the role of catalyst.[8]

The fact that for Yeats this tradition relates to both artistic and lived experience is crucial, and again sets his version of tradition apart from later, modernist, versions. It accounts both for his tentativeness here, and his refusal to restrict his notion of 'ideas' in art. The tradition remains a fertile thing ('begotten'); its translational and cross-cultural continuities (from Provence to 'us', now) can even deceive the senses, so that we greet 'draughty Mays' with enthusiasm. Yeats's version of the relation between tradition and the individual talent, unlike Eliot's more literary later one, includes everyone's everyday responses to the world.

As such, Yeats's reading of tradition and influence predicts what Harold Bloom has latterly described in his discussions of the anxieties of influence as 'facticity', 'the state of being caught up in a factuality or a contingency which is an inescapable and unalterable context'. That context is resultant upon the 'transferences' that take place through the repeated readings of great authors by each generation across history:

> Freud . . . very late in his work, described this investment as the assimilation of the superego to the id, saying that 'some of the cultural acquisitions have undoubtedly left a deposit behind in the id; much of what is contributed by the superego will awaken an echo in the id'. It is in this context that Freud quotes from the first part of Goethe's *Faust*: 'What you have inherited from your fathers, strive to make it your own.'[9]

Yeats's definition of the literary history inherent in our delighted response to seasonal change ('we celebrate our draughty May with a vision made ripe by *more* meridian suns' [my italics]) displays that belatedness which Bloom sees as a 'recurrent malaise of Western consciousness'. Belatedness is integral to the notion of literary influence, and to all writing about literature as sites of anxiety ('criticism' for Bloom is 'prose-poetry').[10] Such belatedness surely underlies the frequently elegiac note of Yeats's poetry and his essays (a note which again sets his work apart from that of his modernist successors, with their constant urge to 'make it new'). From his selection of a sentence from Saint Augustine's *Confessions* as epigraph to his 1893 volume *The Rose* ('Sero te amavi, Pulchritudo tam antiqua tam nova! Sero te amavi.' Too late I have loved you, Beauty old and new . . .) Yeats's writing is haunted by its being, as 'The Cold Heaven' later puts it, 'out of season'. (*CP*, pp. 28, 125) As this book will argue, that note is a principal part of the Yeatsian inheritance, and characterizes also the rage against old age which emerges in his later work, and is then struck again by poets as various as Dylan Thomas, Geoffrey Hill and Robert Lowell.

Bloom's often enlightening exploration of such matters finds its own origin in his *Yeats* of 1970, where he writes that:

the ephebe cannot be Adam early in the morning. There have been too many Adams, and they have named everything. The burden of unnaming prompts the true wars fought under the banner of poetic influence . . . .[11]

But, as Bloom's discussion in the foundational early pages of this book typically shows – with their claim that 'Yeats's immediate tradition could be described as the internalisation of quest romance' – the anxiety of influence in Yeats remains largely for him a matter of literary and textual interaction which disregards the specific historical actualities of 'cultural acquisition' and transference.[12] Yet these actualities (which are also absent from the discussions of Yeats by New Critics and by later deconstructionist critics) must necessarily have a direct effect upon any poet's style and thence upon the nature of their influence on later writers.

The idealized and internalized 'quest romance' which Bloom traces in Yeats back to Blake and Shelley and to their precursor in the form, Spenser, is itself conditioned and burdened by that divided inheritance and gapped tradition which is Yeats's as a writer in Ireland seeking to found a national and distinctive literature in English.[13] Those divisions and gaps then resonate once more behind the work of those, such as the American poet John Berryman in 'Homage to Mistress Bradstreet', who have appropriated Yeatsian form and style in order to review and re-vivify their own nation's origins.

Yeats's historical and cultural context or situation in history, in other words, also largely motivates his sense of belatedness. As this book hopes to show, that context also echoes variously behind the recontex-tualizations his work undergoes when it influences or impresses itself upon the work of writers from his own and different cultures later in the century.

II

The reintegration and rediscovery envisioned at the end of 'Art and Ideas' notoriously remains a difficult and unattainable dream in Yeats. Its grounding in a unified culture rests awkwardly with his acknow-ledgement elsewhere of a *detachment* between art and people.[14] This 1913 essay's cosmopolitan, nonchalant and sunlit delineation of des-cent seeks to transmute and turn away from its own critical recognition relating to the fragmentary detachments of his own age, and to more local drags upon its golden reverie. Within such a light, Yeats seems to

be inattentive to his earlier specific recognition of historical perplexity
in such matters.

In an essay of 1907, 'Poetry and Tradition', he had reviewed the
nationalist ambitions of his youth, and concluded that, with the waning
of the possibility of armed insurrection and the growth of the new
shopkeeping class under the shadow of Parnell, Ireland became out of
step with her artists (an out-of-stepness which was later to result in the
idealization of a single, solitary audience in the 1919 *The Wild Swans At
Coole*'s 'The Fisherman'):

> we artists, who are the servants not of any cause but of mere naked
> life, and above all of that life in its nobler forms, where joy and
> sorrow are one, Artificers of the Great Moment, became as elsewhere
> in Europe protesting individual voices. Ireland's great moment had
> passed, and she had filled no roomy vessels with strong sweet wine,
> where we have filled our porcelain jars against the coming winter.
>
> (*E&I*, p. 260)

Yeats says that he had been aware of a similar failure in that social bond
of artists with the nation's people in other European countries with the
rise of the capitalist classes, but he had hoped that the near-reality of
strife in Ireland might serve to perpetuate it there. 'Tradition', as he had
conceived of it early in his career, was at the heart of the nationalist
impulse of his writing, 'to forge in Ireland a new sword on our old
traditional anvil for that great battle that must in the end re-establish
the old, confident, joyous world'. (p. 249)

Yet, a year later than this, from out of the intensified definitional
debates around questions of politics and nationhood which had derived
from his involvement with the Abbey Theatre, we find Yeats engaged in
a historical discussion which locates the *difficulty* of cultural unification
within a contextualized problematics of reading. Those problematics
then have a crucial effect upon the style which he passes down to
those later influenced by him in English poetry from all cultures. It is
an effect which derives in part from the fact that the problematics that
Yeats describes are themselves dependent upon the inevitable issues of
constraining cross-cultural translation and influence, given his own
historical situation.

In an article in the 1908 issue of the Abbey Theatre's magazine,
Samhain, Yeats reflected on the original ambitions of the Theatre, and
also upon the nature of a distinctly national literature. He looked back
once more to the so-called Young Ireland poetic movement of the

1840s, a movement which had attempted to declare a national independence through literature not unlike his own. But Yeats immediately recognized a complication in the nature of those earlier poets' work: 'those songs and ballads, with the exception of a small number which are partly copied from Gaelic models, and a few... that have a personal style, are imitations of the poetry of Burns and Macaulay and Scott'.

In recognizing the imitational elements in the Young Irelander's poetry, he is in part standing out against the Gaelic League, which was arguing for a distinctive national consciousness founded upon linguistic separatism, a return to the native language of the island. Yeats's riposte is founded upon a very different notion of tradition and influence:

> All literature in every country is derived from models, and as often as not these are foreign models, and it is the presence of a personal element alone that can give it nationality in a fine sense, the nationality of its maker. It is only before personality has been attained that a race struggling towards self-consciousness is the better for having, as in primitive times, nothing but native models, for before this has been attained it can neither assimilate nor reject. It was precisely at this passive moment, attainment approaching but not yet come, that the Irish heart and mind surrendered to England, or rather to what is most temporary in England; and Irish patriotism, content that the names and opinions should be Irish, was deceived and satisfied.

Within literature, for Yeats, then, there is an inevitable translation and retranslation of models from one cultural context and historical moment to another. But in Ireland this seemingly 'natural' situation has been disrupted by colonization. He feels that the English colonization of Ireland has prevented the development of a true maturity in the colonized country. As he put it elsewhere, the result of the invasion is that 'the literature of ancient Ireland is a literature of vast, half-dumb conceptions'.[15] So the country finds itself in an unspeaking, *unresolved* position. It is unable to return to the native models from which it has been cut off before time, and is prejudiced also against those traits and models derived from outside of the country which might actually aid in the development of what he calls 'self-consciousness' or character in art as in nationality. When T.S. Eliot, only fifteen years after this article, sought to delineate a mythic method in modern literature which would counter the 'immense panorama of futility and anarchy which is contemporary history', he acknowledged Yeats's earlier adumbration of it.[16] But Eliot's extreme emphasis upon the allusiveness and *impersonality* of the 'method' is at odds with Yeats's reading of his own futile cultural situation, one in which the nation is still awaiting the emergence of distinctive individual and cultural *personality*. That quest marks, as I will discuss below, the stylistic manner of Yeats's poetry from early to late, a manner which for such historical and political reasons resisted the untrammelled translation of allusions from an original context to a modern one, that free translation which characterizes the writings of the Anglo-American Eliot and also of Ezra Pound.

As the article in *Samhain* illustrates, Yeats was alert to the false visions of nationhood which are fostered by a failure in the modern world to attend to origins and contexts, however romanticized. The patriotic press of the day, by which, of course, Yeats largely means the Catholic press, is to his mind dominated by superficial representations of national culture. If the names of the authors and the situation of the narrative in a novel are Irish, then the work is praised (as a result of similar feelings, he had back in 1894 called for a 'criticism as international, a literature as National, as possible').[17] Yeats even goes so far as to claim here that 'English provincialism shouts through the lips of Irish patriots' and urges his audience rather to look for national traits in places where they are not so obvious:

> It is always necessary to affirm and reaffirm [he continues] that nationality is in the things that escape analysis. We discover it, as we do the quality of saltness or sweetness, by the taste, and literature is the cultivation of taste.   (*E*, pp. 232–4)

Yeats here describes a circle which ensures the valency of his own national cultural project, in moving from nationalism to taste, a taste of which literature is a primary cultivator. As he had proclaimed in an 1892 letter to *United Ireland*, 'there is no nationality without literature, no literature without nationality'.[18]

That combination of anti-provincialism and self-conscious taste was to emerge again two years later, in Yeats's elegiac and summatory essay for his erstwhile colleague at the Abbey, 'J.M. Synge and the Ireland of his Time'. This essay is in effect a defence of Synge, whose *The Playboy of the Western World* had ignited riots in 1907 because of its supposedly sacrilegious portrayal of Irish womanhood. Once more we find Yeats turning here to what he calls 'the substantiation of the soul' as a way to 'fasten men together lastingly'. For while, he claims, 'popular', 'external and picturesque and declamatory writers' like Burns and Scott can but create a province, and our Irish cries and grammars serve some passing need, Homer, Shakespeare, Dante, Goethe and all who travel in their road define races and create ever-lasting loyalties.

(*E&I*, p. 341)

The 'picturesque' models behind the work of the Young Irelanders could but bring about, according to Yeats, a desire for kilts and bagpipes and guidebooks and newspapers, the fripperies of a so-called national identity, rather than that true separateness which resides in the depths of the mind to which the artist appeals. As a result, in both the Synge essay and the 1908 'First Principles', the national culture which Yeats presents is very much one of emergence and confusion. He says in the earlier work:

of course [the Irish national tradition of writing] was not all English, but it is impossible to divide what is new, and therefore Irish, from all that is foreign, from all that is an accident of imperfect culture, before we have had some revelation of Irish character, pure enough and varied enough to create a standard of comparison.   (*E*, p. 235)

The colonizing foreign influence is therefore ultimately destructive of judgement in the culture of the native population, and leads, for Yeats, into a false valuation of the immediately recognizable, an inability to interrogate the nature of the traditional models which underlie it. The Celtic culture offered by the Scottish writers might *seem* to provide graspable points of comparison for Irish writers seeking to establish a national literature upon their distinctive native inheritance. But that is to fail to recognize that the Celticism of Burns and Scott is a matter of surfaces, likely to cultivate a seemingly national 'taste' which is appealing to English tourists, but not to engender a self-contained, self-sufficing national character. Rather, the foreign models that must be adopted are those writers who might truly be taken to have achieved an originating status within their respective national cultures, figures like Homer, Dante, Goethe and Shakespeare whose national ambitions are integral to their artistic concerns.

Such ideas of mixed models for literature; a blending of the native and the foreign, had, of course, been integral to the Yeatsian project from the start. His early dramatic lyrics bear the mark of Shelley and Spenser in representing Irish myths. The Homeric had been correlatively present from the early 1890s, at the height of his Celtic Twilight years, in lyrics like 'The Rose of the World': 'For these red lips, with all their mournful pride... / Troy passed away in one high funereal gleam / And Usna's children died.' (*CP*, p. 36) Conversely, in the *apologia* 'To Ireland in the Coming Times', which Yeats printed at the end of the 1893 collection *The Rose* which contained this lyric, we find him attending to – but finally distancing himself from – earlier attempts to found a national literature:

> Nor may I less be counted one
> With Davis, Mangan, Ferguson,
> Because, to him who ponders well,
> My rhymes more than their rhyming tell
> Of things discovered in the deep,
> Where only body's laid asleep.

> (*CP*, p. 50)

The appeal is once more to a personal dream-life as counterweight to what he calls 'Ireland's wrong'. Yeats's spiritualist interests blend here with his most intimate concerns; the rose, whose red-bordered hem he vows to journey after in the poem, is in part symbol also of his forlorn love for Maud Gonne. At such moments, Yeats is at his most Blakean, 'a symbolist who had to invent his own symbols', as he later put it (at the time of the poem Yeats believed Blake to have had an Irish father).[19] 'His counties of England... are arbitrary.... He was a man crying out for a mythology, and trying to make one because he could not find one to his hand.' (*E&I*, p. 114)

The range of nuance and reference which emerges from such inter-mixing, a referentiality which ranges from the intensely personal to the symbolic and the national, makes each element in the poem hard to decipher, weigh and evaluate. The distinctions between the old and the new, the native and the foreign, are actively disrupted by the phantas-magoric and personal elements, while in turn such disruptions are embraced as being historically conditioned, the essentials of a national lineage of writing. Yeats's poems, even at this early stage, then, are crucibles in which it is hard to decipher the origins of, or to make meanings of, the variously emergent distinctions and emphases.

At the centre of both the political and the personal addresses in the poem, what binds them together, of course, is the sense of hurt and failure. As late as 1929, he was writing to T. Sturge Moore that his conception of the 'one heroic sanction... a gay struggle without hope' had freed him from 'British liberalism'. 'Our literary movement would be worthless but for its defeat.'[20] And, on another level, in the opening sentence of his 1937 'A General Introduction for My Work', Yeats was proclaiming personally that 'A poet writes always of his personal life, in his finest work out of its tragedy, whatever it be, remorse, lost love, or mere loneliness'. (*E&I*, p. 509) Yeats recognizes that, even in *The Rose*, he can only 'sweeten' Ireland's wrong, and that he is destined to be forever in pursuit of the unattainable Gonne, the centre of his personal symbolic system. Yet, as he would put it in an 1899 review of 'The Literary Movement in Ireland', such hurts might in themselves form a distinguishing feature of his national culture:

> Even the [Irish] poetry which had its form and much of its matter from alien thought dwelt, as the Gaelic ballads had done before it, on ideas living in the perfection of hope, on visions of unfulfilled desire, and not on the sordid compromise of success. The popular poetry of England celebrates her victories, but the popular poetry of Ireland remembers only defeats and defeated persons.[21]

And not only the popular poetry, but that of the national literary writing of which Yeats was the founder. Both his own love poems of 'unfulfilled desire', but also his public addresses, from 'Easter 1916' to 'Meditations in Time of Civil War' and 'In Memory Eva Gore-Booth and Con Markie-wicz', meditate upon such defeats and defeated persons.

In adopting foreign models and alien thought as part of the colonizing power's inheritance for the conquered nation, Irish writing in his view therefore ultimately gives back a negative, defeated image. Where any number of contemporary English writers were delighting in praise of the Empire ('the masterwork and dream of the middle class' according to Yeats here), the Irish had been imaginatively preoccupied with the weak and the poor, the collection of whose music and stories Yeats sets as a central feature of the Literary Movement. Where English writing was celebrating a move outward, Irish was using the models imposed upon it to look inward. Importantly, in the 1908 'First Principles' article, Yeats recalls his visits with Lady Gregory to Galway cottages in 1897 as the moment at which 'I escaped from many misconceptions...I began an active Irish life.'

Yeats is, of course, a notoriously difficult and liminal figure to cite in regard to these paradigms of cross-culturalism and its impact upon emergent national consciousness, and (as my next chapter will show) this has led to his work often being treated sceptically by subsequent Irish poets and historians. His Anglo-Irish lineage was something that he increasingly reverted to from his 1914 volume *Responsibilities* onwards, and towards the end of his career it formed the centre of his visionary self-mythologizing. Yeats himself captured that twin pull of identification in the General Introduction for a proposed edition of his collected works:

> The 'Irishry' have preserved their ancient 'deposit' through wars which, during the sixteenth and seventeenth centuries, became wars of extermination.... No people hate as we do in whom that past is always alive, there are moments when hatred poisons my life.... Then I remind myself that... all my family names are English, and that I owe my soul to Shakespeare, to Spenser and to Blake, perhaps to William Morris, and to the English language in which I think, speak, and write, that everything I love has come to me through English; my hatred tortures me with love, my love with hate.... This is the Irish hatred and solitude...that can still make us wag between extremes and doubt our sanity.   (*E&I*, pp. 518–19)

However dubious when viewed by later Irish writers, this sense of double abandonment due to his heritage, this agonized wagging between extremes which cannot be given adequate expression (what Timothy Webb has called a 'civil war within the self'),[22] exacerbates Yeats's sense of the inevitable makeshiftness of the expression of those who have been colonized. His continual desire to acquire a style and syntax that would be adequate to conveying in poetry 'passionate normal speech' is ultimately integral to his project of realizing and giving expression to a vision of national self-consciousness. 'The English mind is meditative, rich, deliberate', he wrote; 'I planned to write short lyrics or poetic drama where every speech would be short and concentrated, knit by dramatic tension'. (*E&I*, p. 521) The quest for 'a style which would not be an English style and yet would be musical and full of colour', described in 'What is "Popular Poetry"' of 1901, continued across his career. (*E&I*, p. 3)

Yeats's sense that the foreignness of the models bequeathed to the Irish poet might be alienating but also reconstituting, the basis for national identification, the creation of 'ever-lasting loyalties', obviously accords at some level with the key terms of Homi K. Bhabha's theorization of the impact of Empire upon colonized native populations.[23] From this plane of literary and cultural imposition and translation, the 'hybridity' which Bhabha describes in his essay 'Signs Taken for Wonders' as deforming and displacing 'all sites of discrimination and domination' can be seen operating in Yeats's recognition of the 'accidents of imperfect culture' which disrupt any reading of Irish texts, and interfere with an ability to discriminate the 'new' and identifiably native from the 'old' and foreign.

At issue is the valency of textual material within what Bhabha elsewhere calls 'that Benjaminian temporality of the present which makes graphic a moment of transition, not merely the continuum of history'. Yeats's inclusion of various mythic materials from a variety of origins alongside hidden personal and Rosicrucian symbols, with no mediation or deciphering of them in the poetry itself, makes this 'in-between' 'now-time' uncannily visible. As will become clear across this book, such considerations also make the *identification* of Yeats's work from the perspective of later writing extremely difficult. Whatever the self-remakings across his own career, he remains, as I've said, both indecipherably modern and also 'dated', 'traditional'. The sense of defeatedness and the concomitant Swiftian savage indignation which Yeats feels late on in his career arise from that very sense of incommensurability which Bhabha claims as the basis of cultural identification in the 'problematic of colonial representation'. Yeats's invention of an eclectic 'tradition' offers a partial form of identification, partial because its oblique take on Anglo-Irish cultural temporality estranges any immediate access to originary identity, be it Irish or British.

III

It is Yeats's consistent emphasis on performative literary *style* – what 'Poetry and Tradition' describes in Paterian fashion as 'continuing, self-delighting happiness' going beyond the conditions of its making – which might be taken as a warrant of what Bhabha calls the 'excess and slippage' inherent in interstitial colonial relationships and, later, in postcolonial national contexts. Yeats had himself identified 'the vivifying spirit' 'of excess' as the unique contribution of Celtic to European literature. (*E&I*, p. 185) His emphasis upon a passionate syntax knit with dramatic tension, a short lyric outburst which does nothing to qualify or mediate itself to any audience (and which would seem alien to English readers), is a mark of the 'in-between' nature of that style, its mixing of foreign and native models.[24] It is also integral to the notion of a particular kind of presence both *within* his writing, and *of* his poetry in later work, a presence that finds variously-heard echoes in later Irish poetry, in the work of W.H. Auden and Geoffrey Hill, and of John Berryman. As such, it needs some further discussion in its original context here.

His model for that style, from 'Poetry and Tradition' to the late 'General Introduction', remained an English one: Shakespeare's tragic heroes and heroines at the moment of their deaths, where 'joy and sorrow are one', as he put it in the earlier essay:

> for the nobleness of the arts is in the mingling of contraries, the extremity of sorrow, the extremity of joy, perfection in personality, the perfection of its surrender, overflowing turbulent energy, and marmorean stillness.   (*E&I*, p. 255)

But that mingling is only momentary, experienced by tragic figures 'when the last darkness ha[s] gathered about them'. Yeats is concerned, however, to argue that this transfiguration of language is something which tragic figures share with their creators. It is a joy, 'always making and mastering' which 'remains in the hands and the tongue of the artist'. (p. 254)

What is again striking in the equation between tragic hero or heroine and the poet is that shared sense of their attaining style 'in the face of death', the suggestion that it is only when exterior fate is at its most contrary that the possibility for personal identity, and – therefore – transfiguration occurs. ('The soul . . . only returns to itself, in both senses of assembling itself and waking itself, becoming conscious, in the consciousness of self in general, through this concern for death', as Derrida has recently contended.[25]) Under this aegis, the act of writing poetry, the quest for style, becomes a quest for immortality; the constant victory, and constantly renewed struggle against completion, stopping, endings.[26] 'What else can death be but the beginning of wisdom and power and beauty?' (*M*, p. 115) As Yeats wrote to Robert Bridges, 'you asked me about my stops and commas. . . . I do not understand stops. I write so completely for the ear that I feel helpless when I have to measure pauses by stops and commas'.[27]

'Style', in this conception, seems itself a mingling of Keatsian 'negative capability' with his 'fine excess'; it is correlative to that notion of 'tragic joy' which many times Yeats related to his discovery of the antithetical Mask – as it is formulated in the memoir 'Four Years: 1887–1891', for instance:

> As life goes on we discover that certain thoughts sustain us in defeat, or give us victory, whether over ourselves or others, and it is these thoughts, tested by passion, that we call convictions. Among subjective men (in all those, that is, who must spin a web out of their own

bowels) the victory is an intellectual daily re-creation of all that exterior fate snatches away, and so that fate's antithesis; while what I have called 'the Mask' is an emotional antithesis to all that comes out of their internal nature. We begin to live when we have conceived life as tragedy.   (*A*, p. 189)[28]

It is out of extravagance and surprise that the conception of 'active virtue' as 'theatrical, consciously dramatic' arrives, with the attendant recognition that 'all the sins and energies of the world are but the world's flight from an infinite blinding beam'. (*M*, p. 334)[29]

Per Amica Silentia Lunae and *A Vision* will later register his attempts to systematize and understand the workings of that 'exterior' fate and our conflicts with it. What seems important to stress here is the daily re-creation of the antithesis which is 'Style, personality – deliberately adopted and therefore a mask – [which] is the only escape from the hot-faced bargainers and the moneychangers.' (*A*, p. 461) 'Style', and the tradition it embodies, is consistently represented by Yeats as an attack upon logic and those grubbers in the tills who live by it. Style's alternative economics, its excess, becomes associated for him at times with a call for a seeking out of organic rhythms, 'which are the embodi-ment of the imagination, that neither desires nor hates, because it has done with time, and only wishes to gaze upon some reality, some beauty'. It is also a call for a continuation of formal qualities in writing, which, as he argued in the 1900 essay 'The Symbolism of Poetry', gives 'a body to something that moves beyond the senses, ... [to] mysterious life, as the body of a flower or of a woman'. (*E&I*, pp. 163–4)[30]

Most tellingly, there emerges out of this continual antithetical re-creation a paradoxical defence of discontinuity, the better to defend those continuing qualities of 'tradition' and 'life'. At the opening of his memoir 'Estrangement', Yeats makes a note to himself about notes:

> To keep these notes natural and useful to me I must keep one note from leading on to another, that I may not surrender myself to literature. Every note must come as a casual thought, then it will be my life. Neither Christ nor Buddha nor Socrates wrote a book, for to do that is to exchange life for a logical process.   (*A*, p. 461)

This note-based casualness of thought, which 'will be life', but which also represents an anxiety about the deathly qualities of books and writing, provides the structuring principle throughout Yeats's memoirs and counters that Victorian rationalism which he hated. (*A*, pp. 157,

168) It also characterizes his literary output more generally.[31] The 'ephemera' of literary production, prefaces and lectures appear among his prose collections. As Paul de Man among others has claimed, many of the longer poems are made up of gatherings of short sections, or the accumulation of poems around a similar subject which do not, by the standard of our instinctive reading practices, resolve themselves into a whole.[32]

This raises the possibility that the Yeatsian poetic of the antithetical mask in fact elevates discontinuity and the fragment, in other words the poetry of the isolated moment, above his much-argued cyclical continuities – and emphasis, as in the essay 'Art and Ideas', upon the continuous unconsciousness embodied in tradition. 'Tradition', like the cycles of civilization and dissolution mapped in *A Vision*, is graspable as an 'idea', but that is not necessarily to say that the 'idea' conveys the actuality of lived experience which is the Yeatsian conflictual 'style'. Once again, the interstitial nature of his national and cultural position seems to discover an incommensurability between actuality and hoped-for resolution. That incommensurability has become 'style' itself. Like 'The Magi', Yeats will remain 'unsatisfied', but perpetually 'hoping to find once more' the 'mystery'. (*CP*, p. 126) His is an emergent, problematic art, rather than a completed, monumental one. It is ever aspiring to a symbolic completion to which it can never arrive.[33]

Apposite examples of this ambivalence can be found even in Yeats's later work, when he would seem to have turned disappointedly and aggrievedly away from Ireland's political development towards a monumentalist visionary world of his own, encapsulated in poems like 'Sailing to Byzantium'. Such tensions continue to resonate, for instance, in a poem like 'The Municipal Gallery Revisited', a poem which is clearly attentive to Spenserian ideas and which models its form on the *ottava rima* upon which Spenser played his own variations in his epic *The Fairie Queen*.[34] Yeats's praise here of Lady Gregory owes much to Spenser's celebrations of his patrons:

> My mediaeval knees lack health until they bend,
> But in that woman, in that household where
> Honour lived so long, all lacking found.
> Childless I thought, 'My children may find here
> Deep-rooted things,' but never foresaw its end,
> And now that end has come I have not wept;
> No fox can foul the lair the badger swept –

(An image out of Spenser and the common tongue).
John Synge, I and Augusta Gregory, thought
All that we did, all that we said or sang
Must come from contact with the soil, from that
Contact everything Antaeus-like grew strong.

(CP, pp. 320–1)

The complicated returns upon the self in the sequence 'Childless I thought, "My children . . . "', but never foresaw its end, / And now that end has come', with its play again upon false imaginings, the thwarting of expectation and surprising responses to the unforeseen, comes complicatedly after the compacted phrase 'in that household where / Honour had lived so long, all lacking found'. Found what, health? honour?[35] Then, with the sudden intervention (exaggerated here by the shortened stanza) of the tone of scholarly footnotes, telling us of the complicated origin of the aphorism 'No fox can foul the lair the badger swept', we move to another plane of tension. The locatable but unlocated nature of the saying seriously qualifies that 'contact with the soil' which Yeats later in the poem celebrates in himself and his friends.

In the 1902 Preface to his selection from Spenser, Yeats had discussed this reference himself. He praises Spenser's Ode for the Earl of Leicester's death as

> more than a conventional Ode to a dead patron. . . . At the end of a long beautiful passage he laments that unworthy men should be dead in the Earl's place, and compares them to a fox – an unclean feeder – hiding in the lair 'the badger swept'. (*E&I*, pp. 359–60)

Yeats immediately goes on, though, to lament that Spenser could not forever have acted as a 'master of ceremony' in 'the elaborate life' of Leicester's court. Instead, he had to be 'plunged into a life that stirred him to bitterness, as the way is with theoretical minds in the tumults of events they cannot understand' – a vividly prescient description of his own career.

This is a remarkable way to describe Spenser's move to Ireland with the colonial army, but it also strikes the tone of condescension which Yeats feels when pondering the fate of Gregory's household at Coole Park, which was sold to the Forestry Department, then pulled down after her death. In a typical manoeuvre for his later work, Yeats evokes what he calls in the last stanza of this poem 'Ireland's history' in order to rebuke what he elsewhere describes as 'the filthy modern tide' of contemporary Irish life. (*CP*, pp. 337) The inclusion of the scholarly footnote, alluding to both Spenser and the common tongue, is jarring. It recalls the beauty of the Elizabethan poet's Ode to *his* dead patron, but also the bitterness and ignorance upon which such beauty is often founded (as he had earlier acknowledged in 'Meditations in Time of Civil War').

But the inclusion also allows for a demotic provenance for the phrase that is itself incommensurably implicated in the suggestion of worthlessness in the Spenserian image. Spenser felt that other, baser, men should have died instead of Leicester. The sense is that the commoners should know better than to think they could destroy the honour of a household when they destroy a house. Yet the allusion to the 'common tongue' might also be there to counter the suspicions, which Yeats was himself exercised by, of Spenserian complicity in the invasion of Ireland. What's foreign and in itself destructive is also potentially 'common' and native through the interminable process of colonization. The foreign model of imagery and form is, therefore, made strangely rootless, complicit with Yeats's rebuke to the unimaginable destructiveness of beauty by his own countrymen, but also dehistoricized, its translation to this context troubling and unresolved. The abrupt and open-ended shifts in the syntax both complicate notions of commonality but also sit uneasily against the elaboration of Spenserian form. (Such disjunctiveness is perhaps the impulse behind the odd *non-sequitur* with which Yeats heralds his discussion of style in his 1937 'General Introduction': 'Because I need a passionate syntax for passionate subject-matter I compel myself to accept those traditional metres that have developed with the language'.) (*E&I*, p. 522)

While not wanting to deny the fact that the implications of this particular example are politically distasteful, what I think the abrupt shifts of register here and elsewhere in Yeats's writing, and the awkward compacting of the literary and the vernacular, seem to show is that liminal excesses of style in colonial contexts are always a matter of performance, of self-creation and self-assertion. Yeats's early syntheses of Homeric, Irish mythic and spiritualist materials into an Irish Literary Movement are wholly his own. In 'The Municipal Gallery Revisited', Yeats, Gregory and Synge are theatrically said 'alone' to stand for that 'contact with the soil' which is a definer of Irish history. Nationhood in Yeats is (as Bhabha claims it to be for all colonized or newly postcolonial peoples in his essay 'Dissemination') a continually renewed performance across his career. What Bhabha sees as 'the historical construc-

tion of a specific position of historical enunciation and address' necessary to 'modernity' is to the fore in Yeats's thinking, *early* and *late*, about
nationhood – to the fore as both proclaimed originatory strength and as
an acknowledged vulnerability.[36]

Such acknowledged problematics of reading, reception (*national* com-
prehension), historically-governed indecipherabilities and their impact
upon a performative, dramatic notion of self (what, in writing of Henley
he called bringing 'life to the dramatic crisis and expression to the point
of artifice where the true self could find its tongue' (*A*, p. 126)), inevitably provided varied and contradictory opportunities for later poets
influenced by Yeats. The unresolved, open-ended nature of his own
historical location opens his work to reappropriation within a greater
variety of contexts, perhaps, than that of his modernist successors
Pound and Eliot. As will become clear from my discussions below, the
greater presence and claims to cultural 'origination' of his work in Ireland obviously lead to problems of identification for later poets there, as
they do not from the relatively remote perspective of later writers in the
States.

In America, the relative 'meaning' and representativeness of his work
seems fairly fixed, and the poets can weigh its valency or otherwise
across their careers. In Ireland, however, the very complexity of Yeats's
inheritance, its tones and overtones, leads to a constantly-shifting process of evaluation and re-evaluation within a single poet's work. In
Britain, in contrast, Yeats seems somehow both present and absent.
The mediate status governed by the 'Anglo-' in Yeats's own heritage
leads to a process of reading by later poets there in which some elements
(often national) of his own work can be resisted, others abstracted – or
seen as abstractions – and so can be appropriated.

While at this stage the map or schema for this book must remain
qualifiable and questionable, the complex negotiations and problems
of reading amidst which Yeats himself constantly wrote allow the issue
of his influence to raise questions of what it might mean to read
'nationally' or 'internationally'. What might be involved in transference
between these two contexts? On one level, Yeats's relative 'presence'
within and over subsequent writing in Ireland might lend him a symbolic status, in which originary splits and complexities are held and
sustained within the figure 'Yeats'. Whereas, in the United States, the
comparatively straightforward and transparent 'understanding' of his
work makes it into much more of a 'sign' of certain ideas and values.

In other words, it might be possible to apply the key terms of Paul de
Man's essay upon conflictual impetuses within Romanticism, 'The

Rhetoric of Temporality' (in which symbolic presence is displaced by allegorical signs subject to time which defuse that simultaneity), within the dimensions of geographical space as well as within historical unravellings of 'meaning'.[37] Yet, on the other hand (or perhaps as a result of this), Yeats's comparative 'absence' from American writing, his comparative representativeness, lends several writers, including Theodore Roethke and John Berryman, to seek to conjure his 'literal' presence, to exchange gifts with the dead poet in ways that no Irish poets have sought to.

The reading of Yeats's influence as a shift from 'symbol' towards 'sign' (values which, in his own work, as I have shown, seem slippery, since his desire for 'unities' is constantly interrupted by situational perplexities), accompanied by increasing geographical and historical distance, remains itself irresolvable and complex, therefore. Such complexity finds its echo in the recognition by Julia Kristeva that *both* elements (what she calls the 'symbolic' and the 'semiotic') 'are inseparable within the *signifying process*'. It is in the dialectic formed between the two that both 'the type of discourse (narrative, metalanguage, theory, poetry, etc.)', and the content or 'subject' emerge. Modern poetry (and for Kristeva once again the 'modern revolution' seems a belated form of Romantic tropologies) becomes the place in which the 'I', the speaking subject, is put most intensely 'in process / on trial'. It is the place where 'the *positing* of the symbolic...finds itself subverted' as syntax and 'grammatical rules' are trangressed.[38]

Yeats's 'presence' within later more contemporary work remains, in accordance with similar recognitions about the questioning of the 'symbolic', variously proximate and distant, resisted and welcomed.[39] Such variousness is in part warranted by the Romantically problematic status of symbolism in his own work. From early to late, the mystic and nationalist Yeats was attentive to the dangers full presence offered to the poet and his personae, thwarting their powers of expression and paradoxically diverting them from 'true' relationships. In the introductory verse to *The Rose* (1893), 'To the Rose Upon the Rood of Time', the speaker enjoins the unifying symbol of that collection to 'Come near, come near, come near – Ah leave me still / A little space for the rose-breath to fill!' The fear is that the symbol will prevent the speaker from hearing 'common things', and so be distracted from his audience and his nationalist purpose. (*CP*, p. 31) At another level, we can see in the poems voiced for Crazy Jane collected in the 1933 *The Winding Stair and Other Poems* the paradoxical confidence and celebration of love which is possible in the *absence* of the loved one. Crazy Jane's lover Jack is dead, yet this enables her, in 'Crazy Jane and Jack the Journeyman', to envisage her own death and burial 'in an empty bed', from which, however, she would 'walk', since the skein of love 'so bound us ghost to ghost'. 'Man [and woman] is in love and loves what vanishes, / What more is there to say?' (*CP*, pp. 258, 208)

For Yeats, as for Rousseau and the Romantic tradition which Derrida has traced coming down from him, 'presence is at the same time desired and feared'. These conflicting emotions then engender for Derrida the supplementary transgression of writing itself, which is able to procure 'presence' 'through the proxy of the sign', but also holds it at a distance and limits or 'masters it'. As a result, desire 'carries in itself the destiny of its nonsatisfaction', an idea with resonance for Yeats's cultural, nationalist and personal yearnings.[40] Full presence, which would cancel the undecidability of the symbol, would prove fatal (something of which Austin Clarke, for instance, would seem exemplary, when thinking through the influence of Yeats upon the next generation of Irish writers, as I will discuss below). The over-near proximity of the rose would steal the breath away. Yet, at the same time, and as Auden acknowledges in his 'Elegy' for Yeats, temporality is, from beginning to end of his career, a destructive force. In 'The Falling of the Leaves' from the 1889 *Crossways*, time duly renders the conventional passing away of love and beauty. (*CP*, pp. 14–15) In the volumes from *The Tower* of 1928 onwards, it brings the rage and frustrations of old age. 'The innocent and the beautiful / Have no enemy but time', as we are told in 'In Memory of Eva Gore-Booth and Con Markievicz'. 'Bid me strike a match / And strike another till time catch'. (*CP*, p. 233) Such recognitions, regrets, desires and fears are central to the work of the poets I will be discussing in this book, in their marking their distance from Yeats's own work.

IV

The reading of Yeats has had a founding impact upon American theories of poetry and influence, from those of the New Critics (to be discussed in Chapter 4, on American writing) to those of the Yale critics Harold Bloom and Paul de Man. In turn, it has had significant resonances within Bloom's and de Man's engagement with French textual criticism. Bloom's 1970 book *Yeats* marked the start of his theorization of literary influence; de Man's doctoral thesis was on Mallarmé and Yeats, and he later only found reason to reprint some of the Yeats sections of the thesis in *The Rhetoric of Romanticism*.[41]

No book discussing literary influence can now be written in ignorance of Bloom's theories. But, as will already have become clear, my argument here discovers some *limitation* in Bloom's tropes of crossing and sublimity, both with regard to his discussion of the origins of Yeats's style and to its own visionary company. Bloom's dismissal of aporetic deconstruction forms an anxious but worthy defence of poetry, perhaps, yet it often misreads deconstruction and misses valuable thinking by Derrida and others about all forms of inheritance. As such, I wish to identify here with some of Bloom's ideas, but, by thinking through some of the implications of deconstruction, I want to distance myself from some of its historical implications and also its implications for the practice of reading through influence. In this last section of the chapter, I want to bring the two sides of the discussion into dialogue, one with the other, and to add my own *caveats*, as this debate has implications for my own practice throughout the book.

As Bloom has claimed, and as Yeats acknowledges in different terms in his essay on 'Poetry and Tradition', 'all poetic odes of incarnation are in effect Immortality odes.'[42] Or, as Yeats told Louise Morgan in 1931, 'If you don't express yourself . . . you walk after you're dead. The great thing is to go empty to your grave.'[43] It is better to discover a full incarnation through expression than to suffer purgatorial unsettledness after death.

For Bloom, the quest by the *ephebe*, or new (later) poet, to overcome the precursor is figured in Freud's conflicting drives, the one toward love or Eros, the other towards death or Thanatos. On the basis of this equation, a poet might be defined as someone who is particularly anxious to counter the drive towards death, to make death a 'figuration rather than a reality':

> the repressed rhetorical formula of Freud's discourse in *Beyond the Pleasure Principle* can be stated thus: *literal meaning equals anteriority equals an earlier state of meaning equals an earlier state of things equals death equals literal meaning.* Only one escape is possible from such a formula, and it is a simple formula: *Eros equals figurative meaning* (original italics).[44]

The drive to create, therefore, becomes the drive to overcome the death of the self by entering the self into union with tradition and history. This is achieved firstly through the relation with a precursor text, and then (when the danger of the belated, new text, forming only a weak repetition of the earlier text's figuration becomes clear) through an overcoming and repression of the precursor and an attempt to reverse history, to 'lie against time', in order to gain priority and thence immortality.[45]

Bloom's defence of the drive towards Eros and figuration, the struggle against death and literal meaning, in effect amounts to his defence of poetry. In *Ruin the Sacred Truths* of 1989, he even went so far as to claim that poetry amounts to a third drive, perhaps without the same cognitive status as Eros and Thanatos, but nonetheless 'primal' and taking 'priority over belief of any kind'.[46] That *compensatory drive* had earlier been to the fore in Bloom's setting out of his six 'revisionary ratios' in *The Anxiety of Influence* and in the following *A Map of Misreading*, in the play of absences and presences conceived there (as it is also in de Man's discussion of the link between later and earlier texts as a 'recuperation of a failing energy by means of an increased awareness').[47] It is through discovering what has been repressed in any text that the possibility for new writing – poetic or criticial – becomes possible. As Bloom formulates it later in *Agon: Towards a Theory of Revisionism*:

> When I speak of repression, in a text, I do not mean the accumulation or aggregation of an unconscious. I mean that I can observe or frequently identify *patterns of forgetting* in a poem, and that these tend to be rather more important than a poem's allusions, even where those allusions are patterned. What makes a poem strongest is *how* it excludes what is almost present in it, or nearest to presence in it. Criticism (strong) begins by finding the Sublime moment which is the most intense Negative crossing in the poem. ... [T]he critic discovers *what* it is that the poem *represses* in order to have persuaded us of the illusion of its own closure. That *what* is, in the first place, necessarily another poem.[48]

That the process of repression and forgetting which forms the Sublime is integral to all writing is inescapable for Bloom, then, even within the process of 'discovery' which is the best criticism. Such ideas govern his central concerns with the misreading, or misprisions of all reading and writing ('Initial love for the precursor's poetry is transformed rapidly enough into revisionary strife, without which individuation is not possible').[49] The Bloomian critic is liberated into fictiveness concurrent with that of the text he or she is 'reading'. A 'scientific', 'historical' or 'linguistic' criticism is *always* 'poetic', and Bloom is amazed that this cannot be seen by those engaged in those other versions of reading and writing.[50]

Bloom's is ultimately an historical position, therefore, since it is predicated upon the fact that, with increasing belatedness, the possibilities of making meaning are diminished (and in this it echoes de Man's readings of Romanticism as moving from the presence of symbolism towards an allegorical and temporal sign):

> The curse of an increased belatedness, a dangerously self-conscious belatedness, is that creative envy becomes the ecstasy, the Sublime, of the sign-system of poetic language.
> ... [B]elated poems suffer an increasing overdetermination in *language*, but an increasing *under-determination in meaning*.
> ... [T]he Wordsworthian or modern poem has an apparent dearth of meaning, which paradoxically is its particular strength, and its demand upon, and challenge to, the interpretative powers of the reader.[51]

'Influence,' as he says elsewhere, 'does away not only with the idea that there are poems-in-themselves, but also the more stubborn idea that there are poets-in-themselves. If there are no texts, then there are no authors'.[52]

But, in terms of my earlier argument, the compensatory economics driving both Bloom's and de Man's theories of influence might seem to rest awkwardly alongside the slippery, excessive, self-creative stylistic and historical positioning characteristic of Yeats's poetry. While themselves compensating for historical repression, Yeats's poems do not always, or between each other, manifest repression in their illusions of closure. 'Byzantium', with its vision of perpetual figurative creation ('Those images that yet / Fresh images beget' (*CP*, p. 249), and the notions of 'casual thought' and self-revision integral to Yeats's poetic, would seem to resist such balancing concluding returns of the repressed as those figured in Bloom's final 'revisionary ration' *apophrades*. Bloomian criticism in particular, with its synchronic version of textual overcoming, would seem finally unable to throw off a New Critical approach to textual completion (however 'illusory'), which is itself a distanced and dehistoricizing reading of Yeatsian problematics.[53] Yeats's irresolution, his historically-unfounded poetic of founding, open his work to a greater range of possibilities as a precursor than the Bloomian model suggests. His impact upon American *poetry*, as Chapter 4 will argue, is, for example, more irruptively surprising than Bloom's particular sense of poetic repression can allow for.

Indeed, Bloom's historical recognitions and reading of tradition, however seemingly consonant with much of Yeats's thinking about the antithetical and belated relationship of the new poet to tradition, make it difficult to read a history of Yeatsian influence across the last two-thirds of the century according to his model. Bloom, at the end of *Yeats*, after all, proclaims his subject 'the last of the High Romantics, the last of those poets who asserted imaginative values without the armor of continuous irony'. His is, in this sense also, an endstopped reading, one whose processes of valuation depend strongly upon the limitation of its sense of historical completion and possibility.[54]

Further, Bloom's 'historical' reading also raises difficult questions about its own context and situation (although he can be rather confusing around this issue, often seeming to see Yeats as the end of an *English* tradition, whereas the American one continues in the texts of Wallace Stevens, Hart Crane, John Ashbery and A.R. Ammons). *Agon*, the book of 1983 that in many ways rounds off Bloom's sequence of works on anxieties of influence, unregenerately proclaims the crossings into the Sublime he has formulated as Emersonian, 'the American religion of competitiveness'. As a consequence, he then argues, against post-structuralists, for a culturally specific reading of texts:

> What is the motive, the drive, for all those problematics of deconstruction, via language, from Heidegger on to Gallic Post-Structuralism? ... An Anglo-American poem is after all a richly confused relational event, from the standpoint of any continental dialectical philosophy. ... Poems, however strong, lie against time and protest place only by being embedded in time, and place, and American poems tenaciously remain texts resembling Walt Whitman and not Stephane Mallarmé.[55]

Anxieties of influence are finally revealed, then, as having their origins and closure in Emersonian self-reliance.[56] As a result, Bloom's *poetic* criticism will not ultimately yield to an explicitly deconstructive sense of textuality as writing, taking its place, instead, in a culturally-dictated prior scene of exchange and self-assertion. From the declarations of *Agon*, it is possible to read this *local*, or nationally-based, influence back to Bloom's first statements against deconstruction in *A Map of Misreading*:

> Tradition, the Latin *traditio*, is etymologically a handing-over or a giving-over, a delivery.... Tradition is good teaching, where 'good' means pragmatic, instrumental, fecund. ... The first use ... of a Scene of Instruction is to remind us of the humanistic loss we sustain if we yield up the authority of oral tradition to the partisans of *writing*....

The human writes, the human thinks, and always following after and defending against another human....[57]

This defence now seems essentially founded upon an intimate, almost personal, translation of tradition-as-tuition into a coming-of-awareness. Yet, importantly here for my purposes, it is upon this recognition of an unexpressed, prior selfhood within and against the transferences of reading and writing, and upon a tradition of continuing, instructive orality whose trace can be found within any literary art, that Bloom builds the foundation of his arguments against the deconstructionists and his prime interlocutor in these matters, Paul de Man.[58] Yeats, of course, continually promoted a sense of the interplay between speech and writing as the basis for his notion of dramatic selfhood and presence ('When I begin to write I have no object but to find... some natural speech'.) (*A*, p. 532) In Bloom's hands, however, that perception of critical and human *loss* in writing, as deconstructionists have done, solely of textuality, rapidly lapses into polemicism and subjectivity.

Bloom feels deeply that deconstruction has had little of value to say about the reading of poetry, and indeed that its reduction of everything to questions of language fails to account at all for the *specific* issues involved in reading and composing this genre as opposed to all others. Most tellingly perhaps, he has attacked the self-proclaimingly anti-rhetorical nature of deconstructive criticism, its claims to reveal the aporias or the hidden undermining elements in textual structures, for being itself a rhetorical ploy:

> When current French critics talk about what they call "language", they are using "language" as a trope. Their scientism is irrelevant... their value-words... are almost wholly figurative. ... They are at least as guilty of reifying their own metaphors as any American bourgeois formalist has been. ... Language is hardly in itself a privileged kind of explanation. ... [My defence against this would be] to look at the language of poets, and not at any theory of language........ A theory *of* poetry must belong *to* poetry, must *be* poetry, before it can be of any use in interpreting poems.[59]

Time and again, deconstruction's focus upon the problematic of language is equated with that literalization of meaning which is equivalent to Freud's drive towards Thanatos, and away from the essentially figurative act of poetic creation which is at the centre of all individuation, for Bloom.[60]

Yet, as I hope has become clear, such individuation as Bloom conceives of it is fraught with situational problems and circularities. If the only criticism of poetry 'must *be* poetry', then the basis for judgement of the success or failure of any particular act of belated overcoming or sublimation of an earlier text becomes shaky. Bloom's criterion of differentiation or distance of the belated from the precursor text relies upon a reading of the repressed that is itself proclaimedly unreliable and subjective. His argument against French criticism's interest in aporias depends upon an acceptence of a model of figuration as Romantic Imagination or Sublimation that is taken to hold for every post-Miltonic poetic text, including 'poetic' criticism. But this leaves major parts of literary history unread and unreadable – the eighteenth century, Anglo-American modernism (Pound and Eliot will be forgotten, we are assured in the Preface to *Yeats*), and much of the twentieth-century. Bloom's liking for Gilbert's saying in Wilde's 'The Critic As Artist' that criticism is 'the only civilized form of autobiography' – a Romantic subjective perception *in* writing – finds its cultural validation in *Agon*,[61] but in the process often undermines our means of speaking about and judging a whole range of either poetic or critical origin or context.

Most obviously, as Sandra M. Gilbert and Susan Gubar amongst others have argued, Bloom's version of literary history figures it as an essentially male entity, founded upon a doctrine of competitiveness alien to women's writing (or, as Hélène Cixous has argued, 'literary history... all comes back to man – ... his desire to be (at) the origin', 'woman... does not enter into oppositions').[62] For this perspective, Yeats's preoccupation with tradition, from which Bloom partly takes his cue, remains an essentially *male* anxiety, however personally, culturally and historically motivated. As will be borne out in my survey and close readings of Yeatsian influence since his death, women writers have rarely been concerned to negotiate with the shadow of past (essentially male) writers – to, as Cixous says, allow death to work and to perform the work of mourning which is integral to constructions of, and writing within, literary history. To that extent, this book is itself limited by the *kind* of history that it seeks to describe.

But it is in relation to issues of origin and context, perhaps, that Bloom most approaches, and most misrepresents, the ideas of Derrida (whose own recent work has often benefited from the thought of women writers such as Cixous and from Julia Kristeva's discussions of intertextuality) and of Paul de Man. These ideas are perhaps better descriptive of the metamorphic, sequential, processional and processive nature of Yeats's poetics and influence than his own. Bloom often misreads Derrida in order to assert his essentialist notion of poetry and self-reliance. As Derrida himself argues in response to a similar attack to those made by Bloom on deconstruction, an attack made upon his paper 'Signature Event Context' (*Sec*) by John Searle:

> *at no time* does *Sec* invoke the *absence*, pure and simple, of intentionality. Nor is there any break, simple or radical, with intentionality. What the text questions is not intention or intentionality but their *telos*, which orients and organizes the movement and the possibility of a fulfilment, realization, and *actualization* in a plenitude that would be *present* to and identical with itself.

While he recognizes that this questioning of a telos makes it difficult to say what 'intention' might mean 'as the *particular* or *original* work (*mise en oeuvre*) of iterability',[63] Derrida decisively here denies that it is possible to locate a thwarting deconstructive impulse *at the moment of transmission* by the author/writer of any text. Rather, the linguistic aporias, which undermine the text's claims to metaphysical meaning, appear as a result of the fact that the *reception* of the text cannot be absolutely guaranteed.

It is the lack of an examination of this inability to guarantee receipt of a text which Derrida particularly bemoans, and which underlies and motivates his own project:

> The absence of the sender...from the mark that he abandons, and which cuts itself off from him and continues to produce effects independently of his presence and of the present actuality of his intentions, indeed even after his death, his absence, which moreover belongs to the structure of all writing...of all language in general... *this* absence is not examined....[64]

From this argument, all reading can come to seem despairingly, poignantly or pathetically to convey a possibly misplaced desire to understand what we might take a text to 'mean', without understanding that we have no coherent identity apart from language (or apart from poetry, in Bloom's view) from which to do so. The very fact that words can and will be repeated in different contexts, what Derrida claims is the essential *iterability* of language, undoes all attempts to tether language to a specific moment, utterer or reading-context in any sense. Indeed, he argues, iterability renders it questionable whether it is possible to establish such a thing as event or context at all. The very absence which shadows all discourse militates against it being possible to say that something occurred once and for all, or that such and such was the originator of a particular way of thinking or writing.

As does Bloom, then, Derrida attributes this absence to the fact of death, a crossing of a border which converts 'proper names' into 'singular common nouns'. As Derrida's *Mémoires: for Paul de Man* recognizes, however, this does not set a limit to our need to 'inscribe' 'figures', because 'they can outlast us'. For him, as for Yeats and others writing in a Romantic tradition (perhaps all of us), the act of writing as memorialization is essentially a projection 'toward the future across a fabled present'.[65] Yet in this as in much else, Derrida hesitates where some of his followers have gone the whole way, into the abysm of irredeemable textual free play in the present (and it is perhaps the Yale School of criticism's version of deconstruction rather than the Derridian which Bloom has in mind in most of his attacks). Derrida has always resisted the notion that deconstruction is a 'methodical technique, a possible or necessary procedure ... unfolding possibilities' in each instance of writing; rather, he does not himself limit the possibilities of various means of engagement.

In his recent work *On the Name* (1993), Derrida specifically asks whether, given iterability and undecidability, we should henceforth forbid ourselves to speak of such a thing as the philosophy of Plato, that is, of such a thing as the origin of all subsequent philosophy? 'Not at all', he replies to himself, 'there would undoubtedly be no error in principle in so speaking'. What *would* be an error, though, is to claim that in so speaking we would do anything other than involving ourselves in 'an inevitable *abstraction*'. 'Plato' would mean 'the thesis or theme which one has extracted by artifice, misprision and abstraction from the text, torn from the written fiction of "Plato"'.

But this does not mean for Derrida that it is arbitrary or illegitimate to categorize whatever is extracted from a text in this way as being readings of 'Plato'. In fact, the whole history of Platonism in Western Philosophy has been legitimated by the presence of a certain level of abstraction in the language of Plato himself, which governs and generates the abstractions to be found in the writings of his followers and those who would seek to 'understand' his thought. We are again, in other words, in the Bloomian territory of the history of reading as an increasing underdetermination of meaning and overdetermination of language. Or, as Yeats's Oisin realizes in returning from his 'wanderings', to re-enter history is to know 'how men sorrow and pass, / And their hound, and their horse, and their love, and their eyes that glimmer like silk.' (*CP*, p. 384)

Yet, however heterogeneous and dominant the 'dream' of a particular text seems to be (and in the case of Plato the texts command the whole history of philosophy), there are forces within the language of the text which maintain, Derrida says, 'a certain disorder, some potential incoherence'. The dominant law of Platonism has held for a certain time, but it has always contained, in the gaps or aporias in its coherence and language, the possibilities of its own deconstruction. It is in a text's 'general tone of denial' that anything other than itself can be true, a denial which generations of readers have had to train the ear and eye to perceive, that the text most exposes its undecidability. Such undecidability for Derrida, as for de Man, would seem to itself deny a reading of successive critiques as *history*, since they remain subject to doubt and tropology. In this, as in much else, de Man is clearly closer in his thinking to the insights of Derrida than to those of his Yale colleague Bloom. To translate this into the terms of my discussion above: Yeats's own reading of native *and* mainstream history as indecipherable for the colonial writer is itself subject to turns that alter and refocus his influence within other contexts.[66] Yet (and here the problems of theory's applicability to the local beginnings of the work itself arise again), at the heart of Derrida's theory of reading, as of Bloom's and de Man's, lies a seemingly compensatory impulse – every signature demands a counter-signature – which liberates the later reader, philosopher or critic into writing.

Derrida in fact accords literature an exemplary role in this training of the ear for tones of denial, since, as he says, 'literature can all the time play economically, elliptically, ironically' with the dissociation language enforces between a self and that self's use of 'I' to relate to itself in any utterance. In literature particularly 'I am always speaking about myself without speaking about myself'. Presence is not necessarily outside the text, but can only be posited within it, or, as Kristeva has put it, the desire inscribed in all texts 'designates the process of the subject's advent in the signifier'.[67]

For Derrida, therefore, philosophy at this stage of belatedness becomes an inadequate way of saying its own origins. The whole history of Platonism in the West from this perspective becomes a curiously arbitrary and dissimulating way of speaking about Plato, and, moreover, one subject to an entropic misprision which we are by now familiar with, whereby given a long enough time that history will itself be proved redundant. Derrida's deconstructive impulse is, to that extent, though, achieving an *opposite* result to the descent into repetition envisaged in literary history by other members of the Yale School, though not by Bloom himself.[68] Their free play of language within the materiality of the text is a result of overdetermination by, his a result of *liberty from*, the dominant discourses of textual history. Both share, however, a sense that reading is involved with the discovery of absences, uncertainties and gaps within the dominant discourse of the text, and attending to the repressions or self-referentiality which undo 'meaning'. For whatever philosophical, negatively theological, or literary-historical reasons, when rendered as the inevitable iterability within language influence becomes merely another unconscious aporia or gap, an arbitrary repetition which reveals nothing in itself, but makes us further aware of the text's literariness.

Yet again, however, Derrida has not gone into this abysm of emptied significance as some of his followers have, and in this his thought remains potentially valuable for a discussion of influence which wants to resist the historical and metaphysical implications of Bloom's model, which is so dependent upon the Sublime. In *On the Name*, Derrida has explored the recognition that the negative theology which deconstructive criticism represents is itself a response to a naming which must take place in order for it to be denied:

> *On the one hand* . . . the principle of negative theology, in a movement of internal rebellion, radically contests the tradition from which it seems to come. Principle against principle.
>
> But *on the other hand*, and in that very way, nothing is more faithful than this hyperbole to the originary ontotheological injunction. The *post-scriptum* remains a *countersignature*, even if it denies this. And, as in every human or divine signature, there the name is necessary [*il y faut le nom*].

In the final essay of his book, then, Derrida seeks a location from which that originary injunction might emanate, and (re-)discovers it, daringly, in a source which had been central to Julia Kristeva's discussions of such matters since the mid-Seventies.[69] 'Khora' (or, for, Kristeva 'Chora') was Plato's name in the *Timaeus* for the place or receptacle that lies *beyond* all binaries and oppositions such as that between 'logos' and 'mythos'. While 'Khora' (a female principle) possesses no qualities, neither is she reducible to the interpretations which have been made across history about her; 'she' is a source and a place which ultimately resides beyond all language and saying, who can only be glimpsed 'in a difficult, aporetical way and as if in a dream'.[70]

Similar possibilities of glimpsing a place or presence beyond all opposition in language have been engaged (in an ungendered way) by

Bloom's erstwhile Yale colleagues J. Hillis Miller and Paul de Man, in their considerations of the rhetorical trope of *prosopopoeia* – the giving of a face or personification to something which might be either (and this is the crux) missing *or* non-existent. Prosopopoeia resides in figurations such as 'the leg of a table', 'the eye of a storm', 'the back of the mountain'. In 'Hypogram and Inscription', de Man has described the problematics but also the poetic possibilities of the figure:

> in linguistic terms, it is impossible to say whether prosopopoeia is plausible because of the empirical existence of dreams and hallucinations or whether one believes that such a thing as dreams and hallucinations exist because language permits the figure of prosopopeia. ... Prosopopoeia undoes the distinction between reference and signification....
>
> The claim of all poetry to make the invisible visible is a figure to the precise extent that it undoes the distinction between sign and trope.[71]

Having glimpsed the possibility of escaping the binaries upon which his whole version of deconstructive criticism is based in this 'undoing', however, de Man retreats at the end of the essay from this notion of an indeterminability and hallucinatory element which defines poetry. He argues that, however prosopopeia might have been figured in a poetic text, the only thing that we can be certain has been revealed is the materiality of the text itself, its inscription. De Man seems to back down in the face of his own recognition, as he does also in his 1979 essay 'Autobiography as De-Facement'.

In his discussion of Wordsworth there, de Man sees prosopopoeia as positing both face *and* voice, that it is essentially 'the fiction of an apostrophe to an absent or voiceless entity, which posits the possibility of the latters's reply and confers upon it the power of speech'. Yet, again, such speech is, because of its very fictional and linguistic nature, 'accessible only in the privative way of understanding. Death is a placed name for a linguistic predicament'. Despite such regretful limitation and demurral, however, Derrida is surely right in his *Mémoires* to see in de Man's discussions of prosopopoeia 'the sovereign, secret, discrete and ideal signature' of his work, while also stating his own belief (one consonant with Yeats's), that 'this voice already haunts any said real or present voice'.[72]

The claim that what the figures of poetry do is to make the invisible visible, to bear the trace of khora in the text, underlies both the encounters and overcomings of Bloomian notions of influence, and also the methodology of a Yeatsian poetry of 'impress' and 'mummy truths'. As J. Hillis Miller has argued, it involves the process of reading in ultimate questions which can never be answered: 'Is it the face of a pre-existent other we encounter through the transport of literature or is that face only invoked by the performative spell of the work, charmed into phantasmal existence by words?' Whatever the answer, and whatever governs the intention of the poet, or the conjuring of the shadow of past writers within the present text, all writing is 'a resurrection and safe-guarding of the dead'.[73]

As ever, de Man himself casts such moments in the light of temporality, and his terms are useful in establishing a counterstrain to that note of embodiment which Miller strikes, which is a note truer to Romantic ambition (including Yeats's), perhaps, than to its achievement – for whatever personal, cultural and historical reasons. De Man argues, rather, that the past, both personal and literary, 'intervenes only as a purely formal element' in texts. Like works of art, it is *actually* irrecoverable. Memory is a 'constitutive act of the mind bound in its own present and oriented toward the future of its own elaboration'. It does not, therefore, establish relationships of temporal continuity, but is 'a deliberate act establishing a relation between two distinct points in time'.[74] Such 'deliberate acts' might be taken to characterize Yeats's poems in memory (in all senses). 'In Memory of Major Robert Gregory' and 'In Memory of Eva Gore-Booth and Con Markievicz', for example, both introject an idealized past, and project a future, through values solely inscribed in the poems' own rhetoric. Such 'deliberate acts' also constitute the haunting, shadowy nature of Yeatsian influence, both seemingly originary and (perhaps) not so; a voice particularly inflected and a voice simply of the past, of tradition. At moments modern or local, proximate and disturbing. At others, remote, abstract, knowable and 'known'.

Such ideas of coming-to-understanding through engagement with the tropology of texts suggest that the rhetorical figure of anagorisis might be set alongside that of prosopopoeia as being central to the work of literary influence. Anagorisis is the figure of recognition, of the dramatic recognition scene as Aristotle perceived it. Terence Cave has argued that, post-Hegel, the figure has been taken to describe the passage from ignorance to *self*-knowledge, and is integral to the recognitions which come to us through reading. The figure can be as disturbing as it is solving and resolving, seeming to bring identity and symmetry, but, in its sheer excessiveness, drawing attention to its own implausibility. It (sometimes tragically) questions our sense of kinship (through its origins in works like *Oedipus Rex*), while also founding and constituting (to adopt de Man's word) our coming to (self-)recognition within a family scene. Anagorisis might be taken, therefore, as a figure for Yeats's relation to his Anglo-Irish forebears, and also as one for the kinds of 'knowledge' and 'understanding' which belated poets enter into through conjuring the ghosts of their forebears. The word 'recognition' recurs many times in the close readings of my subsequent chapters.[75]

In terms of the ideas of this book, that history of the figure which Cave traces from an origin in dramatic narrative towards a vaguer modern self-recognition, might take on specific generic implications which I am anxious to follow in shaping my argument. Put differently, I wish to take *positively* de Man's reading of the distinction conferred upon lyric poetry by its recourse to prosopopoeia, and also the force of that contrast between dramatic and lyric form which, Bloom has argued, developed after Shakespeare: 'As poetry has become more subjective, the shadow cast by the precursors has become more dominant'.[76] If the 'shadow' is revealed through (ghostly) *encounter* rather than Bloomian struggle, and if the 'particular exaggeration of style or hyperbolical figuration' (which Bloom claims that 'tradition' locates in the Sublime) is also returned to its context in historical and cultural circumstance, then the reading of a Yeatsian *traditio* of influence since his death becomes again a possibility, whatever paradigms of overdetermination are set against it.

That historical and cultural circumstance inevitably involves a sense of *poetic form* as the scene of encounter. Bloom's concentration upon tropes of crossing and translation makes him inattentive to formal issues generally; de Man's dismissal of formalist criticism chimes in with the characteristically deconstructive strain in his approach:

> All formalistic theories of poetry sooner or later have to confront a similar problem: their adequation to the phenomenally realized aspects of their topic makes them highly effective as a descriptive discipline, but at the cost of understanding. A monument, per definition, is self-sufficient; it can at most be contemplated but it exists independently of its beholder, even and especially when it houses his mortal remains. Formalism, in other words, can only produce a stylistics (or a poetics) and not a hermeneutics of literature, and it remains deficient in trying to account for the relationship between these two approaches.[77]

Yet Yeats's theory of 'tradition' and poetic practice would surely disprove this. The 'understanding' which poets make of themselves and of their position in the enunciation is partly gained through deployment of particular forms that carry particular expectations, meanings and resonances from the past.[78] As will become clear in my discussion of American poetry from the generation emerging just after the Second World War, for example, experience of familial and cultural dispossession is mediated through adoption of a specific Yeats-inflected form which registers the disorientations of the speaker's position, while at the same time encapsulating a yearning towards settledness and security. Form, as empty shell or vacant room, is unspeaking. But, when deployed and re-read within literary history, it raises the ghosts of earlier inhabiters of the same patterns. It is Yeats's formal variety and alertness to traditional echoes which makes him often exemplary for later poets who pick up and amplify those echoes, in ways that Eliot's and Pound's adoption of *vers libre* has prevented their work from doing.

A further difficulty with applying these theoretical approaches to the reading of specific poems arises in the relation of style to influence. Bloom's practice of setting a single poem by a precursor against one by an *ephebe* works to foreground the rhetoric of sublimity to the exclusion of all others.[79] The deconstructive emphasis upon the indeterminability of language within iterability detracts from any formalist or descriptive discussion of style, the excessive nature of which in Yeats's case acts as both allure and reason for resistance in later poets. Intertextuality works here, rather, to diffuse and resist the location or naming of precursors for belated styles, something that poets have themselves been anxious to do. That work of naming ('our part / To murmur name on name' (*CP*, p. 181)), naming as integral to processes of abstraction as reading, will form a central focus for the book.

Yet, *pace* Bloom, it is often of course the case that literary influence is a multiple process, with several precursors being encountered within a single text. It will, however, be one of the ambitions of this book to dissociate a specifically *Yeatsian* influence from the other possible ones coming down from the first part of the century, and to that extent I have had to avoid prolonged discussion of other precursors. (In addition, Yeatsian features, as James Longenbach has proven, frequently emerge behind 'characteristic' works by Pound and Eliot themselves.)[80] The word or name 'Yeats' might not be imbued with absolute presence as conveyer of certain kinds of truths which are *guaranteed* to be translated to later audiences. Much falls away in the process of transmission and retransmission across time and cultural spaces, in other words of reading and re-reading of his work.

Yet it is only through consideration of the ways in which the writing that appears under that name has variously been refigured in later work that we can begin to understand the parameters which the name 'Yeats' might be working within. The kinds of abstraction, in Derridean terms, which his texts both govern and foresee, as well as the kinds of abstraction from which they are formed. Reading Yeats through the poets he has influenced is another way of re-reading Yeats himself, setting him in different lights and cultural contexts. By reading back through the history of that influence, we can come to a greater understanding of the history of cultural exchange, the forces governing it and the re-readings it requires in response to other historical forces and circumstances across the century. So, for example, as a result of abstractions from that influence in English poetry immediately before and after World War Two (when there was a retrenchment and wariness about stylistic hyperbole because of its possible alignment with extreme politics which caused the war), a reading of Yeats as offering a 'civic' style and concomitant social model emerges. More recently, when that retrenchment started to ease, other poets could take up different characteristic strains in his work, such as the chthonic and the mythological.

Further, and in keeping with the often indeterminate Yeatsian and Bloomian notion of influence as what the latter has called 'facticity', I will discuss works where the trace of Yeats's influence is detectable either despite the authors' actual denial of it or in their silence around the issue. Out of these discussions, I hope, will emerge the features of a Yeatsian face within later lyric poetry. My selection of poetry for discussion, which could never be exhaustive or encyclopaedic in a book of this length, has largely been made to illustrate the generally-shared view in each context of what those features are, and to reveal how, through processes of translation and re-translation, they have become increasingly set, 'known', and *readable*.

The Yeatsian face as it is glimpsed in Britain, Ireland and America has appeared in forms which include elegies, love poems, poems of national founding; poems of debate about the relationship of the aesthetic to the pattern of a life, dialogue poems, poems voiced through personae and antithetical masks, as well as 'occasional', civic or political poems. Centrally, such features further the work of mourning (not least of mourning Yeats himself). Mourning as the personal attempt to internalize a (lost) past, absent from the founding work of modernist poetry, only to appear belatedly in Eliot's *Four Quartets* and Pound's *Pisan Cantos*, texts within and behind which Yeats forms a significant ghostly shadow. The greater presence beyond Ireland of his specific influence in Britain and America rather than (as yet) in other anglophone cultures which have suffered colonization is notable. It perhaps suggests that the governing continuity of a Romantic tradition he alternately tunes into and defeatedly yearns for itself provides the ground for more suggestible receptivity of his characteristic poetic figures and debates.[81]

In deliberately choosing to concentrate principally upon those poets who have either made themselves or significantly *remade* themselves after Yeats's own death in 1939, I have sought to explore the resonances and implications of his final acts of self-remaking and questioning. Questioning around, not least, that notion of reincarnation and resurrection which figures so strongly within both versions of *A Vision*, but which is contradictorily present and denied in 'Under Ben Bulben' and 'Man and the Echo'. Such late poems, along of course with 'The Circus Animals' Desertion', become inscriptions of that indeterminacy and indecipherability which lies at the heart of Yeats's difficult mediation of Romantic inheritance to later work. It is only *after death* that the features of the face become clear, loved and knowable, as they become unknown. It is only after death, as Derrida claims from within his particular debates, that the work of giving and handing on can begin, that the time for it to happen becomes possible.[82]

In the chapters that follow, therefore, I will be deploying a Bloom-informed and part-Derridean discussion of influence, and, where appropriate, I will draw on de Man's particular translation of Derridean speculation into the realm of poetic criticism. I will also remain alert to the ways in which literary influence marks a recontextualization of a particular text within history; it is through literary influence that history speaks back to itself and relocates itself. No-one, at this late stage, would claim that it was possible to recover or resurrect an originary context in its plenitude. To a certain extent, the underdetermination of what we might take as Yeatsian 'meaning' and its historical and cultural motivation is evident in retransmissions and retranslations of his rhetoric, style and preoccupations across the twentieth century. Yet I hope that at each stage an adequate notion of the governing features and forces behind each re-reading and re-nuancing of the original impulse will come across, and that out of that notion might arise a reading of the century from a Yeatsian perspective.

2
'The Terror of his Vision': Yeats and Irish Poetry

Louis MacNeice, Austin Clarke, Patrick Kavanagh, Brian Coffey, Padraic Fallon, Thomas Kinsella, Seamus Heaney, Derek Mahon, Eavan Boland, Paul Muldoon

The challenge of Yeats's work to subsequent writers in Ireland was, for obvious reasons, more immediate than that felt elsewhere. If, as Harold Bloom has characteristically maintained, the 'strength' of a poem is dependent upon its repression of anterior work which is 'almost present in it, or nearest to presence in it', then within his native culture that repression takes on a particular, potentially disturbing inflection.[1] His own ambition to found a nationally distinctive cultural tradition (*'Enfin Yeats vint'* as John Montague has put it)[2] raises urgent issues of appropriation or rejection.

This is especially the case since his later distance from the actualities of life in the new Republic – itself complicated further by his Anglo-Irish heritage – necessarily provoked charged and divergent responses from later writers. His particular reactions to contemporary event, simultaneous establishment of himself (most famously with 'Easter 1916') as national remembrancer, as well as his later visionary preoccupations in despite of the Civil War, have offered both potentially liberating models and, conversely, points of violent disagreement at various times. 'Yeats', as complex founding symbol for a distinctively Irish poetic style, raises issues of identity and identification, communally, politically, aesthetically and in terms of religion amongst writers living in his aftermath on his native soil.

That symbol has also offered a crucial, form-giving example of the possibility for self-remaking within a poet's career which, as will be discussed, forms a central theme of later Irish poets' work. His own self-divisions and changes of style and direction, from the Celtic Twilight period through to the more self-consciously modern writing from *Responsibilities* (1914) onwards, followed by the visionary work of the 1920s and the self-questionings of *Last Poems*, are mirrored in some of the subsequent poetry's perplexities and self-revisions. As Julia Kristeva has pointed out, a symbol is never a single thing – *symbol* is itself etymologically founded upon scission. It is an 'always split unification that is produced by a rupture and is impossible without it'. The mark of this split is the 'break between signifier and signified', while the *symbolic* is a 'sign of recognition' or anagorisis in which we can see the separate parts brought together.[3] Within subsequent Irish writing, from North and South, 'Yeats' stands very much as such a symbol of splits and breaks – between self and nation, between the traditionally-conceived nation and modernity, between hieratic style and the quotidian life of Irish people, for example.

Within this particular inheritance, there seems also a notable, historically-induced and locally-inflected, attention to the kinds of concern which Paul de Man's fragmentary theorizing has explored: the survival of a Romantic problematics within modern poetic and critical texts. The temporality of poetry remains, in de Man's view, convergent with that of the historian 'to the extent that they both speak of an action that precedes them but that exists for consciousness only because of their intervention'. Yet, at the same time, poetry is preoccupied with its rhythms and language to the extent that 'intervention', like every 'deed, word, thought, or text' is, de Man argues, 'a random event whose power, like the power of death, is due to the randomness of its occurrence'.[4]

Within a colonized or newly postcolonial context and inheritance, where randomness and violence are constants within the individual's experience, the question of the relation between text and historical circumstance is continually raised in more recent poetry, as it had been by Yeats himself. Conversely, the desire which was also his, towards envisaging a site of integration and peaceful unity, often through 'resolution' of 'conflicts' within the symbolic space of the poem, is equally strong. Poetry's intervention in this historical and cultural context, and in the immediate context of Yeatsian inheritance, exerts this twin pull towards 'history' and towards 'vision'. As a result, the poetry itself often becomes a conflictual site, a very momentary stay against confusion.

Because of such pressures, later Irish poets have found themselves in imagination returning again and again to the symbolic site of instruction which is Thoor Ballylee, the Norman Castle which Yeats bought in 1917 and which formed the centring-point for his writing from the 1921 *Michael Robartes and the Dancer* through to the 1933 *The Winding Stair and Other Poems*. As an early poem on the tower, 'To Be Carved on a

Stone at Thoor Ballylee', reveals, Yeats was alert to the transient nature of the site of writing he was founding for himself, but also to the comparative durability of text in contrast to that of masonry ('may these characters remain / When all is ruin once again.') (*CP*, p. 190). And yet, as subsequent poems make clear, the fractured history of 'this tumultuous spot' is something which Yeats is anxiously attentive to, as characterizing the nature of the art to be produced there, particularly once civil war broke out in Ireland in 1922–3.

'My House', the second of the 'Meditations in Time of Civil War', forms both contrast and continuity to the first, 'Ancestral Houses', in which 'violence' and 'bitterness' are the bases upon which ordered architectural beauty and the aristocracy's 'self-delight' in life are 'reared'. 'My House' rises upon 'An acre of stony ground / Where the symbolic rose can break in flower', a highly equivocal, vulnerable, and fractious reviewing of his earlier symbolic system. Now, in continuation with the tower's equally beleaguered founder, Yeats must discover in this place 'Befitting emblems of adversity' – of which the tower, of course, outside whose walls war was raging, was the principal emblem. (*CP*, pp. 201–3) Here it was, also, that he fulfilled that quest for a personal symbolism which had been given impetus with the 1917 *Per Amicae Silentia Lunae* and which was to issue in *A Vision*, 'The Great Wheel' section of which was 'Finished at Thoor Ballylee, 1922, in a time of Civil War'. (*AV*, p. 184) The historically and personally determining 'system' which that book describes then underwrites much of Yeats's later poetry. As he wrote in 1927 to T. Sturge Moore, who was designing the cover for the volume *The Tower* which was to appear the next year:

> I like to think of that building as a permanent symbol of my work plainly visible to the passer-by. As you know, all my art theories depend upon just this – rooting of mythology in the earth.[5]

The dual nature of the tower – as both retreat from contemporary event and challenge to it, as both resistant masonry and permeable membrane, as place of writing which reveals its own history, and as originary or 'founded' – resonates through much later Irish poetry. It is both symbol and haven, but also and at the same time a threat of over-burdening, irrepressible presence and completion which, as Derrida has argued within his own discussions of Romantic inheritance, render all subsequent writing mere iteration.

These questions of identification, resistance, and evaluation of the inheritance were, of course, particularly pressing for Irish poets around the time of Yeats's death and again in 1965, the centenary of his birth. In the process of elegizing and eulogizing him, they were forced to look again at their own earlier readings of his work, and also, as a result, to review their sense of the nature and worth of poetry itself, in the national context, at that time. In 1939 particularly, when performing the public and formalized work of mourning through obituaries, poems, or reviews of *Last Poems and Plays* (which appeared in June 1939, about five months after Yeats's death), poets were forced to declare their own sense of his founding project.

Those immediate declarations, their processes of reading the various splittings in Yeats's symbolic presence, then resonate across all subsequent discussions of his influence – and across subsequent Irish poetry itself. As a consequence, in the early sections of this chapter, I want to gather some immediate and divergent responses and interventions following the random event of his death, responses from Louis MacNeice (1907–1963), Austin Clarke (1896–1974) and Patrick Kavanagh (1904–1967), and to discuss the impact of those responses upon these poets' later work. In later sections, once the moment of proximate mourning has passed, I will adopt a chronology (which will be followed throughout the rest of the book) based upon date of each poet's birth.

I

Louis MacNeice's book-length study, *The Poetry of W.B. Yeats*, which was begun in August 1939 (just after the publication of *Last Poems*), and which was published in February 1941,[6] represents the most sustained immediate response to the older poet's career, now that its entire shape and final self-questionings could be seen. The study found its impetus and purpose in both private and public impulses. 'I wished to find out why Yeats appealed to me so much', MacNeice tells us in the 'Preface': 'In a world . . . where the bulk of criticism is destructive, I feel that to express and, if possible, to explain one's admiration for a particular poet is something worth doing.' Yet that expression of admiration immediately translates itself in MacNeice's prose into a wider context, as he continues:

It is perhaps particularly worth doing at this moment when external circumstances are making such a strong assault on our sense of values. . . . If war is the test of reality, then all poetry is unreal; but in that case unreality is a virtue.[7]

Just as Yeats himself retreated into his tower in order to assert the paradoxical 'sweetness' of cultural or artistic artifacts, and to develop the symbolic 'system' which brought 'pattern' to contemporary violent events, MacNeice at the start of World War Two concentrated himself upon the celebration of 'value' he discovered in Yeats.

Yet MacNeice does not immediately develop in the book the theme of poetry and violence, as he would do in a review of *Last Poems*.[8] Rather, his celebration 'at this moment' notably involved MacNeice in a revision of his own earlier notion of poetry as being properly devoid of mysticism, as he asserted in his 1938 book *Modern Poetry*. Rather, he now recognizes, the poet shares with the 'ordinary man' a 'mystical sanction or motivation' in all of his 'activities which are not purely utilitarian' – activities amongst which MacNeice characteristically includes bathing and dancing, alongside the more immediately aesthetic ones such as looking at pictures. Yeats's own visionary concerns in Thoor Ballylee across those years of civil war seem to have directly led, then, to MacNeice's own discovery of further spiritual possibilities in this later time of violence. Yet MacNeice is concerned to sustain within this new aesthetic that 'impurity' which he had sought to celebrate in the earlier book, a sense that poetry is 'conditioned by the poet's life and the world around him.' 'Value', as it is asserted in that book, is worldly and potentially local; 'the only invulnerable Universal is one that is incarnate . . . value [is] inseparable from . . . existence'.[9]

As such, the path of Yeats's career that MacNeice maps is that of a movement towards a value which can mediate between 'unreal' worth and the 'impurities' of the moment. Yeats's origins in an essentially English, Paterian aestheticism of the Nineties, associated by MacNeice with an extreme form of Romanticism, were overcome within a more realistic modernity in the later work. What forces this change in Yeats's work, as MacNeice sees it here and elsewhere, is his Irishness, 'his orientation towards Ireland, who was herself accepted for her romantic and aesthetic possibilities, but who gave Yeats something other than he was looking for'.[10] Yeats's nationalism, and the historical course his country took across his writing lifetime, forced adaptability upon the poet which brought him closer to modern realities.

So, in the later pages of his book, MacNeice makes it clear that it is Yeats's stance towards the modern 'chaotic world' which makes him a valuable example to more recent poets like himself, and also to the English poets Auden, Day Lewis and Spender. He echoes Yeats's own opinion of the subsequent generation to his own, contained in essays like 'A General Introduction for my Work' and the Introduction to his

Oxford Book of Modern Verse, in accusing Eliot of 'a feminine conception of poetry', one which is passive towards experience. Rather, MacNeice asserts, 'it is the poet's job to make sense of the world', not to reflect its disorder. The 1930s poets, in reverting to regular metrical and stanza patterns against the *vers libre* innovation of the modernists, were simplifying and 'putting a shape' to the world as they found it, not allowing it to overrun their work.[11]

Yeats's national identity seems to play a defining, if shadowy, role in MacNeice's reading of his poetry, therefore. On the one hand, identification with his nation brought Yeats back to having to write about the situation in his times. It took him away from an essentially *English* aestheticism into a realistic modernity in which he shared much with his younger contemporaries (MacNeice discusses the diction and literariness shared by Yeats and Eliot). On the other hand, Yeats's systematic thought, evident not only in *A Vision*, but more immediately in the stylistic and formal procedures of his work, sets him apart from the disorderly characteristics of that very modernity. As 'Ego Dominus Tuus' saw it, modernity is equivalent to an egotism which has lost the 'old nonchalance' of creativity and the power to create 'masks'. (*CP*, pp. 160–2) And yet, for MacNeice, that very systematic thought offers a form of engagement which holds good for later committed, but unaligned, poets like MacNeice himself. On this reading, Yeats's formalism derives from a deep reading of the history of his personal situation and that of his times, but is not dependent upon it. Hence, for MacNeice, his more general and translatable value, when compared to the immediate and unmediated responsiveness of such as Eliot.

At the root of such dual identification of trends in Yeats's work lies, as Edna Longley has pointed out, the 'dialectical structure' of MacNeice's own imagination.[12] As he wrote in 'Dublin' (the opening poem of the 1939 sequence 'The Closing Album' which is overshadowed, as the Yeats book is, by the beginning of international hostilities), 'She is not an Irish town, / And she is not an English'.[13] That being-caught between opposed possible identifications marks MacNeice's Anglo-Irishness, and also establishes the essentially dramatic nature of his writing, as it had that of the older poet.

However, Yeats's continuing and various influence would seem to have made the locatable 'value' in his work around the relationship between 'life' and 'art' or 'vision' and 'history', as it is conceived in the critical book on him, more troubling in MacNeice's own poetry, particularly at times of historical crisis. Although in post-war poems, such as 'The Window' of October 1948, MacNeice could cautiously proclaim the paradoxically oppositional continuities between the two poles of art and 'impurity' ('Yet that which art gleaning, congealing, / Sets in antithesis to life / Is what in living we lay claim to'), the run-up-to-the-war immediacy of the 1938 *Autumn Journal* had delineated a Yeatsian disjunction between them, and a concomitant envy:

> Nightmare leaves fatigue:
>> We envy men of action
> Who sleep and wake, murder and intrigue
>> Without being doubtful, without being haunted.
> And I envy the intransigence of my own
>> Countrymen who shoot to kill and never
> See the victim's face become their own
>> Or find his motive sabotage their motives.
> So reading the memoirs of Maud Gonne,
>> Daughter of an English mother and a soldier father,
> I note how a single purpose can be founded on
>> A jumble of opposites:
> Dublin castle, the vice-regal ball,
>> The embassies of Europe,
> Hatred scribbled on a wall,
>> Gaols and revolvers.[14]

Yet such envy, for MacNeice, leads not to the founding of a single purpose in his own political identity, but founders rather on the violent chaos of his country itself ('both a bore and a bitch'), in which a sacrificial heroic nationalism leads nowhere: 'Griffith, Connolly, Collins, where have they brought us? / Ourselves alone!'

But, such is the variousness of MacNeice's own thinking, that he does not rest in the inaction that the rebuttal of such envies on his native soil might imply. Like Yeats's delighted identification of himself with the man-at-arms who founded his tower and concomitant envy of the soldiers fighting the civil war, MacNeice celebrates the necessary connectedness which comes from activity: 'Aristotle was right to think of man-in-action / as the essential and really existent man / . . . Nothing is self-sufficient'. Such recognitions then seem to generate that damning of 'tight and narrow' England which follows in the next section, a condemnation as vituperative as that of Ireland earlier.[15]

MacNeice's dialectical, oppositional identity emerges at this level as both a critical capacity and a self-critical one. He is unwilling to remain within a single position or location while at the same time he recognizes the allure of other possibilities and points of view. But that capacity is modulated also by the variousness which comes from his reading of Yeats's career, and the sense that even the critical systematizing capacity within poetic form has to be open to historical change. As the tour-de-force 'Plurality', itself dating from August 1940, has it,

> You talk of Ultimate Value, Universal Form –
> Visions, let me tell you, that ride upon the storm
> And must be made and sought but cannot be maintained . . .
> No, perfection means
> Something but must fall unless there intervenes
> Between that meaning and the matter it should fill
> Time's revolving hand that never can be still.
> Which being so and life a ferment, you and I
> Can only live by strife in that the living die . . . .

The onward rush of history itself seems to redeem an aspiration in humanity for perfection and universality, which would become redundant without adaptability. The artistic desire to 'transcend and flout the human span' becomes symptomatic of the nature of a humanity 'mad with discontent', a discontent which is directly responsive to the changes wrought by time. Time operates in MacNeice, as it does in Yeats, as a disruptive, disintegrative force. Yet such consciousness of 'the power / of going beyond and above' is itself part of plurality, which includes the countervailing awareness that, for the individual, time will stop. As the last lines of this poem put it, we are:

> Conscious of sunlight, conscious of death's inveigling touch,
> Not completely conscious but partly – and that is much.[16]

In Yeats's *Last Poems*, 'Man and the Echo', 'The Gyres', and 'Cuchulain Comforted' would seem to qualify or revise his earlier faith in reincarnation. Here, MacNeice also sets death as a equivocal limit to 'plurality'. Our partial consciousness of it both forms another possibility and also a haunting border beyond which we, and the poem, cannot go. The final word, 'much', in its fullness resonates back across, and paradoxically empties out, plurality's former plenitude. As a result, MacNeice seems to accept the 'strife' raging around him and personally threatening him at the time of the poem's writing as an essential part of 'Time''s actions within the world. As with late Yeats also, however, that acceptance is formative of 'style and attitude'.

Yeats's ability to clear-sightedly envisage that situation renders the 'tragic scene' itself a ground for 'gaiety', which, as 'Lapis Lazuli' figures it 'I / Delight to imagine'. (*CP*, p. 295) 'World / Is more spiteful and gay than one supposes', as MacNeice puts it in 'Snow'. His delight in variousness is ultimately a version of that 'zest' which he celebrates, in the poems of Yeats's old age, towards the end of *The Poetry of W.B. Yeats.* Many of his own later poems (including 'The Truisms', 'Soap Suds', 'Round the Corner', 'The Taxis' and 'As in Their Time'), move towards that 'peculiar genre – somewhere between epigram and nursery rhyme' which he discovers in Yeats from 'Crazy Jane' onwards; a deceptively light verse which carries 'the same passion and the same ideas that he uttered elsewhere *ex cathedra*'.[17]

Underpinning MacNeice's haunted variousness, then, is a speeded-up version of Romantic tropes of adjustment and compensation, that 'constant modulation from the elegiac...to...praise' which Paul de Man has identified as one of the central features of writing in the Romantic tradition.[18] One result of his increasing move towards a 'peculiar' Yeatsian seeming-nonsense verse, from the 1940 'Autobiography' onwards, is a greater highlighting of this constant interchange. In 'The grey ones' of 1961, for instance, the 'three grey sisters' (clearly some version of the Fates) 'share an eye':

> ... Every such what and where betwixt
> Your fact and fancy stands transfixed
> By that one unremitting stare
> Which cancels what you never were,
>
> Who might have been a prince of Troy,
> A lord of song, a roaring boy,
> Or might have been an idiot mild,
> Who meets his match in every child....[19]

And so on. This syntax of flux, seen first in the 1927 'River in Spate' and instrumental in MacNeice's constantly-shifting and cumulative writing throughout, here issues in a determinist vision which paradoxically (as in the Romantic tradition and in Yeats's visionary 'system') opens the way to yet further imaginings. The final line of the first stanza quoted here is redeemed from its shockingly double negativity ('cancels what you never were') by the brave expression of the possibilities of what 'you' also never were. Those possibilities then in their turn run immediately towards trauma and difficulty by the end of the second stanza.

The inescapability of the nightmarish staring eye checking 'the client next to die' paradoxically makes for the resolutely fairytale imagery and rhythms.

In his 1940 review of *Last Poems*, 'Yeats's Epitaph', MacNeice claimed that:

> Physical violence being a simple thing, the Yeats who honoured it took to writing in ballad forms, while the contemplative Yeats continued to use a grand rhetorical manner and a complex inlay of esoteric ideas and images....[20]

That impact of the reality of the violent physical world upon poetic form, evident in the sudden switches of direction in the contemporaneous 'Plurality' as in the 'peculiar genre' of MacNeice's later writing, is, however, finally unmatched for him by a Yeatsian 'esoteric' possibility. Yet he also sustains a 'critical' stance to contemporary history, and a Romantic awareness of the end to which such violence might lead. Ireland is never so singularly prominent in MacNeice's writing as it was in Yeats, and therefore at this level the measures of the poetry's contact with that 'reality' are less easy to define. His reading of Yeats proffers an identification through origins which his own writing seems to eschew; in consequence, the focus of his own poetry seems paradoxically much more inward-looking, concerned with its own procedures and antinomies within a syntactic continuum.

As a result, his poetry displays a greater allegorizing 'rhetoric of temporality', in which the sign immediately refers 'to another sign that precedes it' – a reference which displays the trace of a true, insightful Romanticism, in de Man's reading of it. Yeats's more discontinuous attention to the relation between sign and meaning, and concomitant dream of Unity of Being and Culture to be captured in the *symbolic* figuration of his poetry, leads him to a kind of blindness which is also a possibility. It is a blindness in which the generic opposites of the ballad and the 'grand rhetorical manner' are somehow reconcilable in ways that MacNeice, as Yeats's primary (Anglo-) Irish poetic reader cannot pursue in his own poetry.[21] As such, the 'value' of MacNeice's writing resides in its variousness, its distance from (and, perhaps, its resultingly greater flexibility in approach to) locating 'reality', whatever its origins – its open acceptance that language is always separate, and poetic language, within its particular syntax, especially so. What he identifies as the salvation of Yeats's work, its nationalist ambition, would be fatal to his own late version of Romanticism.

II

Austin Clarke, whose own poetry found its idiom in the Gaelic tradition, seems to have been stirred by Yeats's death into reviewing the relationship between writing and modernity, as MacNeice had been. But Clarke took a more sceptical line than MacNeice's when it came to viewing the impact of that modernity upon notions of identity and Irish nationhood. For MacNeice, Yeats's value for subsequent writers largely derived from his experience of violence and 'reality' on his native ground. For Clarke (as also for Yeats in some modes), modernity threatens Irish values and also clouds possibilities for national identification.

As his obituary essay for Yeats argues, even when Yeats's style changed after he was fifty (i.e. at the time of *Responsibilities*) and became more acceptably 'English', 'that individual Anglo-Irish note which one finds in Burke and Grattan' is sustained, together with something of 'the earlier *tremuli*'. In this later work, though, Clarke finds only 'a suggestion of a dark revolutionary Ireland'; 'Yeats's attitude to home rule in Irish letters in his later years is somewhat of a mystery.' Here, as elsewhere in his critical prose, Clarke seems to see the internationalizing of Yeats himself – his influence upon the modernism of Eliot and Pound and adoption of a 'barren dry style' – as concurrent with an ending of a particular epoch of Irish attitudes and writing.

The modernization of Ireland itself means that 'In these days of our new materialistic ... state, poetry will have a harder, less picturesque task' than it had for Yeats. As such, it is the task of native writers to look to local continuities, since Clarke asserts that in Ireland 'the artistic tradition of the literary revival has not been broken'. Yeats can only therefore be 'an imaginative incitement and great example rather than an influence'. What emerges from Clarke's re-articulation of the nature of Yeats's impact upon later Irish writing, then, is a troubled sense of the relationship between the modernity which was becoming an economic reality in the country, and a more lyrical native strain, which the older poet's own 1890s writing had tuned into. Yeats's death, for Clarke, marks the end of an epoch, a 'silence which is painful to contemplate', as he concludes his obituary. [22]

His own early attempts to draw upon the Gaelic inheritance in order to bring new musical possibilities to his English versions of Irish myths – as in his 1917 'The Vengeance of Fionn' – gave way by the mid-fifties to satirical comments on contemporary Irish life more in the manner of the later Yeats of the Hugh Lane controversy. But interestingly Clarke's poetic encounters with the shade of Yeats after his death tended to seek to resolve the conflicts between traditionalism and modernism characteristic of the prose tributes in a very Yeatsian fashion. The seeming monumentalizing, and anguished, regretful consigning-to-history of the earlier poet in the obituary, for instance, govern the antithetical and contrastingly ironic responses Clarke made to the 1951 fire at the Abbey Theatre in two poems collected six years apart.

In the 1957 collection *Too Great A Vine*, Clarke had seemed to reflect enmity – an enmity which he felt towards Yeats when the older poet disdained to put any of the younger's work in his *Oxford Book of Modern Verse* – in combination with a vision of Yeats as an extra-historical figure:

> Forgetting our age, he waved and raved
> Of Art and thought her Memory's daughter.
> Those firemen might have saved their water.

The aestheticism and classicism of the Yeatsian pose are set alongside a difficult-to-date sense of Yeats's neglect of his (Irish?) age. As a result, Clarke sees the fire as Time bringing in its revenges. But, in the later poem also called 'The Abbey Theatre Fire', from the 1963 *Flight to Africa*, Clarke forgets 'his' enmity, and details the work his own theatre company had done to keep alive the plays of Yeats in the theatre itself. The older poet's otherworldliness is as a result treated benignly, and history treated as a scene of haphazard pathos: 'Yeats had not dreamed an unstubbed butt, / Ill match, would bring his curtain down', the poem concludes.[23]

A similar note echoes through Part II of the 1965 'A Centenary Tribute: W.B. Yeats', in which Clarke takes up the theme of some of the Coole Park poems in viewing Yeats's own last house at Riversdale and the modernizations made to it, 'improvements' which the poet would have hated. The poem moves towards a wished-for other time, in which such contemporary changes might be overturned:

> Some night, perhaps, the Great Mood
> Will change all in a dream: the house restored,
> Old mortar used again by it as in a story
> That Sato's sword might glitter at the moon.[24]

The elision of two houses, in the transplantation of a central symbol associated with Thoor Ballylee into this house, once more establishes the houses' inhabitant as embodier of a tradition against troubling times, rather than, as in the Abbey fire poems, as a variously-scrutinized monument. Yet, we cannot help but note, the Romantic afflatus of the compensatory ending, its awkward manipulation of key Yeatsian furniture from moods to moons, suggests the fadedness of the tradition itself, its failure to compensate for, and its inability as symbol of perfect presence, to address change.

Whatever the efficacy and importance of Clarke's satires, their bold outspokenness against a Catholic-dominated Irish state in which the taboos of the past are causing frustration and even death amongst those living in the present (as in 'The Pill'), the materialism and lack of fixity in modernity clash for him with poetry's integrational essence. As a result, there increasingly comes into Clarke's work a radical splitting of genres, in which these two forces of satire and symbolic 'resolution' cannot be held alongside each other, as they had been by Yeats from 'September 1913' to 'The Municipal Gallery Revisited'. Clarke's poetry eventually splits between a harsh, Swiftian rage against modernity and a violently Romantic, 1890s, otherworldliness which is palely set against the 'filthy modern tide'. The late poems, including the 1971 'Tiresias', lapse into a classicized eroticism which is unmixed with that galvanic rage which kept Yeats's later 'lustful' poems ever-various.

The dilemma with which the legacy of Yeats confronts Clarke, then, seems to be an unresolved confusion between history, as conceived as a finished entity, and modernity, in which that pastness is either rendered questionable, or in which it has to stand as a Romantically compensatory possibility. The sheer 'complexity' of Yeats seems to defeat Clarke, and self-consciously so. It serves to render his work and the path of his career a fractured imitation of the older poet's, an imitation in which the issue of Irish identity in writing itself remains undeterminably unclear.

III

A more salutary possibility for the Yeatsian inheritance within Irish writing than that translatability immediately recognized by MacNeice, or that overburdened nostalgia which dominated Clarke's work, is perhaps offered by two opposing figures in the generation after Yeats's. That possibility is one, however, which accepts the splitting of the inheritance, rather than seeming to reconcile its conflicting strands. Patrick Kavanagh was immediately responsive to Yeats's death, and Yeats was a central figure in his definition of a distinctive national 'parochialism' to set against modernizing trends both in Ireland and beyond. Contrarily, Brian Coffey (1905–95), whose work I will discuss in the next section, was from early influenced by modernist experimentalism which made him personally and poetically resistant to Yeats. Yet, at a key moment in his career, Yeats becomes a crucial figure in Coffey's debates with himself about modernity and locatability, and so offers a different perspective upon national identity in international contexts.

Kavanagh's difficult engagement with the older poet was often concentrated, though fractiously, around issues of class and national identity. In his centenary tribute, 'Yeats', from the 1966 *The Holy Door*, the begrudging note is still to be heard in his response: 'Yes, Yeats, it was damn easy for you protected / By the middle classes and the Big Houses / To talk about the sixty-year old public protected / Man'.[25] The centrality of Yeats within the national consciousness is envied by the belated poet, who cannot command the same attention, and as a result fears for the sources of his inspiration. 'I Had a Future', as the ironic title of a 1952 poem has it; 'He's finished and that's definitely' is the mischievious-but-felt last line of the 1963 'The Same Again'. Kavanagh's own resultant position of recessiveness is signalled in the 1938 'Snail' (a precursor of Paul Muldoon's 'Hedgehog'), in which the elusiveness of the persona is explored:

> I go from you, I recede,
> Not by steps violent
> But as a snail backing
> From the lewd finger of humanity.[26]

The mildness of this seems itself a rebuff to the later Yeats's interest in the relationship between violent action and artistic creation. The speaker of this poem has a fragile, 'twisted habitation', not a Norman Tower. And yet the disdainful, almost puritanical shrinking away from the 'lewd finger' is not itself dissimilar from the Yeatsian distaste for the masses.[27] 'A poet is never one of the people. He is detached, remote . . . A poet has to have an audience – half a dozen or so', as Kavanagh asserts in his prose 'Self Portrait'. Or, in the memorial essay 'William Butler Yeats', 'I am not one of those who think that a brilliant poet should be accessible to the ordinary people.'[28] For all his parochialism and fellowship with his County Monaghan 'folk', therefore, Kavanagh shares Yeats's Romantic sense of the election of the poet and of the necessary difficulty of the craft in which they are mutually involved.

As a result of such feelings, Kavanagh's comments on Yeats attack the pose ('Insincerity is boring. Masks are boring', as he wrote in 'Signposts'), but also seek to extricate him from his own self-delusions and also his deluded nationalism ('He would have abandoned the anaemic world of petty nationalism...if he had been great').[29] In the essay 'Nationalism and Literature', Kavanagh suggests that the pose and the desire to be part of that 'anaemic world' are inextricably linked. Attacking the myth of Ireland as a place in which creative artists might uniquely thrive, he argues that 'nationalism is seldom based on those sincerities' necessary to the 'spiritual force' of art. Elsewhere, Yeats's attempt to link his art to a national identity is related by Kavanagh to his uncertain status within the country itself, due to his divided inheritance:

> there is one facet of the poet's life that few people have discussed – his desperate desire to be thought Irish and one of the People. Nobody will deny that he was Irish of a certain kind...yet he himself was always conscious of being something of an outsider...he was never at ease.

Kavanagh therefore stresses the unconventional, and individualist sides of Yeats, the 'gay youthfulness and authority' which are the 'marks of the poet', his 'wonderful sense of morality'.[30]

Kavanagh's own writing swings between the two poles of identification with community and an almost anarchic Romantic individualism, both of which poles he locates in Yeats. His advocacy of parochialism in the key essay of 1952, 'The Parish and the Universe', would seem to offer a local country-based correcting vision to that middle-class, abstract, Yeatsian vision of a People. And yet he is forced to recognize that this vision in itself is a Romantic ideal and has no roots in reality: 'In Ireland we are inclined to be provincial not parochial, for it requires a great deal of courage to be parochial.' Ireland looks towards the metropolitan centres for its views, and has no confidence in its local traditions and continuities. As with Yeats, therefore, Kavanagh gestures towards a vision of wholeness which is out-of-step with historical actuality, and which does not exist beyond his own rhetoric.

'The Defeated' claims that 'Lost is the man who thinks that he can scorn / His parish mother's paps', and 'Lough Derg' speaks of the 'Homeric utterances' of the 'meanly poor'. Yet in poems like 'Christmas Eve Remembered' or 'Hope', the association with a native population is as difficult and disconnected as it is in Yeats's dream of the Homeric peasantry in his early prose. As the latter poem puts it:

> We sit huddled, old forlorn folk
> Remembering, striving to hold against the dark-to-come

Some of the ballad-liveliness
When minds were supple
And there were poems hidden under the black oak-couple.[31]

For all his unYeatsian early association of the craft of poetry with the tasks of country labouring – an association of course crucial to the Kavanagh-soaked work of early Seamus Heaney – Kavanagh's intimate reading of the history of his people in that context is one of disjunction and, as 'The Great Hunger' notoriously revealed, of personal frustration and despair.

At this level, Kavanagh's work shares something of the Romantic tropology of Yeats itself. The disruption of a habitat in which poems were discovered as though they were natural products,[32] as also the dream of a parochial unity in some future co-terminous space and time, lead him throughout his career towards that inwardness and irresolvability typical of all Romantic figuration. His turn against the Yeatsian public persona and 'pose', inwards towards some purportedly originary self and original place of generation and writing in his native County, repeats the iterative aspect of the 'Intentional Structure of the Romantic Image', as de Man has memorably defined it:

> For it is in the essence of language to be capable of origination, but of never achieving the absolute identity with itself that exists in the natural object. Poetic language can do nothing but originate anew over and over again; it is always constitutive, able to posit regardless of presence but, by the same token, unable to give a foundation to what it posits except as an intent of consciousness.[33]

Poetry can be posited as part of a natural landscape ('hidden under the black oak-couple') – but no sooner is this done than the lack of integration at the heart of such rhetoric is to be more starkly revealed.

But that authoritative gaiety which emerges with the 1960 publication of *Come Dance With Kitty Stobling* (after Kavanagh's own move to Dublin and survival of a serious cancer operation) seems more playfully – yet also painfully – cogniscent of this strain within the concept of a Romantic figuration itself. The title poem, as Antoinette Quinn has observed, manifests a rare moment in Kavanagh when he dons a Yeatsian mask – Quinn associates the figure of Kitty Stobling with Crazy Jane – while the mention of 'mile-high stilts' perhaps registers the presence of Malachi Stilt-Jack here as well.[34]

Yet Kitty remains importantly a figure *in* the poem, not (as in the Crazy Jane poems) the speaker of it. The injunction contained in the title is in fact, we learn, the outrageous cry 'out-of-sense' to the terrorized crowds 'looking up with terror in their rational faces'. At this level, the poem seems a querulous reworking of the question in Yeats's late title 'Why Should Not Old Men Be Mad?'. It shares both in Kavanagh's continuing modesty, his self-proclaimed unimportance in 'the colourful country', and his poetic situation, removed from the common projections and feelings of his kind, 'the namer not the beloved'. As a result, the poet's dream sees him displacing himself in service of his art through a 'myth that was a lie but it served: / . . . my rhyme cavorting on mile-high stilts'. The implication from the speaker is that the trade he follows is a blight, that he must remain an observer of humanity, and so he adopts circus tricks, not unlike the Yeatsian pose, in order to get himself noticed. The 'crowd' can only confirm him in his 'madness', give it back to him as though they were both simply mirrors of each other. His self-image receives no alteration by being expressed or paraded, and yet, through this reflection, neither is it reified: 'thank you sincerely / For giving me my madness back, or nearly', in the poem's chilling last lines.

This is chilling, not because we find the speaker confirmed in his Romantic image as mad poet, but because the expression of that madness, and the reflection back of it, make him aware of the pose itself, of the inwardness of the serviceable lie which he has no choice but to utter.[35] The crowd did not alter his self-image, but the act of expressing it, displaying it as if it were a circus animal, did. At this level, there is more danger for the poet in the assumption of 'myth' or 'pose' than for the potential auditors of such 'insincerity', to adopt Kavanagh's own term. What mythic writing might expose is the inadequacy of all expression, including that Romantic expression of the self which Kavanagh pretty much everywhere else holds to. Language is always separate, and expression separates the one expressing from whatever integrity they might aspire to or dream of. The injunction 'O dance with Kitty Stobling' remains forever 'out-of-sense to them', the audience, but also to the poet himself, since it reveals the way in which finally he can only speak to himself.

Kavanagh's conclusion to 'William Butler Yeats' ('I am sure that Yeats writing – "And did some words of mine send out / Certain men the English shot" – was not so far off the mark. He was a poet. One knew he was there'), seen from the jarring perspective of this late poem, seems like a serviceable lie. 'No, no, no, I know I was not important', as the poem opens, offers through its assonance a Lear-like renunciation before the 'myth' is entered into, given body in the poem. Here 'An Insult' might be significant, a poem in which Yeats's 'dream great house' seems upheld against the drunkenness and hatreds of the everyday. Kavanagh writes 'there is no golden rule / For keeping out suffering – if one lives'. As he remarks in the essay of Yeats's later work, 'To be old is, to be dead. But can a poet die? More and more I am finding it difficult to imagine the discontinuity of that which once was.'[36]

If Yeats's example leads Kavanagh to seek an origin for his own identity, it also makes him aware of the deathly discontinuities within seeming continuity. Within the Romantic aspiration to the 'beyond' in his work lies the quirkily colloquial, which cannot be reconciled. As he puts it in one of the healing and healed 'Canal Bank' sonnets, 'Canal Bank Walk':

> O unworn world enrapture me, encapture me in a web
> Of fabulous grass and eternal voices by a beech
> .... give me ad lib
> To pray unselfconsciously with overflowing speech....[37]

The 'eternal voices' which speak through nature in this version of prosopopoeia can only be pleaded with. The 'ad lib' and 'overflowing speech' might not be allowed or expressed. There is a randomness and gratuitousness about the encomium which manifests both the poem's strength and its defeat. The natural setting (like Yeats's tower) represents an idealized space beyond history, including literary history, in which the zestful musicality ('enrapture me, encapture me') might make itself heard. Kavanagh, like MacNeice, recognizes the dangers of nationalist engagement, particularly of a Yeatsian kind, for the political and poetic aspirations, the wished-for identification of his work. The original, 'natural', and located place towards which the poetry repeatedly gestures *ends with* the gesture. The presence of the poet ('One knew he was there'), or of poetry, is haunted by the lack (in all senses) which that poetry itself seeks to gesture beyond.[38]

IV

The expatriate Brian Coffey's determinedly modernist stance would seem to eschew such testings and troublings of native Romantic inheritance as those of Kavanagh. And yet, latterly, his work would seem to have displayed an antithetical possibility within that inheritance itself – one which troubles accepted critical definitions of it. Coffey's outspokeness against any influence from Yeats upon his own work was initially severe ('a power-hungry seducer who gathered a right gang of praisers around him, and who blocked off the kind of talent he didn't like' is one, perhaps rueful, early comment).[39] But there is some sense that, from the early 1960s, Coffey moved towards a kind of accommodation with the older poet's legacy – indeed, that Yeats became a central figure in his own debates about the relation between poetry's wisdom and its own formal procedures. At the start of his 1967 Gauss seminars, de Man found the polemicism of various anti-Romantic attitudes, similar to that of Coffey's dismissal of Yeats, to be embued with a Romantic problematics which blurs definitions. It is those problematics which I want to discuss in their relation to modernity in Coffey's later work as they inflect Yeats's own concerns in this area.[40]

In the 1962 *Missouri Sequence*, Yeats is named by Coffey as the prime exemplar of an intractable debate and dilemma between the native and the international, in this case between the twin pulls of America and Ireland, the former being where Coffey stayed because his children were happy growing up there. In the opening section of the poem, that dilemma opens in its turn the question of the relation between 'wisdom' and 'love' as they are to be figured in the work:

> Pain it was to come,
> pain it will be to go.
>
> *   *   *
>
> Not just to go,
> not just to stay,
> but the act done in wisdom's way
> not impossible
> if one is wise.
>
> Our William Butler Yeats
> made island flowers grow
> that need as much
> the local rain
> as wind from overseas
> to reach their prime.
> He struggled towards the exact muse
> through a sunless day.
> No servant, the muse
> abides in truth,

> permits the use of protest
> as a second best
> to make clean fields,
> exults only in the actual
> expression of a love,
> love all problem,
> wisdom lacking.[41]

The formality in giving Yeats's full name in the meditation here sparks a tension in the use of the possessive 'our'. Yeats's own refusal to allow Ireland itself to be the judge of Ireland's poetry was present from early in his work, as I indicated in the last chapter. But, as a result, he is himself figured as writing from a benighted and frozen situation similar to that of Coffey's writing this section of his poem (the title of which is 'Nightfall, Midwinter, Missouri'). Yeats, Coffey maintains, also writes under the demands of a precision of inspiration which perhaps counters the superficially Romantic image he is often seen under. The rhetoric of a poetry of 'protest' is seen by Coffey as only minimally effective, in a turn which echoes Yeats's frequent (regrettable) laments about the involvement of Maud Gonne and others, including Eva Gore-Booth and Con Markiewicz, in the world of active politics.

This poem's exultation of 'the actual / expression of love', therefore, follows a typically Yeatsian process of thought. Yet, in *its* turn, 'love' cannot at this point in the sequence be brought into continuity with 'wisdom'. Indeed, it seems to run counter to it. By the end of this quoted section, the 'example' of Yeats's interweaving of nationalism and internationalism has been pursued towards another question, in which 'love' supercedes 'protest', but does not resolve the lack of 'wisdom'. Rather, it highlights that lack. Coffey's thinking is trapped in that dilemma described by an ageing Yeats, sitting by the fireside with the love of his youth in 'After Long Silence': 'Bodily decrepitude is wisdom; young / We loved each other and were ignorant.' (*CP*, p. 265) Yeats seems to offer a vision of the career of poetry with which Coffey might share, but seems at this point to represent a typical failure at the heart of Romanticism, in that he is unable to reconcile the 'knowledge' which poetry conveys with its emotional content. Coffey, like Yeats, goes on, however tautologically, believing in the possibility of wise action 'if one is wise'. But how to know 'if one is'?

The next section of the sequence, which describes the turn of seasons and reawakening in 'March, Missouri', however, approaches these questions ('problems') directly. Coffey's poetry of process comes startlingly close to imagining the possibility of 'death, / its gift of closure', with the painful Eliotic awareness of the repetitiousness of seasonal patterns which awakening brings: 'Easy it would have been to yield / me where snow blanketed the unfurrowed field.' In what seems a re-rendering of the possibilities in Yeats's 'The Choice', Coffey immediately expresses the antithetical dilemma involved even in the resistance to such Keatsian ease, however; as if 'yielding me' were to enter a formlessness which is antipathetic to his being:

> That perfect self sages praise –
> its fruits graced with reason in love –
> who shall shape it, who describe
> what every image would circumscribe
> more strictly than one's hand one's glove?
>
> It grows mastering the unthought-of change
> love's way in unrestricted range.
> But is one ever perfect here and now?
> One is all too sure that one is not.

Such lack of completion prevents the realization of wisdom's perfectability 'here and now'. The wise, are, indeed, indistinguishable 'from others in daily life', until 'questioning event / requires exact response / ... when love alive alone proffers / love's unpredictable reply'. That 'exact', of course, echoes the demands of Yeats's muse, 'when it is wisdom to avoid / the routine answer'.[42]

The exceptional language of poetry seems 'alone' capable of exactingly and self-originatingly responding to 'event' ('love ... proffers ... love's). 'Wisdom' resides in resistance to 'the routine answer' alone. Poetry might seem to offer 'shape', and also unpredictability before event, which is lacking in self and the self's wisdom 'here and now'. As Yeats saw it in 'Blood and the Moon', 'wisdom is the property of the dead, / A something incompatible with life.' (*CP*, p. 239) 'Love all problem', as Coffey had put it in the opening section, but also all that we can know and strive to perfect.

That 'wisdom', or the awareness that it is impossible to be wise 'here and now', builds across the closing half of the sequence. The elegy in section 3 for his friend and international modernist Irish contemporary Denis Devlin, whose own work was occasionally also marked by a Yeatsian antinomianism,[43] finds comfort in the other poet's 'never perfect work / its own reward. // This much is certain / ... he must not escape from here and now.' Across the closing pages of the concluding

section, in which the poem has itself reached an opposite pole of seasonal and ontological possiblity, we are enjoined to

> ... seek wisdom wholly always,
> refuse as you must
> the shape that will not feature you,
> nothing withheld give,
> give love.

And then, in the closing moments, Coffey returns to the integration of
poetry with this giving:

> And poetry, what of poetry,
> without which nothing exact is said?
>
> Poetry becomes humankind.
>
> Only it charms us
> knowing in loving
>
> Any living soul may share
> what the rose does declare.
>
> The habit of withholding love
> unfits us for poetry. . . .
>
> Never was despair imperative,
> never are we grown so old
> we cannot start our journey
> bound to find
> an eternal note of gladness
> in loves true for men,
> the source whence they flow,
> the ocean whither they go.[44]

The double potentiality of poetry here, both exactly predicting 'humankind' and also charmingly becoming it, opens out its democratic potentiality. The Yeatsian symbol of the rose is perhaps demystified in Coffey's
more humanist poetic, but the confluence of 'knowing in loving'
which poetry offers is finally figured in the traditional Romantic
trope of a river. The temporality of poetry finally comes to stand in

for the process of 'our journey', which leads to its own inevitable end ('bound to find'), yet which gains its 'gladness' in an eternal musicality which harmonizes 'loves true for men'. The repetitiousness of seasonal return, with its own form of closure, is here translated by the proffering of a linearity which is 'eternal', but experienced by each human. 'Love all problem' is refigured across the process of the poem as 'loves true for men'. In what *seems* a drawing together of 'The Choice''s opposition of art to life, poetry's 'love' receives its response from 'any loving soul'. It is the Derridean 'gift', which 'allows something to which it appears unrelated to be thought'.[45] The dissolution of each life in the 'ocean' perfectly coincides with the ending of the poem itself.

The assertively modernist difficulty of Coffey's earlier work is here, therefore, transposed or re-envisaged through a Yeatsian questioning about his own situation, Irish but international, into further examinations of the notion of selfhood and selves-in-relation (a feature of his earlier work discussed by J.C.C. Mays in his introduction to *Poems and Versions*) – examinations which are realized through Yeatsian antinomies. Coffey's acceptance of a rhetoric of temporality which is also a shaping figuration of origins and ends reveals an alertness to the kinds of continuity between the Romantic and the aggressively modernist which are discussed by de Man. He makes a poetic issue of modernity here, and in doing so discovers a dialogue with Yeats.

The playful reversal at the end of *Missouri Sequence* of the 'eternal note of sadness' which Matthew Arnold hears in the withdrawing 'Sea of Faith' on 'Dover Beach' paradoxically lacks, in Coffey's rendition, the note of desperation in the earlier poet's turning to his particular beloved: 'Ah love, let us be true / to one another!'[46] Yet Coffey's 'resolution', with its wittily self-involved intertwining of key terms like 'love' and 'wisdom', discovers in its final acceptance of a traditional trope for the course of life the limitation of its own possibilities. Coffey's river here has little sense of that 'exteriority' which is traceable in, say, Wordsworth's use of such natural forces as poetic symbols. This late in the tradition, it shares that 'emblematic' quality which de Man, in 'Landscape in Wordsworth and Yeats', discovers in the latter's description of rivers, the metaphor masking an 'esoteric text' 'without earthly equivalence'. Or, as Yeats himself wrote to his father in 1916, art 'uses the outer world as a symbolism to express subjective moods'.[47] The very abstractions through which Coffey's poem operates, its resistance at each stage to implications from the 'outside' world, as for example the feelings inspired by the turn of the seasons, paradoxically mark the success and inevitable failure of the sequence, its late Romantic desire for an ontology which it can never achieve.

Such reliance upon an imagery gleaned from a Yeatsian palette or range of literary reference increases within the later poems. In the second section of the 1975 'Advent', a 'Sailing to Byzantium'-like urge towards an 'Eden enduring' is figured through a vision of swans 'At verge of lake by gaunt wood'. Coffey conceives of a gnostic's discontinuity between the humanity of this vision and its pastoral shaping and voicing:

> ... the swan of how clear green of lake covers sunken head...
> time after time white to green light green to white change
> no stasis passage out no return like dart in flight...
>
> ... fear of no future absolute...
> tempts to assure naught all naught now inverted hybris
> naught what has pleased ear and eye what pleases now
> only some abstract where of thinking for Beauty pure...
>
> And Beauty that other inferred so often desired in gift of none
>
> is to be longed for but where may it be seen
>
> Silent the star-lit night the sun-lit day
> till shepherd's harp gave voice to star and sky...

But the pastoral, elegiac, origins of poetry have been superceded by present abuses of nature ('man... soils the sea... ravishes maternal earth'), which seem here to blend with the fear of ageing and death into an assurance of 'naught all naught' which makes Beauty unlocated and unlocateable. There is not even an actual 'where' from which to think it. History would seem to have destroyed an original symbolic link between man and the world which is man's actual expressiveness; 'who shall inscribe in sand man's secret heart', as the last line of this section of the poem has it.

Such deprived temporality, and potential for a loss of placing and attendant definition, of course haunts Yeats's 'The Wild Swans at Coole': 'All's changed... But now they drift on the still water... / Among what rushes will they build, / By what lake's edge or pool...?' (*CP*, pp. 131–2) Former and present plenitude are poised above a future void in nature. For Coffey, the temporality ('no stasis') of the natural image underpins the impossible desire for Beauty. In section 4 of his poem, the possible advent of the gods ('all changed changed utterly') can only be figured as a trashy piece of science fiction, with its furniture of a 'mile-high sphere' and 'numinous shield'. 'What we had always wanted' can only be envisaged as a debased version of what we already know, as if at this belated stage Coffey cannot credit the transformational possibilities Yeats discovered, in works like 'Easter 1916', in history itself.

As such, these late Coffey works also display a yearning for an original expressiveness, which is the note sounded again and again in early Yeats. In the 1979 sequence 'Death of Hektor', Homer's own unlocatability is not read as a source of disjunction, as it had been in Coffey's reading of history in 'Advent':

> Homer where born where buried of whom the son
> what journeys undertaken not known His work
> abides witness to unfaltering sad gaze constrained...
> His ear open to spoken word and words down time like wind-blown
> sand...
>
> swirl of sound continual mixed in a perfect ear
> surfacing coherent true than history all and everything....[48]

Homer's lack of location or poetic heritage is taken as opening his work to both orality and the resonance of words through history.[49] As the more anxious last lines of the poem show, Coffey is aware of the 'constraints' which are nevertheless potentially present even within such 'swirl of sound continual', Homer's necessity of leaving 'unsaid' in his 'innermost heart' what might have displeased his patrons and therefore prevented his access to history itself, 'our raddled selves'. As if in answer to Yeats's Castiglione-founded vision of aristocratic patronage (*A*, p. 545), Coffey clearly sees poetry constrained by such original circumstance.

Yet there is a former, unmediated relation posited here between the poet and the world ('Light we suppose once had entered eyes to brand memory') which is at once Romantic vision of an ideal poetic situation and also a recognition that that vision might itself be determined by the belated poet's own late-Romantic situation in history ('we suppose'). At the same moment as he is offered as an extra-historical (textual) entity, therefore, Homer is seen as an idealized result of an historical reading. While he is defended against the visions of authorship by Coffey's modern Irish precursors Joyce ('not indifferent') and Yeats ('not masked'), Coffey has to again acknowledge his *own* situation within a history which renders location, symbolic unity and their lack as pressing contemporary problems – problems also shared by both of those precursors in varying forms.

V

In the poems on Yeats by Padraic Fallon (1905–1974), there is little of the modernist apparatus of Coffey's writing, but a strikingly similar debate about the nature of identification, and about the location for Irish poetry, in the aftermath of Yeats. Fallon, who has often been seen as a mere imitator of the older poet,[50] actually liberatingly dramatizes the destabilizing nature of the proximity of his symbolic presence in later writing in ways which question the bases of poetry's own subjectivity and completion, just as Coffey's treatment of modernity had forced him to do.

The symbolic completion and wholeness of Yeats's vision becomes literally a matter of terror for Fallon, since it confirms the inefficacy of poetry in times of war. Visiting the tower at Ballylee, which was then in ruins, at the time of war in Korea, Fallon sees it as a place turned from its original brutal purpose into one of 'dream' and 'phantasy' in which 'the boy who brooded on book and paint / Long mornings in his father's study' at last found a home. The isolation of the tower, surrounded by fertile fields, confirms for Fallon that 'earth... cares for nothing but its seasons', as Yeats recognized in gazing upon the wild swans at Coole. Earth cares least of all for poetry. As a result, as he climbs to the top of the tower, he recognizes the inevitable failure of poetic aspiration before the brutal realities of war:

> I know the terror of his vision now:
> A poet dies in every poem, even
> As blossom dies when fruit comes on the bough,
> And world is endless time in which things happen
> In endless repetition, every man
> Repetitive as a pattern, no soul
> But the sprawling spirit of the whole
> Massing upon the careless earth like frogspawn.[51]

Fallon's retention of a metaphor of natural process, even in describing the constantly-repeated death of the poet, is a mark of the mixture of determinism and the consequent dearth of expressiveness which for him is inscribed in Yeats's 'vision' itself. He seems to want to establish the repetitiveness of the poet, the 'fruiting' of poetry at the expense of the death of the living poet, as of a different order to that 'endless time...endless repetition' within which the 'world' exists. The poet's personal death in fact ensures both his 'soul' and his absence from his personal symbols ('nothing is here but the wind'). The 'terror' of his death, its inexpressiveness, is all that might be learnt by revisiting symbolic places like the tower itself. Fallon recognizes that other 'terror' in the fact that Yeats is perpetually absent from his own words, and that, rather than establishing the symbolic value of poetry, Thoor Ballylee confirms its ideal emptiness.[52]

Fallon elsewhere strives to write out the consequences of this recognition, in which the self is not present within language so as to be expressive, but is rather something which only language itself can bring about. In the final section of 'Johnstown Castle', another building in which the poet feels himself something of an intruder, he registers an inability to escape out of 'a poem' into 'poetry', to overthrow the self and establish the connection of words to world since 'Always my own monologue / Intrudes'. And yet that monologue itself is acknowledged as a potential way towards a truer level of self which otherwise would not exist, allowing the poet to meet

> ...the major and delicate
> Evasions of his ghost
> Who is the host
> To every massive feeling and must live it.
> Create me, says the poet, I am a body
> For every word, the large word that was lost
> And the word you'd throw a dog....[53]

The poet is only ideally an actuality, a body, therefore, insofar as the language is incorporated within him- or herself, and insofar as readers resurrect that 'ghost'. The organic analogies which the poetry makes are themselves subject to such mixed and various linguistic bodyings-forth; the 'me' which might be encountered travelling 'towards infinity' might be decipherable or not, as the poet, like Yeats had, 'dies in every poem'. 'The soul...only returns to itself...through this concern for death', as Derrida has recently argued.[54]

This varying closeness and absence in the act of writing is most fully dramatized by Fallon in 'Yeats at Athenry Perhaps', a poem which ponders the idea that Yeats might have come into Fallon's home town, and therefore into proximity with the poet as a young man, since he had to change trains there on the way to the tower at Gort. The conclusion ('No, he'd have sat by the line and waited')[55] registers again both Fallon's belief in the integrity of Yeats's vision and the unavailability of that vision, other than through its confirmation of the poet's death and absence, for later writers.

The relation of that confirmation to the 'monologue' in which Fallon feels caught, condemning him to 'a poem' and preventing him from entering 'poetry', remains perplexing across his work, rather than the settled thing which other critics have perceived it as. That perplexity then leaves the relation of the poet to the poetry unresolved. Is poetry merely a personal outpouring or an objectively finished work? How can we ever know if it is the latter, since the poet remains both determined by an endless repetition (iterability) and therefore absent, unspeaking, from his works. As with Yeats himself, poetic symbolism has a way of being rendered through death and history as a series of mere signs. The absolute, idealized call to 'create me' cannot be realized unless the perpetual ('always') monologue can be perpetually interrupted, a crisis which can only occur through and within every poem. Fallon's is as much a struggle with an overcoming of the 'self' and its habitual voice as it is the Bloomian one of overcoming the precursor. To that 'wonderful mixture of awe and shyness' which Seamus Heaney, in his Introduction to the *Collected Poems*, notes in Fallon's approach to Yeats, might be added a continual questioning about the nature and presence of 'poetry' itself – its presence and memorability.

All of this, as Heaney notes, is conveyed within an 'overall security of tone, an assumption of common ground and easy access between audience and voice'.[56] That security is partly attained through Fallon's sense of himself as of the generation of 'Irish Irish' writers who succeeded the Anglo-Irish divisions of the Revivalists. And yet Fallon's Yeats poems also reveal *uncertainties* of identity and tone, of location, proximity and distance, which derive from the encounter with Yeats's ghost and with his mythic sites. Most questioned is the status of the voice of personal experience and reflection in the poem, that quality which Yeats saw as central to all poetry and later asserted against the 'passivities' of Pound and Eliot. Fallon is ever-sensitive to the ways in which the conditions which informed the poetic voice need to be superceded in order that the personal might be translated into 'poetry'. The identifications of that personal voice seem continually thrown into doubt by the presence, and more significantly, the way presence confirms the possible *absence* of the representative of 'poetry' near Fallon's native regional ground, Yeats.

VI

Thomas Kinsella (1928–) is another Irish poet who, like Brian Coffey, has learned much from the precepts of international modernist experimentation. Yet he shares with Padraic Fallon a horrified sense of the ways in which poetic symbolism can be rendered through time into a mere system of signs. 'Death in Ilium', his centenary poem for the older poet, casts Yeats himself within a process of reading which establishes the irredeemability of the originary presence as a result of organic process. What is significant is that Kinsella casts this process of irredeemability as pertaining *both* to the poet and to his readers. 'Truth deserts the body', we are told in the second line, as though the process of physical decay is essentially also an ontological one. And yet the dog-like 'shadow-eaters' who close in once the hero is gone ('Hector... / Drops dead') 'eat, but cannot eat'. The poet himself has canine features in his bowels and face; 'He grows whole and remote.'[57]

It is as though the process of tearing apart the body of the fallen posthumously engenders a reciprocal fierceness in the commemorated poet himself. The paradoxical process whereby wholeness and remoteness might be achieved through such tearing and defence, so that the poet commented on is distanced by the very critical attempt to get the 'truth', suggests that the effects of criticism only serve to confirm the integrity of the original text. As for Derrida in *On the Name*, the process of reading itself becomes one of increasing abstraction across history – an abstraction which responds to the gaps in the original text, but which also removes that text increasingly further away from us.[58]

Unlike Yeats's own fragile mockery in 'The Scholars', Kinsella seems to believe that 'truth' disappears with the death of the poet to be replaced by an irrecoverable formal completion and distance in the process of critical exposure and reading which follows. As such, 'Death in Ilium' sets Yeats within a slightly different hermeneutic dynamic than that of Thomas Kinsella's paper 'The Irish Writer' of the same time, in which Yeats's 'isolation' is seen as a matter of his 'special selection' in founding an Anglo-Irish tradition 'at a graceful elegiac height above the filthy modern tide'.[59] While Kinsella famously sees this distance as a calculated refusal to come to terms with the shaping vitality of modern Ireland (and therefore argues for Joyce as the only possible example from this period for subsequent Irish writers), the vision of remoteness in the

essay is founded upon notions of ideological choice rather than processes of reading, as it is in the poem. There, the Greek-like heroism of
the author is acknowledged only to establish a natural dissipation of
'truth' with time and consequent critical re-reading.

As Derrida has argued when considering de Man's phrase 'the rhetoric
of temporality', there remains something 'non-totalizable... defying all
reappropriation' about the traces left to the living by the dead. It is art's
role to embody this 'absolute past – that is, the immemorial or unre-
memberable'.[60] Kinsella sees the writing which comes after Yeats, and
which seeks to take him into itself, as saying something other than him
('eat, but cannot eat'). Decay is endemic in language, as it is in the
absent dead.

That interest in organic process which is also a process of loss of power
and dissemination (resistant to poetry even, in its integrated remoteness) is something which, perhaps surprisingly, figures as a central
system of tropes in Kinsella's consequent work. His increasing interest
in the frequently nightmarish life of the psyche founded largely upon
Jung has further opened his poetry to processes of emergence and decay.
As the Peppercanister pamphlet of 1985 has it, these 'Songs of the
Psyche' enact exactly that process traced in the transmission and reception of Yeats's work in the commemorative poem 'Death in Ilium':

> ... it *is* a matter
>   of negative release...
>
> By normal process
>   organic darkness would summon
> Self firstly into being,
>
> an upright on a flat plain,
>   a bone stirs in first clay
> and a beam of light
>
> struck and snaked
>   glittering across a surface
> in multi-meanings and vanishes.
>
> Then stealers of fire...[61]

As a parable of the emergence of humanity as the emergence of the
individual consciousness, this 'normal process' is inevitably one of

dispersal. The Promethean act leads to 'ultimately the Cross', passionate sacrifice yet a solely singular, one-off, meaningful act, remote from the original Adamic stirring of the bones or 'beam of light'. In a curiously Foucaultian moment, in a last stanza to this last (and thirteenth) poem of the sequence of 'Songs', Kinsella suggests an alternative possibility, that everything is based on sexuality or power.

The dismissiveness of this gesture, mirrored in other later works as in the coda of *Her Vertical Smile* (also of 1985), seems to acknowledge the void beneath all such processes (a void also stared into by Coffey). The Romanticized 'Self' in this sequence is envisioned as both natural product and, by the same token, as vulnerable to forces of decay. The poem itself seems vulnerable to various acts of theft, in which the originary moment or voice or 'truth' is inevitably lost through time. Kinsella's vigorously unYeatsian, international–modernist poetic, as did Coffey's, in fact serves to open the work to those perpetual processes of recycling and loss which had figured in his review of the literary reception of Yeats, and to which Yeats's own poetic, with its constant remakings of the self, was also vulnerable.

Earlier in his career, such features had seemed to operate also in the acts of cultural recovery in which Kinsella was involved. His attention to the Gaelic inheritance within what in one essay he called 'The Divided Mind' of his country, an attention which provided another reason for his favouring of Joyce over Yeats in the 1960s, led him into a process of translation of those original mythic cycles which provided Yeats with his dreams of Romantic heroism through figures such as Cuchulain – as though Kinsella wished to recover those 'sources' from that Romantic aura. Yet, within his own work outside the translations, Kinsella's sense of such distinctive original impulses has perhaps surprisingly not yielded a wholly different sense of 'normal process' to that contained in the cycles of birth and decay of Self.

In 'Finistère' from 1974, which is a version of a passage from the Gaelic 'Book of Invasions' about the original colonization of Ireland by travellers from Brittany in France, Kinsella dramatizes the voice of Amhairgin, the poet who accompanied the colonists on their voyage:

> We drew close together, as one,
> and turned inward, salt chaos
> rolling in silence around us,
> and listened to our own mouths
> mumbling in the sting of spray:
> – Ill wind end well

mild mother
on wild water pour peace

who gave us our unrest
whom we meet and unmeet
in whose yearning shadow
we erect our great uprights
and settle fulfilled
and build and are still
unsettled, whose goggle gaze
and holy howl we have scraped
speechless on slabs of stone
poolspirals opening on
closing spiralpools
and dances drilled in the rock
in coil zigzag angle and curl
river ripple earth ramp
suncircle moonloop . . .
in whose outflung service
we nourished our hunger
uprooted and came
in whale hell
    gale gullet
salt hole
    dark nowhere
calm queen
    pour peace

What is notable in this version of a founding poem for Ireland is its curious 'nowhereness', to adapt a word from near the end of the section quoted here. Finistère, the place of the poem's title, is the place of setting out, not the place of arrival; it remains a foreign elsewhere into which Ireland's myth of origin and derivation is forever shifted. It is also a curious condition of in-betweenness, timelessness and iteration; 'we went further than anyone had ever been', Amhairgin tells us, only for a parenthetical voice, itself of uncertain origin (is it meant to be his or Kinsella's own?), to interject that 'I had felt all this before'.

Once the 'bad dream' of the journey is over, and the travellers do arrive at a nameless somewhere which we take to be Ireland, the founding song which Amhairgin sings on the beach simply open things out even further. Kinsella ventures towards an irresolute, quasi-spiritual questioning (not unlike Yeats's rhetorical summations, as in 'Among School Children', but also there in the original of the poem, 'The Mystery of Amhairgin', however) which can never achieve an answer: 'Who goes in full into / the moon's interesting conditions? / Who fingers the sun's sink hole?/ (I went forward, reaching out)'. The poem ends on a posture of overreaching its own boundaries, straining towards a history in which the questions will remain unanswered but also in which, as we are told, the 'spear springs / and pours out terror'.[62]

Rather than the promised return to origins here, then, what we in fact have ultimately is a perpetual shape-shifting and boundary-crossing in what Homi K. Bhabha, speaking of the modernity of postcolonial interstitial spaces, has helpfully called a Benjaminian nowtime, a nowtime in this case of continual uncertainty, unfulfillment and hurt. The poetry can never reach back to its own beginnings, as we witnessed also in Coffey's treatment of the pastoral in 'Advent', and can never therefore enter into the history of the place which it seeks to describe. Although shed of the somewhat Pre-Raphaeliteish dream-worlds of Yeats's poems of national founding, like 'To Ireland in the Coming Times', what with its attention to specific cultural and historical artifacts (the 'coils' in the rock), Finistère does not free itself of its particular Jungian trappings. As with Yeats's poem, in which the future of Ireland is intermingled with obscure, unstably-intermixed references to his life with Gonne and his Rosicrucian symbolism, what Kinsella's poem of founding involves us in is essentially a problematic of reading (which, as I have argued in the first chapter, Yeats felt as a result of colonization). This is a problematic which Kinsella's alertness to the divided inheritance of his country has merely exacerbated. Yet he does not repeat Yeats's appeal to an un-located future as a resolution to such irresolvable, unlocatable subject matter ('I cast my heart into my rhymes, / That you, in the dim coming times, / May know...' (*CP*, p. 51)), such is his alertness to the inevitable process of dissipation within such self-dissemination.

Such themes resonate at a more aesthetic level across *Her Vertical Smile*, which reveals how a Mahlerian conductor makes 'sensible figures in the air / so the blood might beat at our temples / with pulse of order', even if only as the work is being played. Yet the possibilities of a reciprocally-sensed 'order' rapidly becomes elided in the sequence into a vision of a self-preening portrait of the artist, for whom history is not so much insignificant as unedifying:

> For what shall it profit a white gloved
> and glittering bellied elder

puffed sideways at the camera

that mile after drowsy mile
    with bell towers and canals of still water...

should darken against themselves,
    and iron animals clambered
in staggered series

up out of the creases and folds
    in our spirits onto dry land
and turn it to mud under us...?[63]

At first sight, this preening buffoon shows some characteristics which Kinsella attributed early on to Yeats, but the remoteness of this historical setting enables him to make a more neutral assessment of the relation of art to history. Kinsella's adoption of a historical perspective in this sequence might mark a rare deployment of a Yeatsian mask, yet perhaps the more recent history of violence in the North of Ireland had also made him attentive again to Yeats's response to that history on his own soil.

At the time of the Irish civil war, Kinsella has written of Yeats, 'there was an outbreak of understanding in the poetry, of the place of violence and the random at the heart of vital processes'.[64] Kinsella's attention to such processes, as the 1976 *A Technical Supplement* illustrates, have always been more concise, close-to and bloody than Yeats's, yet it shows also the necessarily analogous basis of the poetic which he shares with the older poet. However much the quest in both for a Romantically symbolical unity between the processes of poetry and the processes of the world is constantly thwarted, and seen by both as impossible from the outset (in all senses), both continue to seek similar effects in their writing. The 'wholeness' and 'remoteness' seemingly instantiated by the history of critical reading in 'Death in Ilium' is constantly both challenged and confirmed within the tradition's constant quest to re-establish itself in different terms.

VII

Seamus Heaney (1939–) has also more recently come to value Yeats's authority as a representative of poetry which challenges and strives to overcome the conditions of its own making. In the early Eighties he had, along with some of his fellow directors of the Field Day Theatre Company, attacked Yeats for his aristocratic mystification of Irish life, favouring as Kinsella had earlier the Joycean possibility for subsequent Irish writing.[65] But, in his more recent lectures and prose writing, Heaney has frequently set Yeats alongside the Russian poet Osip Mandelstam as crucial examples for his own later vision of a poetry of untrammelled imagination.[66] In the 1990 Oxford lecture 'Joy or Night: Last Things in the Poetry of W.B. Yeats and Philip Larkin', he sets Larkin's late 'Aubade' against 'The Cold Heaven' and 'Man and the Echo' in order to show the 'entrapment' of the Larkin poem (however we might agree that it is an incredibly moving piece), within the sceptical, scientifically-ratified, thinking of its times. By contrast, the Yeats poems reveal that 'the mind's options are still open, that the mind's constructs are still vital and reliable'.

While admiring the technical skill of Larkin, Heaney seems to imply that it leads literally nowhere, whereas Yeats's rhymes have an ontological function as well, not only telling 'of what the spirit must endure':

they show also *how* it must endure, by pitting human resource against the recalcitrant and the inhuman, by pitting the positive effort of mind against the desolations of natural and historical violence. . . .

In an indirect extension of similar valuation of Yeats by MacNeice, Heaney claims here that rhyme, 'which surprises and extends the fixed relations between words', and metre, which 'provokes consciousness into new postures', are a certain good 'on the side of life'.[67] The implication of Heaney's weighing of these two poets would seem to be that the more admirable work is that which is most extensive and provocative in resisting the desolations of human realities, that which creates 'an energy and an order which promotes the idea that there exists a much greater, circumambient energy and order within which we have our being'. Heaney is, in other words, concerned now to celebrate that 'excess' and (to adopt Derrida's term) 'surplus' to be found in poetry generally, and particularly for him in Mandelstam and Yeats.

Heaney has come to accept a visionary Yeatsian dimension to his own thinking which (as it had for Yeats) has political and historical resonances also. Having been dogged by the comparisons made between himself and Yeats, and having seemingly in the early 1980s denied Yeats's indomitability in essays and in poems like 'The Master' from *Station Island*, Heaney's thought has latterly come into closer proximity with the later stages of the older poet's work. In speaking of Larkin and Yeats from the lecturer's rostrum, just after the end of his fiftieth year, Heaney acknowledged an openness to the kind of experience recounted by Yeats in the fourth section of 'Vacillation' and elsewhere, when, 'My fiftieth year come and gone', at a café table in London, for 'twenty minutes more or less / It seemed, so great my happiness, / That I was blessèd and could bless.' (*CP*, p. 251)

The awkwardness, the self-consciously singsong nature of this admission by Yeats, is a mark of that healthy scepticism, that lack of naivety in spiritual matters, which Heaney praises him for in 'Joy or Night'. The banality of the setting and the clumsily literal treatment of time are caught up by the 'less / bless' rhyme, in which the uncertain ('seemed') event achieves a reciprocally-sanctioned translation within another order of things. Such awkwardness is a feature also of Heaney's own admission in 'Fosterling' from the 1991 *Seeing Things*:

> Me waiting until I was nearly fifty
> To credit marvels. Like the tree-clock of tin cans
> The tinkers made. So long for the air to brighten,
> Time to be dazzled and the heart to lighten.[68]

'*Nearly* fifty'; 'cans' (which is 'rhymed' with an earlier 'happens') rests uneasily against 'brighten'. Heaney's more recent accession to the realms of the marvellous remains as 'undeluded' as he feels Yeats's sense of 'illumination and visitation' to have been in 'The Cold Heaven'. Although he accepts in the next poem in this collection, the opening of the sequence 'Squarings', that 'there is no next-time-round', that Yeatsian visionary reincarnation is impossible within his own 'illumination', the hauntedness and ghostliness of that sequence clearly owe much to the ghost of the mentor to whom he puts 'set questions' in poem xxii.

The questioning of Yeats in that poem is about the kinds of locatability and concomitant identifications to be made which have been a feature of earlier Irish interactions with Yeats. 'Where does spirit live? Inside or outside / Things remembered, made things, things unmade?', the piece opens.[69] Does nature preordain the spirit or is it resultant upon it, as it is according to Yeats's Neo-Platonic idealism? Does it reside in the 'perfected form' of art, can such forms even ever be 'inhabited'? Or is it, *sithe*-like, with the 'windy light'? Is it in a jackdaw's nest (not a stare's) at Thoor Ballylee or on the terrace at Coole? By accepting such questions as inevitably rhetorical, Heaney gains access to the Yeatsian 'spirit world', after visiting which the human can appear coarse, clumsy and a let-down.

In poem xxxiv, which opens with a (slightly reworded) quotation from Yeats to that effect, 'The face I see that all falls short of since... could have been one of the newly dead come back' (so perhaps there is a 'next-time-round', if only in poetry?). But the face, in fact, belongs to a remembered 'Vietnam-bound' youth on the bus from San Francisco Airport.[70] For Heaney, as for Yeats, the assurance of poetry's access to 'higher' things is always vulnerable to historical accident and event. So, in poems like 'Keeping Going' and 'The Flight Path', he has followed Yeats's example in parts V and VI of 'Meditations in Time of Civil War', by giving reported encounters with the threat of violence. Yet this latter Heaney, 'visionary rather than political', as he called Yeats in interview, prefigures a liberated future as Yeats and the Romantic tradition had done. As such, his later work forms a model of active consciousness which performs what de Man has called the 'main task' of Romantic ontology:

> temporal structuralization... a phenomenology of temporality (since it is the description of consciousness) as well as a phenomenology of language (since the manner in which temporality exists for our consciousness is through the mediation of language).

The given time of the poem has become a time in which the memories made present or given presence engage a future.[71]

Heaney's attempt, mentioned in the last of the Oxford lectures, 'Frontiers of Writing', to 'sketch the shape of an integrated literary tradition' for Ireland through the figure of the quincunx which joins the mythic sites of Spenser, Joyce, Yeats and MacNeice, envisages a time in which the internal border separating the North from the South of the island will be totally transparent, if not actually invisible. He also acknowledges the continuing presence of the 'Anglo-' within any Irish tradition, as 'a given of our history and even of our geography... in the language... where the mind of many in the republic lives also'. Therefore he enjoins the minority Catholic population in the North towards a Yeatsian leap of consciousness, to 'make their imagination press back against the pressure of reality and re-enter the whole country of Ireland imaginatively, if not constitutionally'.[72] (As such, in this envisaged future, we could perhaps say that the border shares the qualities of the Derridean concept of the 'hymen', place both of deferral and difference, of potential misunderstanding, yet also creator of meaning and plenitude.[73])

When Heaney commemorated Yeats in the Belfast magazine *Fortnight* during the fiftieth year after Yeats's death, he was eager to emphasize this mediatory inclusiveness as the basis for the earlier poet's 'spiritual height and depth':

> One can argue that in spite of the Anglo-Irish flourish of [Yeats's late collections of poetry – the books of his which Heaney clearly most admires], the cothurnus raises him above the caste. Yeats the poet both endures and embodies the whole field of forces active in Ireland and beyond, and is as responsive to the apocalyptic side of himself as to the elegiac.[74]

Through the rhetorical gambit of rescuing the late Yeats from his own identifications ('in spite of'), Heaney is able to envisage him as a writer in whom the normal defining and tribal fastnesses have broken down. The line between the domestic and personal and the public reach of the poetry has disappeared. Under this aegis, Yeats is figured both as an unfettered Romantic individualist, writing 'utterly from himself and for himself', and as an exemplary interweaver of all of the cultural threads of his country. Evidence of Heaney's own late interest in such interweaving is present in his inclusion of Spenser within his vision of a 'quincunx' integrating all traditions, an inclusion which shows a renewed interest in the kinds of accommodation which Yeats was eager to make in his Preface to his selection of that poet written in 1902. In earlier poems, particularly 'Traditions' from *Wintering Out*, Spenser had figured as a representative of the brutal colonizing force in Ireland. Heaney has not withdrawn from that view, but now also points to the inescapability of the Spenserian music in Ireland, 'linguistically, culturally, institutionally'.

Such counterstrains and unconstrainedness had become evident from the early 'Eighties, when Heaney himself began to celebrate the untrammelled Romantic imagination. His version of the medieval Irish poem *Builhe Suibhne* as *Sweeney Astray*, which appeared in Derry in 1983, in which the hero is changed into a bird because of his lack of reverence for a priest, is clearly an exploration of the imaginative freedoms to be gained from native institutions on a level with Yeats's own realization of similar magical and mythical possibilities in *The Wanderings of Oisin*, a text which, as he acknowledged in a letter to Olivia Shakespear, provided the key to all of his subsequent work.[75] The influence of ghostly spiritual messengers (central to Yeats's esoteric beliefs) had been dramatized in the Dantean title sequence of the 1984 *Station Island*, but only achieved full impetus in *Seeing Things* and the 1996 *The Spirit Level*, where it had an impact upon the shaping of subject matter in the poetry which I want to discuss below.

Yet, earlier, Yeats had figured under a different guise in Heaney's work, one which was intent upon holding fast to his native inheritance on his own ground. The mythical fatalism of the 1975 collection *North* has been much criticized, but it marked a close engagement with, and reworking of, another version of Yeatsian 'vision' from that more recently embraced and used as a kind of map for the poetic career as unaligned and exemplary. Under this aegis, Heaney seemed to be working with an improvised version of Yeats's complex 'system' of historical determinism in *A Vision*, rather than the kinds of communion with the dead which Yeats also engaged with there, as reflected in the poem which stands as the book's 'Epilogue', 'All Soul's Night' – a communion in which the recent poetry often finds its instigation. In its vertiginous swings from a poetry of historically-sanctioned and inevitable violence to a poetry of love, *North* re-embodies some of the most characteristic procedures of one strain of Yeatsian thought. The two poems of dedication which open the book celebrate an absence and a silence which counters, much as Yeats's 'Long-legged Fly' (and retreat into the tower) did, the noisiness and violence, the objectivity of historical events.[76] As the first of the poems ends,

> . . . here is a space
> again, the scone rising
> to the tick of two clocks.
>
> And here is love
> like a tinsmith's scoop
> sunk past its gleam
> in the meal-bin.[77]

The space of the mythic poems which fill the first part of the book is that of ground containing the bodies of sacrificial victims across history, including those of the recent violence in the North of Ireland. As such, it is this different kind of 'space' which Heaney is able to recall in dedication – the domestic sphere of his past life, with its fruitful connection to time conceived in the second poem 'The Seed Cutters' as the turn of the seasons ('O calendar customs!') – which has been violated. At moments in these poems of Part I of *North*, Heaney famously strikes a vein of Yeatsian vocabulary in order to describe that lack which history enforces:

> Now as news comes in
> of each neighbourly murder
> we pine for ceremony,
> customary rhythms:
>
> the temperate footsteps
> of a cortège, winding past
> each blinded home.[78]

Yeats's vision of a ritualized domesticity for his daughter in his 'Prayer' for her resonates behind these lines, as Neil Corcoran has written, although we cannot be sure that the echo is as 'ironic' as Corcoran claims it to be.[79] Yeats's question towards the end of his poem, 'How but in custom and in ceremony / Are innocence and beauty born?' (*CP*, p. 190), is, after all, a version of that Shakespearian question which Heaney felt so pertinent in Belfast in 1972, 'How with this rage shall beauty hold a plea...?'[80]

For Yeats, that sense of the fragilities of transcendent modes of perceiving and living within the disruptions of violent history is conceived, as in 'A Prayer for My Daughter' and many other places from 'Meditations in Time of Civil War' onwards, as essentially a threat to the personal, familial and domestic space. This is a strain in Heaney's response to renewed violence in the North of Ireland from the late 1960s onwards. As 'Whatever You Say Say Nothing' later in this book has it, 'In blasted street and home / The gelignite's a common sound effect'.[81] The clumsy yet historically-attentive rhythms of many of the earlier poems in *North* ('As news comes in / of each'), which have the voice speaking the poem fall over itself, are obviously more mimetic of the violence beyond than the ultimate Spenserian formal cohesiveness of Yeats before and against history. But the dreamt-of possibility of an idealized 'space' in both past and future is essentially the same for both poets.

To this extent, these poems in the first part of the collection seek a centre which will 'hold', like that bogland 'I grew out of' as described in 'Kinship'. Heaney's strategy is in part a weighing of the Yeatsian perspective upon history within this dramatic quest for places and spaces, silences beyond it. 'Keep your eye clear / as the bleb of the icicle', the 'ocean-deafened voices / ... of violence and epiphany' enjoin him in the title poem, in a reimagining of the epitaph on Yeats's tomb. But they go on to urge him to 'trust the feel of what nubbed treasure / your hands have known'.[82]

That Yeatsian distancing from event is clearly essential to Heaney's dangerous transhistorical vision of continuing sacrifice and violence at this stage of his career. Yet, at the same time, it seems inadequate to the intimate processes of decay mapped in the 'Bog Poems', and to the self-diagnosed artful voyeurism which Heaney registers before the female victims in 'Bog Queen', 'Punishment' and 'Strange Fruit'. While 'Belderg', the first of the poems set on Irish soil in this first part of the book, signals the persistence and the congruence of both the British and the native inheritance in Ireland (so foreshadowing the conclusions of the later lecture 'Frontiers of Writing'), Heaney was at this stage wary of a stance which is remote from, as he notoriously puts it at the end of 'Punishment' itself, 'the exact/and tribal, intimate revenge'.[83]

When, in the second part of the book, therefore, Heaney moves to a mode of writing more influenced by the improvisational poetics of Patrick Kavanagh, he makes his own difference from Yeats clear in the epigraph to 'Singing School' from *Autobiographies*, in which Yeats recalls himself as a youngster dreaming of dying fighting the Fenians.[84] It is an ambiguous and potentially unfair passage from Yeats to select, suggesting perhaps the ways in which the adult self might overcome early prejudices in accepting a larger vision, while also reminding us of the original political and religious difference of Yeats from the experiences with which 'Singing School' is concerned. The Yeatsian patterning of *North* comes ultimately to seem, therefore, quite a volatile thing. Its weighing of beauty and atrocity through mythic patterns, and its urges towards a 'space' beyond, directly adopts the manner of Yeats. But the various *caveats* entered along the way reveal Heaney's own unease with such procedures, as though in anticipation of the objections of critics and later readers.

When, in recent poems, Heaney has moved towards a more ghostly and spirit-haunted poetry, the influence of Yeats has been more evident in the indirections and abstruseness of the work, rather than in that earlier acceptance and interrogation. Then, Heaney was anxious to declare his own solidarity with the oppressed minority on his native ground. Latterly, that renovative idea of Romantic self-transcendence which Heaney finds in Yeats works in the *The Spirit Level* along with a notion of stamina, just 'Keeping Going' (as one title has it), and of that labour in perseverance which Heaney has also discovered in the older poet.[85] Once again, Heaney is preoccupied by the allure of spaces beyond history, in which the poetry can establish its own temporality. Rather than a temporality of historical determinism, however, this is now often a temporality like that 'in-betweenness' which Homi

K. Bhabha has followed Benjamin in identifying as a defining feature of modernity, but also, as in Heaney's case, as defining the particular situation of a colonial state moving to a condition of postcoloniality.

So, in the central sequence of this book, 'Mycenae Lookout', the opening poem is voiced by the watchman waiting on the roof of Agamemnon's palace for news of the ending of the Trojan War, news which, as he knows, will bring tragedy through the revenge enacted upon the king by Clytemnestra for his sacrifice of their daughter as he set out to the war. 'My sentry work was fate', the watchman tells us, 'a home to go to, / An in-between-times that I had to row through / Year after year . . .'. The moment of the speech is a moment between a past and a future which are equally blood-steeped. He is 'balanced between destiny and dread'.[86] But, in the fourth poem of the sequence, 'The Nights', we learn that his distance from all that he surveys from his roof-top look-outpost is a culpability also. He is guilty of allowing fate to work its way towards tragedy through not speaking out, through not telling the king of Clytemnestra's affair with Aegisthus, and her consequent resolve to kill him upon his return from the war.

The bad-faithed urge to cause no trouble by speaking the truth is pondered also, in a seemingly more personal way by Heaney, in 'Weighing In' ('I held back when I should have drawn blood');[87] here, it seems an unresolved complicity with fate. A Yeatsian distance from event seems condemned in this watchman's casting of a cold eye, yet he lacks also Yeats's repeated determination to stand up against the 'inevitable'. Heaney's voicing of the sequence through the remote watcher once again involves him in exploring the ambiguities of that space 'beyond' or 'outside' historical events. But it also interjects two poems in which that perplexity is eventually overcome through a recourse to that unity with the *natural* world so sought-after by Romantic poets as a resolution to historical dilemma. The third and fifth poems, 'His Dawn Vision' and 'His Reverie of Water', cast the temporality of the sequence as a whole at that irresolvable cusp between Romanticism and modernity upon which Yeats's work often discovers itself. In the former poem, the 'vision' of 'little violets' and 'star-lace' does not lead beyond circumstance, but, rather, deeper into it: 'it was more through them // I felt the beating of the huge time-wound / we lived inside.' Yet, in 'His Reverie of Water', a very different interjection occurs, with the celebration of 'fresh water' and 'the old lifeline', the secret ladder up the Acropolis which allowed the beseiged to survive:

> ...the ladder of the future
> and the past, besieger and besieged,
> the treadmill of assault
>
> turned waterwheel....

And with this metamorphic vision of survival and temporal transcendence ('Of what is past, or passing, or to come' (*CP*, p. 194)), there emerges a curious spatial and historical dis-location of the voice of the poem. The final three stanzas offer another memory which seems more directly personal to the poet, relating as it does to his early arterial poems such as 'Personal Helicon': 'And then this ladder of our own that ran / deep into a well-shaft...'. [88]

The shifts of focus across the sequence resolves itself, then, in an interjected lyric note which challenges the historical dramatizing and voicing of what has gone before. As a 'resolution' it leaves the reader deeply uncertain, throwing open once again the question of distance and intimacy in the poetic note which has been there from the start. The sequence becomes an embodiment of that notion of poetry which Heaney in his Nobel lecture *Crediting Poetry* describes himself as straining towards: 'As if the ripple at its widest desired to be verified by a reformation of itself, to be drawn in and drawn out through its point of origin.' It is an effect which he finds, he says, in Yeats's refrain from 'Meditations in Time of Civil War', 'Come build in the empty house of the stare', with its balancing of 'strength' and 'dissolution'.[89] Yet the 'point of origin' in such poems is difficult to locate, abruptly and even randomly interrupting the continuities of perspective we have been persuaded to establish.

Other poems in *The Spirit Level* are more content in their invulnerability, unsubjected to the process of drawing out and in because of their Yeatsian perspective 'beyond'. 'Tollund', written at the time of the renewed peace process in September 1994, sees the revisiting of the site of a central bog poem as now a sanctioning place 'Outside contention'. 'Poet's Chair' plays some Byzantine games with the statue of that name by Carolyn Mulholland, and the way its sprouting of 'two bronze and leafy saplings' sanctifies those who sit upon it: 'Once out of nature, / They're going to come back in leaf and bloom / And angel step. Or something like that.'

This mini-sequence also surprisingly ends with a personal reminiscence, of his father ploughing a field with the young Heaney leaning 'all-seeing' against a tree, and transhistorically witnessing again, 'all foreknowledge . . . of the chair in leaf / The fairy thorn is entering for the future'. (This new interest in short sequences perhaps itself is Yeatsian.) 'At the Wellhead' swings rapidly and vertiginously from present to past as it enjoins the poet's wife to 'sing on. . . . dear far-voiced veteran, // Sing yourself to where the singing comes from, / Ardent and cut off like our blind neighbour' (from his boyhood, Rosie Keenan). The last poem in the collection, 'Postscript', celebrates a place 'neither here nor there' in which a vision of swans throws the poet out of habitual modes of seeing.[90]

As ever with Heaney, the collection establishes from poem to poem a constant, and definingly Romantic, oscillation between the elegiac ('Damson', 'A Dog Was Crying Tonight In Wicklow Also', 'The Sharping Stone') and the promissory, wished-for future. The particular facts of violence in his past experience are more explicitly spelt out 'for the record' than ever before, but so also is the sense of 'the good' of poetry. The effect of the 'in-between-time' of the collection which results is curiously Berkleyan as he was perceived centrally by later Yeats ('he did not exalt in place of perception some abstract thought or law but some always undefined apprehension of spirits and their relations' (*E&I*, p. 410)). We find Caedmon, in one poem set in the curious two-placed nowhere 'Whitby-sur-Moyola', 'just bogging in / As if the sacred objects were a herd / That had broken out . . . / Caedmon was the real thing all right'.[91] The 'in-between-time' at such moments becomes freighted with spiritual possibility (which is also political possibility) while remaining earthbound. That complex interweaving of resonances is what establishes the magisterial tone of Heaney's work since his fiftieth year, gathering, as in *Fortnight* he said Yeats had, the 'different strands in his make-up and different endeavours in his career in order to ply them into [a] mutually ratifying set of attitudes and prejudices . . .'.

VIII

The tonal values of the poetry which derive from this interweaving are something which Heaney's later work shares with that of Derek Mahon (1941–), the dedicatee of *Seeing Things*. Mahon is clearly the model for the more concerted and complicated return to writing in rhyme which forms the character of the poems in the first part of that book, and of some of the recent work (the watchman's couplets in 'Mycenae Lookout' echo Mahon's use of them in his recent work, for example). Mahon's work throughout has been more drawn than Heaney's to those MacNeicean metamorphoses which open the way to more sacredly-sanctioned possibilities. And, as Mahon told Dillon Johnston, 'only a lobotomy could remove from his mind the Yeatsian line, which he, like MacNeice, exorcises by placing elaborate diction within ironic sentences.'[92] Yet, like MacNeice and Heaney, Mahon feels the allure of places beyond or away from human action and the events of history. In *The Yellow Book*, his recent meditation upon cultural decadence at the millenium and its relation to similar decadence at the end of the last century, he sees that trait, as the epigraph from 'Palinurus' shows, as 'but one technical problem the more which the writer has to solve':

> Chastely to write these eclogues I need to lie,
> like the astrologers, in an attic next the sky
> where, high among church spires, I can dream and hear
> their grave hymns wind-blown to my ivory tower.

Mahon recognizes the equivocal potential for delusion in such a pose ('my thoughts blazing for want of a real fire'), yet at the same time revels in the fastness which the technical challenge (which is also, in this poem as elsewhere, partly one of translation) affords him. He acknowledges also that this has been his habitual approach to his subject matter across his career ('up to my usual tricks'). [93]

Yet he also, in 'Remembering the '90s', acknowledges that the 'technical problem' remains continually to be re-solved (as it has for all writing after Romanticism), that he shares much with the decadent '"tragic" (pathetic) generation' eulogized by Yeats:

> Owning like them 'an indolent, restless gift',
> fitful, factitious and at best makeshift,
> burning without warmth or illumination,
> each verse co-terminous with its occasion,
> each line the pretext for a precious cadence,
> I keep alight the cold candle of decadence.[94]

The elaborateness and irony of this, such as they are, admit also that the writer is entrapped by the style which he would overcome or 'solve'. The Fallon-like co-terminousness of the poetry is its essential strength as well as its weakness, a limitation endemic in Yeatsian style itself, and in the adoption of masks. In establishing the accelerated cultural decline at the end of this century compared to that of the last ('... time spares / the old beeches with their echoes of Coole demesne; / foreign investment conspires against old decency'[95]), Mahon reconfirms the value of 'the infantile imagination', building 'my faerie palaces in the night'. The poet is embroiled in the situation which he would distance himself from, and his solving of it becomes, in Yeatsian fashion, a reliance on style as the foundation for an ennabling position above and beyond what is inescapable. Rather than revealing, as Peter McDonald has claimed, an irony and anxiety about form which see him 'fighting shy' of Yeatsian procedures, the stylistic and formal fastnesses of this more recent work would seem to see Mahon self-consciously but necessarily delighting in the precious and the Byzantine.[96]

As with Yeats's work, in fact, the various demurrals and uncertainties do not fundamentally challenge the formal exactions of the poetry, as they have never done in Mahon. While remaining alert to the human costs of any kind of transcendence, or stepping beyond the normal rhythms of life (as in 'Tithonous', in which the visionariness of a figure like that of Yeats's bird on a golden bough dreaming of the past, future, 'Even of the present', is subjected to the torments of the action of time upon the body[97]), Mahon has continually acknowledged also the Yeatsian urge towards form within himself. He has, indeed, frequently adopted versions of the eight-line stanza which Yeats made his own in his most famous later works:

> Why am I always staring out
> of windows, preferably from a height?
> I think the redemptive enterprise
> of water – hold it to the light! –
> yet distance is the vital bond
> between the window and the wind
> while equilibrium demands
> a cold eye and deliberate hands.

While this poem, 'The Sea in Winter', like many others, acknowledges the doubts over such perspectives which are yet central to the work itself ('The shouts / of souls in torment round the town / at closing time make as much sense'), the consolations wrought by such self-epitaphing 'fine views' continue, and continue to be desired. As 'Beyond Howth Head' had put it, 'our afterlives' might be 'a coming true / of perfect worlds we never knew', and yet the intimations of such worlds are the stuff of Mahon's poetry from 'The Snow Party' and 'The Last of the Fire Kings' onwards, and of the masks he adopts within it.[98] While knowing, as the first of these poems shows, that 'Elsewhere they are burning / Witches and heretics...', the continuous present tense of these poems offers its continual challenge to such actions.[99] The duration of the poem offers an illusion of the present as wished-for presence *here* which renders atrocities *elsewhere* as lacking in form and therefore in meaning. Mahon's belatedness and humanity allows, as most famously in 'A Disused Shed in Co. Wexford', for a voicing of common suffering, while his Yeatsianism continues to deploy an elaborateness of language and syntax, as well as a self-aware formal inscrutability, in order to both manage and register such sympathy.

IX

As such, Mahon's work continues to reveal those stylistic and formal qualities which he has found present in 'the Yeatsian influence' upon Eavan Boland's earlier poetry:

> the peremptory, hieratic note, the assumption of exalted purpose and manifest destiny . . . the sometimes quaint language . . . and a powerful sense of history conceived as theatre . . . .[100]

And indeed, the identification made by Boland (1944–) in early poems between herself and Yeats was a startlingly absolute one, which has endured within her subsequent explorations of a specifically women's experience and history. In that early work Boland casts herself both as the upholder of a threatened poetic possibility (presumably partly in response to the attacks on the Yeatsian inheritance from Kavanagh through to Kinsella), and as a belated temporary escaper from historical circumstance, 'Outside History' as her more recent sequence-title has it.

'Whatever I may learn / You are its sum, struggling to survive' as she put it in 'Yeats in Civil War' from her 1967 first book, *New Territory*, 'A fantasy of honey your reprieve'.[101] The querulousness of this empathy, whereby the summary possibility Boland casts for her own ambition is itself 'struggling to survive', a temporary act of mind achieved in 'a Norman keep' whilst 'Vandals' rage outside, emphasizes her awareness of her own situation as a woman when 'Irish poetry was predominantly male'.[102] The honey-bees, which represent a dreamt-of procreative sweetness amid strife in Yeats's tower-poem 'The Stare's Nest By My Window' (which is also important for Heaney), offer a sense of poetic possibility in Boland's re-envisioning of them. They are a trope of personal survival in times of trouble, poetic and personal endurance becoming irrevocably the same thing.

For all her early alertness to the exclusions rendered by 'great art' as 'From the Painting *Back from the Market* by Chardin' puts it ('Hazard and death. The future and the past. / A woman's secret history and her loves'[103]), Yeats's endurance seems to link him into, rather than to exclude him from, this vision of 'men and women / ...linked / By a common instinct to survive.' That sense of both 'hazard' and of temporariness have, over the next few collections, an increasing effect upon the loosening of form in Boland's work, as 'increasingly I came to regard each poem', as she puts it in the Preface to the *Collected Poems*, 'not as a series of technical struggles, but as a forceful engagement between a life and a language'.[104]

Yet, within that engagement, that bringing closer of the poetic to the facts of her daily experience as a woman raising children in a Dublin suburb, the Yeatsian Neo-Platonist in her continues to be heard. The sequence written mostly in couplets, 'Suburban Woman' (which concludes Boland's next collection *The War Horse*), opens with a mythic or dream landscape in which domestic and personal violence clearly mirror the resurgence of the Troubles in the North, but closes with a moment in a kitchen after the speaker's child is asleep:

> Her kitchen blind down – a white flag –
> the day's assault over...
>
> And on this territory, blindfold, we meet
> at last, veterans of a defeat
>
> no truce will heal... ...
>
> ...Defeated we survive, we two, housed
>
> together in my compromise, my craft –
> who are of one another the first draft.[105]

The uncertain relation between the pronouns in this poem, which manifests the uncertain relationship between the subject (the suburban woman), and the author (suburban woman but also poet), capture that querulousness mentioned earlier. As with versions of Yeatsian mask, the relationship, or comparative distance, between the voice in the poem and the poet's voice remains unclear. In the lyric they are always versions of each other.

For Boland, as for Yeats, the craft itself is always a compromising of experience and a displacement of it within self-mythologizations.

And yet that compromise manifests the only possibility of respite from the inevitable strife and continual defeats of any relational situation. The unstable relation between the public and the domestic private world is figured as the difficult-to-judge distance between the personal voice and that of its mask in this poem. Boland's exploration of these shifting boundaries accords with similar ideas in much recent Irish poetry.[106] Yet her use here ('first draft'), as frequently elsewhere, of metaphors drawn from the practicalities of her 'craft' marks a more foregrounded and honest consciousness of the aestheticization of experience involved in any poetry-making than that of many other writers'. Her preoccupation with the political poems of the embattled Yeats at the time of the Civil War ('Meditations' is, she has written, 'the Irish political poem as it should be'; it 'takes a public reality of fixed meaning and destabilizes it through the intensity of a private world'[107]) lends her an alertness to the radical opposition between the formal and stylistic qualities of poetry and the repetitions of historical violence beyond. In the process, poetry is valued by her for its 'unpredictability', a quality which goes along with an intense vigilance. Boland's dialogue with Yeats is to that extent a wresting-from and overcoming, a refiguring of the tower poems on different ground, and with a sexual politics alien to his. Yet Boland's continuing scepticism about the political efficacy of poetry within the male public world goes along with a Yeatsian intentness upon the work involved in her own craft.[108]

'Formal Feeling', from the recent *The Lost Land*, captures the vulnerability, watchfulness and consequences of this aesthetic. The poem opens by seemingly retelling the myth of a god who visited a woman in the night on the condition that she did not make a light to look upon his nakedness. When she does, he flees.

> Into the dark. Into the here and now
> and air and quiet of an Irish night,
> where I am writing at a darkening window
> about a winged god and his lover
>
> watching the lines and stanzas and measures,
> which are devised for these purposes,
> disappearing as the shadows close
> in around the page
> under my hand.

Boland at once captures the temporal threat within which all devising and recounting survives, while at the same time acknowledging 'The power of a form' which has a woman still addressing 'the work of man in the dark'. The myth is so charged that it constantly seeks new interpretation, and therefore new forms in which to express itself – that sense of repetition and re-reading which intensely haunts all of the Irish poetry I have been discussing in this chapter. Boland's bringing-us-to-awareness of the 'here and now' (that phrase again) within which the myth is being rewritten in turn draws our attention to the vulnerability to remaking of myth itself. The poem ends with an address to Eros, the original promulgator of the myth: 'This time – and this you did not ordain – / I am changing the story.'[109] The absence of authorial control over language is enabling for later interpreters of narrative and history, especially for those who recognize the repressions and silencings being carried out within them.

The gaining of power over myths by women resides in the revelation of those myths' historical longevity and transience, their being brought from a realm of symbolism into a rhetoric of temporality and allegory. 'And where does poetry come in?' Boland has asked in her essay 'The Woman The Place The Poet', 'it enters at the point where myth touches history'.[110] If her more recent poetry has sometimes brought itself closer to 'history', as signalled by the ending of the sequence 'Outside History' and the following 'Writing in a Time of Violence', she is attentive also to the painful limitations which prevent us crossing from the mythic into that other realm. 'Our children are our legends', she tells us in 'Legends', a heartening poem because of its surety that her daughter will 're-tell the story'. Yet, in a later poem from *In a Time of Violence*, a poem whose title, 'Time and Violence', suggests its closeness to the collection's key themes, a random assortment of injured mythic figures ('This is what language did to us') plead with the poet:

> Write us out of the poem. Make us human
> in cadences of change and mortal pain
> and words we can grow old and die in.[111]

Boland's sense of a Romantic problematic, in which the poems' mythologies represent both strength and limitation, and her consequent vigilant preoccupation with their own procedures, is itself heightened and made more painful by her sense of the difficulties of writing as a woman, often a projection of man's consciousness and stories. Her attention to the 'history' of her own body, its ageing, is bolder because more intimate than Yeats's late rage: 'neither young now nor fertile, / and with the marks of childbirth / still on it'.[112] Yet at the same time, and particularly in the liberating poems of the early 1980s, she remains alert to the brutalities enacted upon women's histories and bodies by men who would make them in their own image: 'He splits my lip with his fist, / shadows my eye with a blow / ... What a perfectionist! / His are a sculptor's hands...'.[113] Boland's constant attention to the demands of form and its exclusions, both for good and bad, make her a powerful dramatizer of Yeatsian achievement as dilemma, both the source of something and its denyer.

X

That extreme formal self-consciousness, the constant attention Boland both gives and draws to the underpinning technique of her work, have recently been matched at a different level in the work of Paul Muldoon (1951–). In the 1987 *Meeting the British*, Muldoon had repeated Auden's sniping at Yeats's self-importance, in poems like 'Man and the Echo', as part of an inconclusive debate with 'MacNeice' on the Heaneyish subject of the efficacy of poetry. The 1990 *Madoc – A Mystery* presented a *Vision*-like dissection and indexing of history,[114] *The Annals of Chile* (1994) and *Hay* (1998), show him involved in a complex formal whimfulness as a means of containing a seemingly unmanageable and intractable range of experiences. Although, as Bernard O'Donoghue has pointed out, the 'hermeticism' which attends such complicated formal practices is essentially part of the Irish literary tradition, from Old Irish to Joyce, in its 'preference for form over substantial assertion and for logic over facts',[115] there are many points at which the poetry enters into debate with Yeatsian formal procedures, and therefore with the subject matter which those forms are set to contain.

'The Point', from *Hay*, dramatizes a direct confrontation between the aestheticized hierarchism of Yeats's beleaguered writings from Thoor Ballylee and the everyday damage done by growing up. Rejecting the 'unsullied, keen' Sato's sword as fit subject from the outset, 'what everything in me wants to articulate', is the 'little bit of scar' the speaker received at school when being stabbed in the *'thigh / (not, as the chronicles have it, my calf)'* by a schoolroom enemy.[116] The poem seems to stand up for the vernacular and quotidian against the mythologized symbolism of Yeats's imaginings. That setting-up of the tower with its historically violent associations as a place of writing by Yeats becomes the seemingly simple memory of the child's fight.

And yet . . . Muldoon's poetry is, as ever, wary of the ways in which the recording of any experience is potentially a misrecording. 'The chronicles' (the memories of the children? the schoolroom punishment book?) have it wrong and, further, the scar on Muldoon's leg proves it so. Or does it exist at all? There is obviously a smack at the increasing authorial and historical resonance adopted in Heaney's later poetry here ('The annals say . . .'[117]), but also a complicating of the dialectical possibilities which the sonnet seems to posit. 'What everything in me wants to articulate' expresses a truthful and continuing desire, in other words, rather than a satisfied completion. *This* chronicle, the poem, might as well be as faulty as Yeats's earlier one. The 'mark' on Muldoon, which is 'proof' of the fact, remains merely a mark on the page, set there by the (*absent*) author. Muldoon is testing, as did Yeats, the ways in which seemingly 'natural' embodiments of experience in poetry often actually have a non-natural, emblematic, character.

Hay, perhaps more than any of Muldoon's previous collections, seems preoccupied, in other words, with that issue of what constitutes 'normal' subject-matter and speech when rendered into poetry, an issue which of course continued to preoccupy Yeats from the early 1910s onwards. 'Symposium', which in many ways seems central to the procedures of the collection, dramatizes the ways in which the kinds of authority and knowledge traditionally invested in non-poetic speech are themselves founded upon logical absurdities, and the poem gains its own energies by replacing those absurdities with others of its own:

> You can lead a horse to water but you can't make it hold
> its nose to the grindstone and hunt with the hounds.
> Every dog has a stitch in time. . . .[118]

What Muldoon seems to Romantically feel here, as in the title sequence of *Madoc – A Mystery*, with its 'poems' 'spoken' by various philosophers, is that the 'philosophical' or 'logical' basis of truth is in itself absurd, and that, as with Boland and Yeats, one of the achievements of the best poetry is to reveal that absurdity. The veerings of the poem, and the playings fast and loose with tenses and syntax, are a manifestation of this central imaginative drive, shared also by Yeats. What it reveals once more is that it is the structure of language's temporalization, its syntax, which makes for all ontological 'meaning'. 'Symposium' 'makes sense', but then, Muldoon wryly seems to ask, what is that?

' "Let us now drink", I imagine patriot to patriot cry / after they've shot / a neighbor in his own aftermath, who hangs still between two sheaves / like Christ', 'Aftermath' begins.[119] Similar swift and odd shifts of tense and image appear when Yeats considers the nature and questionable success of martyrdom in 'Easter 1916':

> Was it needless death after all?
> For England may keep faith
> For all that is done and said.
> We know their dream; enough
> To know they dreamed and are dead;
> And was it excess of love
> Bewildered them until they died?
> I write it out in a verse ....

> (*CP*, pp. 181–2)

The 'needless' floats as a continued syntactic possibility here. Knowledge might satisfy, but has its limits ('*was* it excess...?'); the temporal complexities and perplexities of this are dropped ('Was it...may keep...We know...enough / To know...was it') before the final change of direction, back upon the only task a poet might have, 'I write'. The imaginary speaker in Muldoon's poem goes through similar tense shifts ('shot him...in his own aftermath') and syntactic ambiguities ('hangs still').[120] Out of both poems there arises a conflicting sense of the intransigent processes around death. These processes are uneasily described, in temporal terms which are potentially confusing, a skimming back and forth between past and future which makes the present action ('now') disturbing. Muldoon's archaicizing inversion ('Let us now drink') itself distances and estranges us from the event 'described' (when is this? where?). Such difficult transitions between specificity and generality are also at the centre of Yeats's response to events.

What the later Muldoon seems to have intensified, then, is his sense of the formal complications and possibilities involved in writing out such difficult and historically painful material. With his elegy 'Incantata' for his former lover Mary Farl Powers, which adopts the form of 'In Memory of Major Robert Gregory', Muldoon started a process of sound- and formal-patterning-through-rhyme of the extremest complexity and absoluteness. The rhyme sounds from the elegy then reappear in 'Yarrow', which closes *The Annals of Chile*; then, in the same order, in 'The Mud Vision', the opening poem of *Hay*, 'Third Epistle to Timothy', and again in the cycle of sonnets with which the collection ends, 'The Bangle (Slight Return)', firstly in the same running order, then in reverse.[121] Such writing exhibits the supreme clash between a Thomism or Neo-Platonism, 'all...composed', as 'Incantata' itself puts it, against a sense of its opposite, a meaningless detritus, 'all composed of odds and ends', as Muldoon's next phrase immediately tells us.[122]

Whereas the subject matter of lyric poetry contains shards of experience and draws our attention to the ways in which that 'experience' is itself founded upon imaginative possibility, not 'reality', the traditional formalism of the poetry establishes all as part of a continuum. The tragically random event of Powers's death (a randomness which the poem informs us that, as a Thomist, she would never admit of) is matched by a seeming randomness of rhyme patterning, which Muldoon's subsequent treatment turns into an absolute, unforgettable, un-get-roundable. (We are reminded again of de Man's definition of poetry as 'a random event whose power, like the power of death, is due to the randomness of its occurrence' – but, then, death *is*, definingly, inevitable.) Powers's death is indeed writ over all, sounds out through all of Muldoon's recent work. The loss of her 'unifying' vision of everything, as Gregory's had for Yeats, exposes the world to error, the poet to 'Errata', as one of the most surprisingly moving poems in *Hay* is called, or, in a rare visionary moment from Muldoon, to that straining towards a

> ... spirit-troop
> of hay-treaders as far as the eye can see, the coil on coil
> of hay from which, in the taper's mild uproar,
> they float out across the dark face of the earth, an earth
>   without form, and void.[123]

Yeats's cyclical vision would never allow him to look into such substanceless eternity of interpretation and reinterpretation. Yet that standing upon the edge of the abyss is what Yeats's poetry, in its constant urge to remake itself, constantly forces itself to do. Man, as Yeats contends in 'Man and the Echo', and as Muldoon might himself reflect, 'till his intellect grows sure / that all's arranged in one clear view, / Pursues the thoughts that I pursue'. (*CP*, p. 346)

XI

Extrapolating from Martin Heidegger's existential analysis of death, Jacques Derrida has recently controversially claimed that it is in the time and space of mourning that the metaphorical bases of politics might be said to lie. The self's relation to the other, which underlies all political interaction, will, for him, 'never be distinguishable from a bereaved apprehension'. In responding to the death of someone close to us, we recognize both how little of them we can ever embody, and also our susceptibility to them as other. They remain both closed and beyond us and (through memory) open to us, and in this process of response to altereity, the self, including the political self, is therefore (partly) defined.[124]

In performing the work of mourning and remembering Yeats, subsequent Irish poets have frequently had to articulate and refine their own sense of political, national (and tacitly religious) identification. They have also had to express their ideas of the relationship of poetry to Irish society and history, as part of describing what aspects of his writing they find sympathetic and redeployable or, alternatively, as to-be-resisted. The various splittings within Yeats's proximate symbolic presence have therefore enabled Irish writers, as we have seen in the work of MacNeice, Kinsella, Coffey and also Heaney Boland and Muldoon, to take up various aspects of his work at different moments in their own development. In a 1908 uncollected poem, Yeats noted that in remaking (or revising) one of his poems 'It is myself that I remake.'[125] Padraic Fallon has noted, too, how, terrifyingly, the poet dies in each poem only to be remade in the next. The proximity of the would-be founding presence of Yeats within Irish poetry would seem to contribute to bequeathing the Romantic notion, therefore, that in each poem, as Paul Muldoon has said in interview, 'One has to try to begin all over again and re-invent the activity.' 'It's very difficult and alarming to do that, but necessary to try'.[126]

As with Yeats, that process of self-remaking is inextricable from processes of national founding. Declan Kiberd's comment on Yeats holds for all of the work I have discussed here:

> The project of inventing a unitary Ireland is the attempt to achieve at a political level a reconciliation of opposed qualities which must first be fused in the self.[127]

The 'in-between-time' of historical dislocation which Kinsella, Heaney and Boland have made explicit in their work is a frequent feature of all of the poetry discussed in this chapter, from Muldoon's own complex play on tenses, to Mahon's use of ghostly presents, and Kavanagh's deathly discontinuities. Those undecidabilities in their turn mark the processes of emergence of a politics, a vision and identity for Ireland itself. The haunting symbolic presence of Yeats in subsequent writing, whether embraced or variously resisted, offers no single 'truth' or 'meaning', yet continues to challenge later poets variously to inflect their work according to his legacy.

3
Inevitable Abstractions: Yeats and British Poetry

W.H. Auden, Donald Davie, Thom Gunn, Ted Hughes, Geoffrey Hill

The plenitude of possibility, sometimes terrifying, sometimes remaking and enabling, which the near-proximity of Yeats's presence opened up for subsequent Irish poetry, becomes very evidently more divided, emptier, when translated into subsequent British poetry. The opportunities for identification and rejection, on political, cultural and religious grounds, offered under the multivalent name 'Yeats' in his native country, became in Britain both seemingly more knowable and therefore more 'readable' for later poets. Beyond the immediate historical and cultural context which lay behind his own revisions and indecipherabilities, the divergent values and qualities expressed in his work became, elsewhere, more readily subtractable the one from the other. 'The infinity of a totality', Paul de Man claims, constitutes the 'main attraction' of symbolic presence within Romantic and post-Romantic writing, and is founded on 'an intimate unity' between word and 'actuality' or 'truth', a unity obviously lessened beyond an original cultural context.

In Yeats's case, this process of translation from Ireland to Britain gradually moves his symbolic presence towards a more allegorical meaning. To adopt de Man's useful terms again, it becomes more 'a sign that refers to one specific meaning and thus exhausts its suggestive potentialities once it has been deciphered'.[1] The multiple and conflicting possibilities which Seamus Heaney derives from Yeats's visionary reading of history at various points in his career, for instance, reveal a consciously varying responsiveness to the strains and counterstrains in the earlier poet which is unmatched in later poetry from Britain, where the 'anxiety of influence' is less immediate.[2] Yet it is also true that, as both Julia Kristeva and de Man himself have acknowledged, the relationship between the symbolic and signs in texts only ever reveals changing emphases. Sign and symbol are inseparable, and the symbolic is never entirely drained away, merely made subject to different modes of articulation.[3] The shift of weight from the latter towards the former in that process of translation which is literary influence – within a single language but in different cultural contexts – is (as my discussions of the poetry below will illustrate) a matter of *degree*, in which the marks of symbolic presence retain a continuing trace even within their absence.

The processes of reading, and identification with, Yeats in Britain have most often centred upon a deciphering of, and resistance to, perceived 'Irish' qualities in the work. There is a sense that there remains much which speaks to subsequent English poetry (the Anglo element of Yeats's 'in-between' inheritance, perhaps). Yet there also remains much – often dismissed as mystical, or of-the-past – which was not appropriable. While the political effectiveness of Yeats's nationalism and acts of cultural founding are often acknowledged, they are decontextualized within a wider concern around matters of poetic diction and form. In the process, Yeats is figured as a hieratic (and often modernist) poet, as an unlocated, disembodied, universal. As a result of these re-readings, he emerges as a more singular, reduced poet, one whose 'example' is unquestioned (since more easily refutable, perhaps) as it had not been within later writing from Ireland itself.

Such emptyings-out of meaning through the process of reading remind us that, as George Steiner has tellingly argued, reading *within* as well as across languages is transformational, and involves us in issues of translation where, however, 'the barrier or receptor between source and receptor is time'.[4] But the reading of Yeats's influence in later British contexts reminds us also that the 'barrier', even within the same language, is *cultural* and historical; that, as Jacques Derrida has argued, 'we will never have ... to do with some "transport" of pure signifieds ... that the signifying instrument would leave virgin and untroubled'.[5] It is the abstraction in language itself, the distance between sign and signified which all literature (but particularly the intensity of poetic form) dramatizes, which makes reading into a process of translation, *especially* across contexts. What is emptied out, in this instance, is that unsettling, aporetic abstraction involved in Yeats's own quest for foundations of national consciousness, his particularly-inflected Romantic urge to imagine a separate Irish culture in an unidentifiable future from the traces of distinctiveness in its past.

Yeats himself, of course, argued generally, in essays like the 1913 'Art and Ideas', against all forms of abstraction. 'By reintegrating the mind', he claimed, it would be possible to rediscover 'our more profound

Pre-Raphaelitism, the old abounding, nonchalant reverie', and so over-come modern solipsism and abstraction. (*E&I*, pp. 353–5) He objected to certain qualities in modernist art on similar grounds, complaining, for example, in a letter to his father in 1916 about a rhetorical element in Wyndham Lewis's Cubist pictures 'arising from his confusion of the abstract with the rhythmical. Rhythm implies a living body, a breast to rise and fall...'.[6] And yet British critics, including C.H. Sisson, have been eager both to abstract certain qualities from their reading of his work, and to identify as both strength and weakness 'a curious passion for generality in Yeats which contradicts his declared hatred of abstraction'.[7] It is abstraction – in *both* these senses – which underpins later poets' absorption of certain resonances in Yeats while resisting others. Curiously and significantly, the 'inevitable abstraction' which Derrida finds to be the basis of all interpretation here takes on specific, *actual*, cultural and temporal characteristics.[8]

Yeats's complex, unresolved, engagement with history in his own country becomes in Britain a more settled vision and integration, a more 'resolved' version of Romanticism from which certain stable meanings can often be read. Such issues are figured most complexly in the work of W.H. Auden (1907–1973), and so I will spend a larger time at the start of this chapter discussing their implications for him, before following similar ideas in the work of later poets.

I

The arrival of Auden in the United States in early 1939 famously brought about an almost immediate revision of his earlier commitment to political issues, a commitment which had been ever-present in his writings during the past ten years on his native soil. That arrival, and that revision, also famously involved Auden in a renegotiation – or what Stan Smith has called 'Oedipal dialogues'[9] – with the ideas of Yeats. Auden commemorated the older poet's death on 28th January of that year both poetically, in an elegy, and in an article for *The Partisan Review*, 'The Public v. the Late Mr. W.B. Yeats'. In both poem and essay, Auden worries through what were to become continual themes of his own later writing: the relation of the artist as human being to his or her work; the relation of the aesthetics of art to the politics of the age in which it is created; and the efficacy of the work of art in its relationship to history.

Such themes are, of course, themselves centrally Yeatsian. The question about the danger of commitment to active politics resurfaced again and again from his early poems to Maud Gonne to, for example, his

1927 elegy 'In Memory of Eva Gore-Booth and Con Markiewicz'. His notion of style, conveyed as late as the 1937 'A General Introduction for My Work', emphasized the central role of uncommitted personality in art, echoing his father's words of decades before.[10] The late poem 'Man and the Echo' finds him asking about the 1902 *Cathleen Ni Houlihan* 'Did that play of mine send out / Certain men the English shot?' (*CP*, p.345)

Soon after Yeats's death, Auden also wrote a magazine article on him that takes the Yeatsian form of a confrontation of antitypes. The case made by the younger poet's 'Public Prosecutor' against the dead man is easily paraphrased. Yeats failed as a poet, since none of his lines are memorable. He did not have a very profound understanding of the age in which he lived, since he retained a feudal attitude towards the peasantry to the end and was hesitant about his declared commitment to the cause of Irish independence. Thirdly, he was foolish with regard to the progressive thought of his time because he loathed science, believed instead in fairies and Irish myths, and was near the end of his life a Fascist.

Auden's 'Counsel for the Defence''s arguments in reply to these charges are more subtle and complicated. He initially distances the artist from any professed social views, saying that, provided the poet genuinely holds them, the poetry can be valued for its own sake, regardless of the political opinions expressed. He then moves on to claim that Yeats's particular situation in Ireland must be taken into account. It was an 'economically backward' country in which class struggle was less to the fore than in the rest of Western Europe, so Yeats's attitudes were perhaps understandable. And, further, even if he was not physically involved in the Nationalist struggle himself, the Abbey Theatre had played some part in bringing that struggle about. Yeats's odd beliefs in fairies and folk heroes were all about binding his society together; his later personal mythology was simply a transposition of that ambition to a universalized plane.

Then, famously, the 'Defence Counsel' in Auden's article sums up the case, attacking the central premise of his opponent's arguments:

> art is a product of history, not a cause. Unlike some other products, technical inventions for example, it does not re-enter history as an effective agent, so that the question whether art should or should not be propaganda is unreal. The case for the prosecution rests on the fallacious belief that art ever makes anything happen, whereas the honest truth, gentlemen, is that, if not a poem had been written, not a picture painted, not a bar of music composed, the history of man would be materially unchanged.[11]

Finally, there is for this Counsel one field in which the poet is a man of action, the field of language. Here Yeats's 'ideas', however 'false or undemocratic', are overcome, since 'his diction shows a continuous evolution towards what one might call the true democratic style.... The diction of *The Winding Stair* is the diction of a just man', and therefore 'just men will always recognize the author as a master'.

I have rehearsed these arguments again at some length. Due to the much-remarked-upon consonance of the 'Defence Counsel''s summing-up with the conclusions of section II of Auden's elegy 'In Memory of W.B. Yeats' which was added after the poem's initial publication, several of the other aspects of the defence argument have been overlooked.[12] The first of these is the insistence, not devoid of condescension, on a cogniscence of Yeats's Irish context in reading him, that his 'silliest' beliefs (to adopt a word from the elegy) come to make a kind of sense when read against that parochial, backward context (and this was an insistence Auden was making as late as a review on Yeats in 1955).[13] In the poem in memory of Yeats, the dead poet has *become* his nation's poetry. The 'Irish vessel' must 'lie / Emptied' of that poetry after his death. 'Mad Ireland,' we are told in the second section, 'hurt you into poetry', but the ridiculousness of Yeats's beliefs is not seen here (as it was in the article) also to have derived from his historical and national situation. Rather, 'You were silly like us', a universalizing inclusiveness which governs the poignant sense of Yeats's dispersal after his death amongst his readers.

So the pain of his nation's history is seen as guaranteeing the particular nature of Yeats's beliefs in Auden's eyes (if only potentially – the difference between the prose and the poetic context reveal continuing uncertainty). In making those beliefs 'understandable', Auden also distances them. The comradely manoeuvre deracinates Yeats, shrouds him against his own absurdities, while also governing the recognition that he has now become his admirers ('Now he is scattered among a hundred cities / And wholly given over to unfamiliar affections'[14]). In death, Yeats is disseminated into places unknown to him and transformed into the object of desires he would have been unaware of. As he himself put it when addressing 'My Descendants', in distastefully hieratic terms alien to Auden's more democratic if modern and mundane version, 'it seems / Life scarce can cast a fragrance on the wind... / But the petals strew the garden plot'. (*CP*, p. 203) As Auden here suggests, and as post-structuralist theory of course later maintained, the author's absence becomes a mark of the possibilities of his text's reinterpretation and iteration in other contexts, but at the cost of its original integration and suggestiveness.

Yet what is far more startling, given the critical consensus that the Yeats elegy marks Auden's retreat from politics, is the ways in which the Counsel for the Defence in the essay seeks to assimilate Yeats to a Socialist cause, partly because 'Nationalism is a necessary stage towards Socialism', but more surprisingly through his diction:

> The social virtues of a real democracy are brotherhood and intelligence, and the parallel linguistic virtues are strength and clarity, virtues which appear ever more clearly through successive volumes by the deceased.

Such 'social virtues' in Yeats presumably warrant the traditional comparison of the dying poet's body to the body politic in section I of the elegy: 'The provinces of his body revolted, / The squares of his mind were empty, / Silence invaded the suburbs.' The introduction of the cityscape seems slightly inappropriate where Yeats is concerned, in these terms significantly more English than Irish, yet it establishes the civic responsibility of the older poet, his 'true perception of a social evil' as the 'Defence Counsel' claims.[15] Poetry's 'way of happening' might be 'a mouth', as section II of the elegy puts it, but, through its 'parallel virtues' to 'real democracy' in its diction, poetry is implicitly given an active role to play in clarifying and defining 'real intelligence and brotherhood'. 'Every poem, therefore', as Auden put it in one of his lectures as Oxford Professor of Poetry, 'is an attempt to present an analogy to that paradisal state in which Freedom and Law, System and Order are united in harmony. Every good poem is very nearly a Utopia'.[16]

Auden's biographers and critics have been for the most part eager to follow him in his frequently-repeated assertion that, from around this point in his career, he came to recognize that Yeats's early influence upon him had been pernicious. That influence, he felt, made him into 'a symbol of my own devil of inauthenticity'.[17] It is as though Auden was drawn by the dangerous glamour of the foreign and outmoded in Yeats, and also able to identify it, limit and overcome it in a Bloomian trope of repression – a trope complicating, if not actually disproving, Harold Bloom's own assertion that the British are only 'revisionists' when it comes to issues of influence, whereas the Americans are the true competitors.[18] And yet, while not wishing to ignore the force of Auden's assertion of the need for distance from Yeats, it would be true to say that his continued wrestling with the themes and debates of his elegy and magazine article following the death of Yeats was consistently dominant in his later output, perhaps primarily so in its own quest for a language and a location of 'social virtue'. Within his quest we find Auden frequently responding to the models of that virtue offered by his forebears, amongst whom the shade of Yeats remains frequently – if more often than not implicitly – present. Although in the early Sixties Auden was in various ways seeking to debunk the significance of Yeats's influence upon him, in the years between the 1939 elegy and then he several times, in various forms, rethought or reiterated his ideas about the earlier poet. But, as part of this process, the dangerous symbolic value of Yeats was consistently itself voided, refigured, *brought home* to England in ways that render his work exemplary but non-difficult, disentangled from its location.[19]

In the process, the re-readings of Yeats follow the trajectory of Auden's own self-revision across his career. The politicized, even bizarrely socialist Yeats of the 'Defence Counsel' in the obituary article, soon becomes elided with one who focuses the younger poet's debates around mythic concerns. Auden's humorous dismissal in his major essay of 1948 'Yeats As An Example' of Yeats's spiritualism for being 'so essentially middle class – or should I say Southern Californian', and his praise of Yeats for transforming the occasional poem, and for releasing English poetic rhythm from 'iambic monotony', have been much remarked upon. But less notice has been taken of his recognition of his subject's pragmatic solutions to the dilemmas presented to him by his age, and to Auden's remarks on the *differences* between Yeats's age and his own.

The conflict of Yeats's time was 'between the Religion of Reason and the Religion of Imagination'. For Auden's, as he saw it, it was 'between the good and evil will . . . between the integration of thought and feeling and their dissociation, not between the individual and the masses but between the social person and the impersonal state'.[20] This should not, however, in Auden's view lead Yeats or later poets to radically different poetic solutions to these central 'conflicts':

> any poet today, even if he deny the importance of dogma to life, can see how useful myths are to poetry – how much, for instance, they helped Yeats to make his private experiences public and his vision of public events personal. He knows, too, that in poetry all dogmas become myths; that the aesthetic value of the poem is the same whether the poet and/or the reader actually believe what it says or not.

Aesthetic value is somehow abstracted from myth, which, as a mark of its modernity, has itself been extracted from communal or national origins, in ways that Yeats, both early and late, would not wish to recognize. Myth here becomes any system of signs. What matters is, rather, that the myth involved must be a 'personal one', that 'it involves your emotions'. Yeats, 'like us', was faced with 'the modern problem, that is of living in a society in which men are no longer supported by tradition without being aware of it', and by accepting that fact as 'a working condition', he is 'an example to all who come after him'.

As with the article 'The Public v. the Late Mr. W.B. Yeats', therefore, Auden feels that it is allowable to utilize any type of mythic material, provided that the personal significance of that material is visible in the poetry and that the purpose of its use (i.e. its answer to 'the modern problem') is allowed for. What had been a definer of the essential difference of Yeats's poetry earlier, the Irishness of Yeats's mythical interests (and Auden continued in his other comments on Yeats to assert that difference), is here universalized as archetypical of the problems confronting the writer in the modern world. Following from this, criticisms of the nature of that mythic material by later generations might be 'objectively correct', but should not create 'subjective resentment' in later poets which prevents the criticized poet from becoming a significant influence. To do so would be

> a dangerous hinderance to our own poetic development, for, in poetry as in life, to lead one's own life means to relive the lives of one's parents and, through them, of all one's ancestors; the duty of the present is neither to copy nor to deny the past but to resurrect it.[21]

As I showed in my opening chapter, such visionary (and latterly familial) resurrections provide central metaphorical force within Yeats's own descriptions of the relationship between the poet and the past as it is embodied in, and as it embodies, literary tradition. But Auden's synthesizing here, his transposition of issues of literary influence to 'life' and family history is one step beyond, even, Yeats's more self-conscious and self-assertive recourse to his own ancestor's stories from the introductory poem of his 1914 collection *Responsibilities* onwards. It partakes more specifically of that rhetorical figure of anagorisis or recognition, which, as Terence Cave has argued, is always surrounded by issues of kinship.[22]

Indeed, that notion of resurrection had, of course, found a very particular and personal mythic charge for Auden later in the year of Yeats's death.[23] From its first tentative expression in the concluding prayer of *New Year Letter*, Christianity was implicated with his political and artistic ambitions:

> Convict our pride of its offence
> In all things, even penitence,
> Instruct us in the civil art
> Of making from the muddled heart
> A desert and a city where
> The thoughts that have to labour there
> May find locality and peace,
> And pent-up feelings their release,
> Send strength sufficient for our day,
> And point our knowledge on its way,
> O da quod jubes, Domine.[24]

The imagery of this invocation recalls that in 'In Memory of W.B. Yeats', completed the year before, and this seems acknowledged by the fact that a wind blows 'among quiet reeds' in lines just before these. The 'city' of the poet's dying body retains a ghostly presence here, while, more explicitly, the elegy's final invocation of the spirit of Yeats resonates behind these ones ('With your unconstraining voice / Still persuade us to rejoice ... / In the deserts of the heart / Let the healing fountain start'). The current European 'nightmare of the dark' in *New Year Letter* Part One is felt as strongly as it is in the elegy ('The Jew wrecked in the German cell, / Flat Poland frozen into hell'[25]), and the yearning towards a solving figure beyond is expressed in very much the same imagery. At issue again is a debate about the relation between civic order and a 'locality' where, after a Yeatsian 'labour', 'thoughts and feelings' may be expressed. The unstable and again very generalized conjoining of 'a desert and a city' shows the Eliotic uncertainties that underpin such desired 'making'. Void or plenitude: the unknowability of what might be translated 'there' leads to an antinomianism at the heart of Auden's most orchestrated imprecations. As he put it in 'Horae Canonicae' of 1949–54:

> For the end, for me as for cities,
> Is total absence: what comes to be
> Must go back into non-being
> For the sake of the equity, the rhythm
> Past measure or comprehending.

Within this analogous or parable-based art (as for Yeats amid similar uncertainty), what remains constant for Auden is the role of the personal speaking voice as active interpreter or centre of the world expressed. And yet, at the same time, it is as true of Auden's notion of parable as it is of his response to Yeats's death, and also true of de Manian post-Romantic allegory – a process of dissemination is entered into, whereby the 'meaning' made through the 'I' of the poem is *displaced* onto the reader, while also remaining the poem's symbolic centre at some removed, untranslatable level.[26] De Man himself saw this dilemma as being at the heart of post-Hegelian aesthetics, making it impossible to discuss hermeneutics and poetics at the same time.[27] Auden recognizes that his essentially mediatory, *interpretative*, role renders the transmission of experience extremely complex and difficult. Any approach to a 'civil style' (as he calls it in 'We Too Had Known Golden Hours') involves him in that 'existential historicism', or need to relive in the present the deeds of the past, which James Longenbach has seen as one of Yeats's most significant inheritances to his modernist followers Pound and Eliot.[28]

In *Dichtung Und Wahreit (An Unwritten Poem)*, we find Auden troubling through the possibilities of poetic expression in precisely these terms:

> If . . . I attempt, as I should like to do in this poem, to express what I mean by this thought [*I love You*], I turn myself into a historian, faced with a historian's problems. Of the documents at my disposal (memories of myself, or You, of what I have heard on the subject of love), some have probably been doctored, some may even be downright forgeries. . . . Even were I gifted with total recall, I should still be faced with the task of interpreting them and assessing their relative importance.[29]

As with Yeats's use of myth, or his later visionary attempts to 'order' the chaos of his times, this locates even the most meaningful and intimate statement within a late modern context of historical perplexity. Yeats, in 'The Second Coming' but especially in the cyclical gyres of *A Vision* (itself later dismissed for abstraction, since its 'harsh geometry offered an incomplete interpretation' of imminent unities of being (*E&I*, p. 518)), felt that he could find a standing-place within history -however momentarily – from which he could prophecy the future from within the present. Auden's belated and therefore stronger sense of the personal and historical difficulties of expression, however, made him more hesitant.

In the poems of the 1950s in which Auden writes out such hesitations about, and concomitant feelings of liberation within, history, this failure of expression is ever to the fore. In 'Secondary Epic', Virgil is chided for presuming to claim knowledge over historical process ('Hindsight as foresight makes no sense'). In 'Homage to Clio', the reticence of the Muse of History is seen as opening space for personal human remembrance and interest ('to chirp like a tearless bird, / As though no one dies in particular / And gossip were never true, [is] unthinkable'). While himself more reticent about the individual's (and perhaps especially the poet's) ability to control and express the larger rhythms, Auden retains throughout, then, the sense that, as Yeats did, history must be read, if it is to be read at all, personally.

He does not, in his own deployment of mythic materials, finally give up, either, on the sense that in works of art we might read truths which we might not have been expecting, but which nonetheless will actually happen. In 'The Shield of Achilles', the goddess Thetis's visit to Hephaestos, the smith to the gods, yields the opposite result to that she had expected:

> She looked over his shoulder
>   For ritual pieties,
> White flower-garlanded heifers,
>   Libation and sacrifice,
> But there on the shining metal
>   Where the altar should have been,
> She saw by his flickering forge-light
>   Quite another scene.[30]

Yet this shockingly unKeatsian shield, with its 'artificial wilderness / And a sky like lead', its 'weed-choked field', is, as her final cry of dismay recognizes, truer than her 'poetic' imagining; her son *will* die young. Auden's attentiveness to the extra-poetic register of the sign is once more seen, through the process of mythic narrative, as having a valency which counters both the symbolic and the pious.

Yet the drabness of the shield is also concurrent with the dull and unpersonalized world – a negative consequence of generalization – in the poem: 'Out of the air a voice without a face / Proved by statistics that some cause was just / In tones as dry and level as the place.' Whilst eschewing a falsifying (Keatsian/Yeatsian) world of poetic 'fine excess', therefore, Auden would also seem to be bemoaning *as a poet* unpoetic dismalness which we might also take to be as signature of the modern.

The featureless, timeless landscape of this poem is one which in 1968 Auden was to characterize as remarkably similar to the 'primary world' as it has been conceived by *modern* historians:

> a de-sacralized, depersonalized world where all facts are equally profane. Human history becomes a matter of statistics, in which individual human beings are represented as faceless and anonymous puppets of impersonal forces.

That union of poet and more imaginative historians which had existed until 150 years ago has been broken, and the poet has retreated into a 'secondary world' of narcissistic 'private subjectivity'. Whilst, in the context of this discussion, the self-regardingness of modern art seems to be read negatively, at the end of the lecture series from which these quotations are taken, personal freedom assumes a more positive tone:

> Poetry is personal speech in its purest form. It is concerned, and only concerned, with human beings as unique persons. What men do from necessity or by second nature as individual members of society cannot be the subject for poetry, for poetry is gratuitous utterance.... The artist is a maker, not a man of action.... [T]here is no comprehensible relation between the moral quality of a maker's life and the aesthetic value of the works he makes. On the contrary, every artist knows that the sources of his art are what Yeats called 'the foul rag-and-bone shop of the heart', its lusts, its hatreds, its envies....[31]

Auden's emphasis on the personal enables him to engage, therefore, that excess of utterance which is Yeatsian style, as I described it in my opening chapter, to translate a version of it from its originating conditions into his own aesthetic. As such, therefore, the goddess Thetis's hopes and dreams in 'The Shield of Achilles' are not to be derided. However 'untrue' to reality, they at least offer a personal expression which counters the world of historians or the economics of 'The Managers', whose dumb labour on reports proves that 'In the bad old days it was not so bad'.[32]

The liberating divorce which art offers its maker from the necessary constraints of the world is of course figured most resonantly in Yeats's delineation of possibilities in 'The Choice', a poem which surely resonates throughout all of Auden's considerations of the situation and nature of poetry. What we find from 'The Public v. the Late Mr. W.B. Yeats' through to these 1968 lectures is that Auden is persistently willing to forgive the messiness or objectionableness of the artist's life in order to proclaim the aesthetic value of the works. As Richard Ellmann has noted in passing, Auden is able to dismiss 'The Choice' ('This is untrue', he writes of the intellect's proposed decision between two perfections, that of the 'life' or 'the work': 'perfection is possible in neither'). Yet he is also able to compose a libretto with his lover Chester Kallman, *Elegy for Young Lovers*, on this theme.[33]

That libretto of 1959–60 is based, as the co-authors acknowledged in their note on the 'Genesis of a Libretto', upon 'a local embodiment of...myth'. The hero, an 'artist-genius of the nineteenth and early twentieth century' is 'a genuine myth because the lack of identity between Goodness and Beauty, between the character of the man and the character of his creations, is a permanent aspect of his condition', best summed up, we are told, by 'The Choice' itself. The details of the 'hero', Mittenhofer's, life (his reliance upon spiritual 'messages' from his wife for his work and his rejuventating injections), all suggest that the 'artist-genius' who partly forms the model for that character is Yeats, and that Auden has in mind late Yeats poems like 'Sailing to Byzantium', 'The Spur' and 'Politics'.[34]

In this libretto, the rift between life and art is absolute. In order to complete his elegy, Mittenhofer has to send the 'real' young lovers, Toni and Elizabeth, out to die on the mountain. Elizabeth had earlier been Mittenhofer's young Muse. Yet he gives her away to Toni, largely perhaps out of his inability to make her understand the absolute responsibilities and horrors of art. In lines which it is known from the manuscript were drafted by Auden alone, he sings:

> But you cannot know,
> Have any conception
> Of what it is like
> To be a poet,
> Of what it means
> Never, never
> To feel, to think, to see, to hear,
> Without reflecting: 'Now,
> Could I use that somehow?
> Would it translate
> Into number and rhyme?'
> Until in time
> One no longer knows
> What is true and false
> Or right and wrong.[35]

The monstrousness of Mittenhofer's destructive actions, his ability to sacrifice anything so that the poem may reach completion, is tempered somewhat by such pleas regarding his own *lack* of choice. The Good and the Beautiful are never identical in this world. But, what is more striking in this context is the fact that the other branch of possibility, 'life', is shown to be equally complex and brutal.

In the final scene, a duet between Toni and Elizabeth which we know was also drafted by Auden alone, the young lovers review what might have been their lives had they been allowed to survive. From a childish-pretend perspective of old age they 'review' their marriage – a bourgeois existence with three sons and the husband's adultery, a marriage in name only. 'Not for love were we led here', they and the opera conclude,

> But to unlearn our own lies,
> Each through each, in our last hour,
> And come to death with clean hearts. . . .
>
> God of Truth, forgive our sins,
> All offences we fools made
> Against thee. Grant us Thy peace.
> Light with Thy Love our lives' end.[36]

From the extreme perspective of these two about to die, therefore, we do not receive that 'ecstasy of vision' or 'tragic joy' which Yeats found in Shakespeare's heroes and heroines, and which he saw as the basis for his 'style and attitude'. Rather, what we receive from this 'truth' is the resignation of imperfectibility before the full realization thereof.[37]

Auden's dismissal (cited by Ellmann) of 'The Choice' in his 1956 Oxford lecture 'Making, Knowing, Judging' because 'perfection is poss-ible in neither' life or art seems qualified by these lines therefore. Life is undoubtedly imperfect, in that love itself seems momentary, and the life of the artist is (at least for the purposes of this drama) destructive of other lives and happiness. Yet the work of art produced from the action of the opera is unquestioned and unquestionable, rendered literally so by Auden and Kallman's decision that Mittenhofer's 'poem', when it is finished, be represented by 'orchestral sound and pure vocalization', as they tell us in 'Genesis of a Libretto'. Since it is 'impossible for the audience to distinguish between the verse he gives his hero to speak as a character. . . and the verse he gives him to recite as a specimen of his work as a poet', the librettists display that work (which, for the 'dramatic and moral point of the opera', the audience must be convinced is 'a very good one') in non-verbal ways. The poem remains *untranslatable* into the medium of this work of art. Its *condition as music* renders it immune to the opposing possibilities of 'The Choice', and (temporarily) eludes the post-Romantic dilemmas at the heart of Auden's aesthetics.

In a narrative in which 'life' is frequently judged by 'truth', therefore, the work of 'art' defies verbal articulation. In its turn, this elusiveness of the 'poem' in *Elegy for Young Lovers* might itself be implicated within the medium. After discussing the libretto in his lecture 'The World of Opera', Auden concludes that

> as an art-form involving words, opera is the last refuge of the High style, the only art to which a poet with a nostalgia for those times past, when poets could write in the grand manner all by themselves, can still contribute....[38]

With the representation of Mittenhofer/Yeats's 'elegy' non-verbally, Auden's own nostalgia for a symbolist age seems momentarily at least to the fore, and his distance from it simultaneously confirmed.[39]

Yet, however Yeatsian he might become in the operas, Auden's dialogue with Yeats continues by other means in the poetry. *Elegy for Young Lovers* dramatizes the individual and the personal *in extremis*, the necessity driving the artist's completion of the work as inhuman. The Nietzschean landscape for the drama, the equally unresponsive and inhuman mountains, is utterly the opposite of that 'inconstancy' valued in 'In Praise of Limestone', with its benevolent attitude toward human failings for what they are, rather than the brutal revelation of their dismalness in the closing aria of *Elegy*:

>   ... to become a pimp
> Or deal in fake jewellery or ruin a fine tenor voice
>   For effects that bring down the house, could happen to all
> But the best and worst of us...
>   That is why, I suppose,
>   The best and worst never stayed here long but sought
> Immoderate soils where the beauty was not so external,
>   The light less public and the meaning of life
> Something more than a mad camp.

Yeats's lamenting recognition of a world turned upside down in 'The Second Coming', where 'The best lack all conviction, while the worst / Are full of passionate intensity' (*CP*, p. 187), is seemingly rebuked here.

Such extremity of attention is immediately allied to the political extremism fostered by 'granite wastes' or 'clays and gravels'. Yet 'In Praise of Limestone' is itself an inconstant poem, evasive and intensely vacillating, to use a Yeatsian word. Having dismissed and ridiculed 'Intendent Caesars' and the 'really feckless' who seek no landscape at all other than 'the oceanic whisper', the (for the first time in the poem first-person speaker) pulls himself up short:

> They were right, my dear, all those voices were right
> And still are; this land is not the sweet home that it looks,
>   Nor its peace the historical calm of a site
> Where something was settled once and for all . . . .

This is, in other words, no 'locality' of lasting 'peace' or 'release'. Having raised the possibility of the 'backwardness' and 'provinciality' of nostalgia for a limestone landscape (here that of Auden's holiday island Ischia, but also the Pennines Auden explored in his childhood – as well as those similar characteristics earlier attributed to Yeats's Ireland, in the article at the time of his death), the last section of the poem goes through a series of self-splittings. The political efficacy of the analogy provided by limestone is reasserted (it 'calls into question / All the Great Powers assume'), only for the sentence then to conclude 'it disturbs our rights.' In another turn, a further rebuke of unlocated origin comes to 'the poet . . . [who] is made uneasy / By these marble statues which so obviously doubt / His antimythological myth'. Then 'I, too, am reproached, for what / And how much you know'. The poet comes then to seem a public figure, *separate* from the private person whose faults and mode of address are somehow intimate and non-poetical. After a further series of speculations, increasingly religious ('But if / Sins can be forgiven'), the limestone landscape is reasserted as the earthly vision of an imagined 'faultless love / Or the life to come'.[40]

While not wanting to deny that, as Anthony Hecht has acknowledged, 'the entire poem is a *paysage moralisé*', one crucial to Auden's aesthetic, what I would want to argue is that its honest inconstancy recognizes the allure of the immoral and the politically abhorrent, yet feels rebuked by them to the extent of asserting once more a Yeatsian splitting between 'the poet' and 'I'.[41] The sole constancy within the poem is the belatedly-appearing address of the speaker to the beloved, the sense that it is only through such an address that the dangers and temptations, as well as the ignorances, within inconstancy can be articulated. As much as it is a moralizing and moralized poem, or a political and civic poem, therefore, 'In Praise of Limestone' ultimately is a 'foul rag-and-bone shop of the heart' poem, one in which the desires and envies of opposite landscapes and habitats to its own are irresolvably integral to its nature.

Auden's poems of the early 1960s in praise of the habitat of his house at Kirschstetten in Austria re-gather some of these tensions and themes. Yeats's own later retreat into a personal and also Anglo-Irish mythologizing had led him to remake the country house tradition of poetry in English. The beleaguered poems from *The Tower* in a time of Civil War, and those later celebrations-cum-elegies for Coole Park from *The Winding Stair*, whose 'social virtues' the 'Defence Counsel' praised in 1939, find him situating his aristocratic, traditional, personal and political vision in a suitable location. Auden's sequence 'Thanksgiving for a Habitat' both continues and negotiates with that legacy. Kirschstetten is a modern house. It carries none of the resonances of sanctity and loveliness of Yeatsian 'emblems'. But it does enable the poet to represent a kind of self-mocking lordship ('I...at last am dominant over three acres') which is raised into a kind of eminence from which to survey, as Yeats does from his tower in 'Meditations in Time of Civil War', the world around ('Territory, status, // and love, sing all the birds, are what matter').

In the 'Postscript' to the opening poem of the sequence, this locatedness leads him to assert 'The frontier of my Person', resurrecting that preoccupation with bounds and boundaries which had figured in his work since the Thirties. 'Beware of rudely crossing it', we are warned. The privacy and frontiers particular to each room of the house are a marked theme of the sequence as a whole. Auden's workroom, 'The Cave of Making' (an elegy for MacNeice), is 'an antre / more private than a bedroom' (so sharing, if you like, the transitional qualities of the Derridean site of writing, the 'hymen' as 'cave', 'antre', inter'[42]). The activities in the toilet are an 'ur-act of making / Private to the artist'; the bathroom 'has only an inside lock', and our ability to withdraw into it is 'a political right'. As an 'unwilling celibate', Auden's bedroom is his own space. Guests are cordially invited in, but the guestroom itself is a curious no-place, 'Ours yet not ours'.

Like Yeats's Thoor Ballylee and Coole Park, Auden's and Kallmann's house is curiously outside history yet permeable in 'neutral Austria', 'the Country of Consideration'. While the poem 'Thanksgiving for a Habitat' itself, and the final poem 'The Common Life', register the threat of death through nuclear war or 'History's criminal noise', in the house the two inhabitants are 'oddly' untouched. The celebration of commonality in that final poem, a celebration of domestic life with Kallmann, is typical of the whole sequence, whose assertion of the frontiers of the person, which a house makes actual, goes along with a comity expressed in the dedication of each poem to an individual friend or to other couples.

Yet such acts of friendship are marks, to adopt again Auden's terms of differentiation between his time and that of Yeats, of 'the social person' rather than of the 'impersonal state'. In the address to the ghost of Plato in 'Grub First, Then Ethics', sociability, 'a good dinner', is set against the apocalyptic upheavals ('the night...when comets blaze and meres break') which might be necessary to allow 'our City' to 'become / Her own Vision' – to become an ideal Republic. This is a company which, like that of his inheritors as Yeats imagines them in 'The Tower', is 'Bound neither to Cause nor to State'. As with Yeats's 'Coole Park, 1929', what the Austrian house provides is 'A scene well set and excellent company'. (*CP*, pp. 198, 243) Like *his* visionary tower, on which we paced the battlements, we are told by Auden in 'The Common Life' that 'every home should be a fortress, / ...versed in all ancient magic' which will stand against the ignorant and (what Yeats called) the 'filthy modern tide': 'Any brute / can buy a machine in a shop'.[43]

What we find in both Yeats's and Auden's later poems about their houses and habitats, therefore, is that they are established as fastnesses of sociability, but more importantly as places which establish the frontiers of self, within and against the potentially threatening and brutal realities of the state in the modern world. The houses are each in their ways caves of making, whose celebrations of creativity, friendship and conversation offer a rebuke to the world outside. Such company might stand as an analogy for the unrealizable ideal state, but it might also stand in its use of language and diction as an example for civic order in the world as it is. As Auden wrote in his 1938 'Introduction to "Poems of Freedom"', 'the medium of poetry is language, the medium in which all social activities are conducted'.[44] The house both becomes synonymous with that 'medium', and also a resistance to its uses in contemporary 'common life'. It is a 'locality' (at last) of peace and exchange which remains cogniscent of the symbolic allure of such spaces even as it seeks to demythologize them. The emblematic drive at the heart of Yeats's resurrection of this particular genre is replaced by a functionalism in Auden, yet something of the resonance of the older poet's vision threatens to give a befitting, emblematic aura to this 'Grub First, Then Ethics' culture.

II

Similar concerns to these were essential to Donald Davie (1922–1995), in his wrestling with the issue of the nature and function of poetic diction and syntax in the earlier part of his career, and also in the self-revisions he made around those views from the late 1960s onwards. Often these debates – as Auden's had – centred upon the nature of a civic or social utterance in poetry, and Yeats's shifting profile within them is symptomatic of Davie's own shifts of allegiance when expressing a politics through discussion of literary-critical issues.

In the paired books of the early 1950s, *Purity of Diction in English Verse* and *Articulate Energy*, Yeats's example had been taken as a corrective to a symbolist poetics which could be derived from Pound and early Eliot (i.e. everything he had written it seems, barring *Four Quartets*). Symbolist writers allowed their poetic imagery to outstrip their conceptual thought, and were therefore both poetically 'impure' and socially irresponsible; they tended to be lax about syntax and metre. In the essay on 'Berkeley and Yeats: Syntax and Metre' from towards the end of the later book, *Articulate Energy*, Davie spells out the implications of an adherence to those virtues:

> there is force in Peter Allt's suggestion that, where authentic syntax appears in modern poetry, it is a sort of tribute paid by the poet to 'the beautiful humane cities'. Systems of syntax are part of the inheritable property of past civilization, and to hold firm to them is to be traditional in the best and most important sense. This seems ungracious to both Pound and Eliot, who have both insisted upon the value of the European civilized tradition, and have tried to embody it in their poems. Nevertheless it is hard not to agree with Yeats that the abandonment of syntax testifies to a failure of the poet's nerve, a loss of confidence in the intelligible structure of the conscious mind, and the validity of its activity.[45]

For Davie at this stage of his career, it is Yeats's adherence to the 'normative' traditions of poetic syntax and its concomitant impact upon the retention of traditional rhythm and poetic form (issues which form the subject of a 'debate' by the later poet Geoffrey Hill, to be discussed below), which anticipates and manifests his later, Berkleyian, sensibility. This is a sensibility attuned to what happens in the world being perceived, but also to the process of registering that perception upon his own consciousness, itself an 'intelligible structure'

(Davie's phrase here echoes one of Richard Ellmann's).[46] Unlike Pound and Eliot, who have wandered in what Malraux called 'le musée imaginaire' of modern art, drawing examples from here and there without an eye to an audience, Yeats in these ways kept faith with an audience. He even kept faith with the fact that 'the artist is still determined by his society to some extent' so that some of his most abstruse analogies, like that between 'the noble culture of Japan' and his own country, must derive from his finding 'some points of contact' between them.[47]

In the essay he wrote which confronts the issue of Yeats's influence upon subsequent poetry directly, the 1964 'Yeats, the Master of a Trade', the older poet's Irish nationality is initially described by Davie as a mark of his difference, of the untranslatable element in his work for later writers, just as it seems at least partly to have been in Auden's estimation. Yet it is also Yeats's very poetic traditionalism, which seems in the essay to float free from those origins, which for Davie makes him a powerful example. Yeats teaches that 'hackneyed, conventional images' are better than 'unprecedented ones' – again a keeping the faith, presumably, with audience expectation. The effort to be 'original, distinctive' is a 'wasted labour'. Unlike the basis of Pound's Imagist aesthetics, Yeats's writing shows that abstract words, as in 'A Prayer for My Daughter', can be powerfully used; they are, after all, to be found in 'common speech', upon which Yeats's poetry is founded. Davie then expands that sense of commonality through abstraction to include '*civic* speech'. He agrees with Padraic Colum that Yeats's use of a kind of journalese in the later work (like the phrase 'The Roman Empire stood appalled' from the play *Resurrection*), represents a major innovation in poetry, a sense that a language which has gone dead within journalistic *reportage* can be revivified by poetic energies. Therefore, although Yeats's influence had been dominant in the 20 years since his death in getting poets to return, after modernist interruption, to writing in traditional forms, Davie in this essay believes that he should be taken as *the* model for twentieth-century poetic diction. In his later work, Yeats sometimes 'took liberties' no-one else could afford to take in this area, but more recent poets had much to learn from *The Wild Swans At Coole* and *Michael Robartes and the Dancer*.[48]

The two collections singled out here of course display 'common speech' in both private and public spaces, since they include the most famous of Yeats's political poems on the 1916 Rising, as well as personal meditations upon inheritance in the Gregory elegies, 'In Memory of Alfred Pollexfen' and 'Upon a Dying Lady'. Yet, only a year after 'Yeats, the Master of a Trade', Davie was starting to revise his attitude towards him. With a stronger interest in the nature of a Poundian poetic coming through the 1965 *Ezra Pound: Poet As Sculptor*, Yeats seems to lose some of his Berkeleyan credentials, being seen (unlike Pound, who is praised for his recognition of the objectiveness of the world) as a poet centrally in the symbolist vein.[49]

By 1968, when Davie's own distrust of a politically 'extremist' British intelligentsia was hardening during his difficult latter days at the University of Essex, Yeats is being compacted by Davie with Pound and Eliot for his lack of wisdom about politics and history, a lack which Davie claims underlies their adoption of 'right-wing positions' in the Thirties. Davie was by that time working towards the position which, in the 1973 *Thomas Hardy and British Poetry*, would issue in the proclamation of a native tradition founded upon poems about 'landscape and the areal, relations in space', such as Auden's 'In Praise of Limestone'. These are poems which form a check upon a poet's 'manipulation of the historical record' for his or her own extremist purposes. Yeats is here grouped with Pound under the banner 'right-wing mythological politics'.[50] After such an assessment, Yeats's role in Davie's critical explorations of the relation of poetry to politics, or of poetic modernism, would never again be as important, although he continued to discuss the work of Pound particularly.

Like Auden, then, Davie comes to see Yeats's work as dangerously 'inauthentic', while also seeking to read it away from, and even against, its origins. The 'inheritable property of the past' which Yeats had earlier seemed to truly tune into, in contrast to the symbolist Pound and Eliot, becomes grounds for a wider dismissal, underpinned by a sense of the superiority of native, British, poetry free of extremist political overtones. In substituting a particular version of spatial relations for the earlier poets' diachronic relations, Davis makes anti-symbolism complicatedly inherent within a delineation of a separate, non-Irish, non-American, national character, one founded upon the reduced but homely qualities of post-war British domestic life.

Yet Davie's own poetry, while it never adopted the dangerous mythic and intellectual approaches of the latterly-questionable moderns, never adopted either the provincialist outlook of those British poets like Graves and Larkin who resisted all notions of 'le musée imaginaire'. When, in *Thomas Hardy and British Poetry*, Davie famously described the 'shabby second-hand' of Larkin's poetry of 'lowered sights and patiently diminished expectations' as establishing him 'for good or ill' as the 'effective unofficial laureate of post-1945 England', the reluctantly compromised tone reveals a different ambition behind his own establishment of a level, normative, voice as his own poetic voice.[51]

Davie's sense of civility shares none of the pietistic, Betjemanian nostalgia of Larkin's. It is from the outset innured to the random dogged survivals of an earlier order. Gazing down on Plymouth in the 1955 'Among Artisans' Houses', the poet adopts the posthumous tone of passing familiar from Yeats's late celebrations of the culture of Coole Park, but to different ends:

> And if civility is gone,
> As we assume it is, the moulds
> Of commonwealth are broken down,
> Then how explain that this still holds,
> The strong though cramped and cramping tone
> Of mutual respect, that cries
> Out of these small civilities?

Davie is alert to the dissentient voice crying 'Provincialism!' even as he asserts what 'holds'. The 'civility' / 'civilities' chimes across the stanza show the cussedness of the gesture, but also display that centrality of abstract words which characterizes Davie's poetry, as it had Auden's, from early to late. Plymouth's maritime tradition, 'sanctioned by the use of time', might have established a continuity which allows such claustrophobic (if strong) social virtues to endure. But, like Yeats's Coole Park, these artisans' houses stand out against history, and are therefore paradoxically vulnerable to destruction. Davie even limits their ability to speak to the present ('There is no moral to the scene, / Curious relic from the past'); whatever rebuke the houses have to offer to the modern world beyond, it is a muted one.[52]

Despite this drawing of continuities that might seem in line with Davie's critical admiration for Yeats in the early years at least, Yeats already figures ambiguously in these early poems, and sometimes in ways that predict his later recantation of that praise. Most notably, when writing from and about his own time living and working as a lecturer in Ireland, Davie comes to envisage Yeats as complicit with ideas and feelings which are alien and threatening to him. Yeats seems a dangerous Romantic, whose intensity is aligned with extreme political movements that threaten English 'small', if 'mean', 'utilities.' Watching an Orange Order parade in 'Belfast on a Sunday Afternoon', Davie has his urge 'to scoff' erased by the sheer hugeness of the display, before turning and returning upon the 'worry' that it causes him:

> Some brawny striplings sprawled upon the lawn;
> No man is really crippled by his hates.
> Yet I remembered with a sudden scorn
> Those 'passionate intensities' of Yeats.

Yeats's own excited early friendship with a stable-boy who had a book of Orange rhymes ('when I had begun to dream of my future life, I thought I would like to die fighting the Fenians' (*A*, p. 14)), and frequent recognition of hatred as central to the colonized Irish character, gather a fearful afterlife in the hands of this English poet. When witnessed in action on the Belfast streets, the political resonances of Yeats's Romantic rhetoric receive a fierce but troubled response. The scorning of Yeats is synonymous with the anxious rebuttal of an alien militantism which the self-consciously English poet is unable to accommodate or assimilate.

In 'Hawkshead and Dachau in a Christmas Glass', another poem from this first collection, *Brides of Reason*, however, the dismissal is calmer because viewed from a more distant, and celebratory, perspective: 'At Dachau Man's maturity began / . . . At Dachau Yeats and Rilke died.' More subtly though, in 'Evening on the Boyne', the Yeatsian emblem of the swan disturbs the tranquil sun-filled time by this river of the crucial battle in Ireland's history. Davie is forced to ask in Yeatsian terms about the fact that the tranquil 'sweet arrangements' of the world might be founded upon falsity: 'O bleak and lunar emptiness, / How many eyes were then belied?'[53] In their contrasting contexts, these poems of Davie's first collection therefore celebrate a post-war tranquility, safe from the apocalyptic historical upheavals of the war, but deeply traumatized by the ambiguous possibilities of an unspecified resurgence of violence for which Ireland itself seems to offer a forewarning.

Davie is, even here, in the anxiety and rhetorical questions, attentive to the fact that, as he was to put it in his later essay 'Yeats, Berkeley and Romanticism', the Romantic basis of poetry in arguments with the self is probably unavoidable, even in 'pure' dictions.[54] Such an understanding was to become a *method* in the title poem of the 1977 collection *In the Stopping Train*, which adopts Yeatsian anti-types in order to castigate the weaknesses and failings of the poet as man. But, even from an early stage, he was also aware that the historical bases for controlling that inevitability could be celebrated in a critical prose, but were already alien to modern poetry. As he spells it out in 'Pushkin. A Didactic Poem', again from his first collection *Brides of Reason*:

Self-consciousness is not a fault
In itself. It can be kept
Other than morbid, under laws
Of disciplined sensibility, such
As the Seventeenth-century Wit.
But all such disciplines depend
On disciplines of social use,
Now widely lost.[55]

Such 'discipline' was not, of course, unknown to the Yeats who in *Responsibilities* appropriated Ben Jonson in order to adopt a more modern, unRomantic persona.[56] Davie's contention that such virtue was to be found more recently in only a 'few men' such as Pushkin perhaps displays a fascination – despite himself – with 'gifted, or / Especially heroic' personalities.

In these and later poems, where he consciously resists the self-dramatizing extremity of a Romantic selfhood, Davie sometimes paradoxically deploys a strikingly Yeatsian imagery. In the title poem of his 1957 collection *A Winter Talent* (a poem which anticipates the question at the centre of his late collection *To Scorch or Freeze?*), Davie acknowledges that some have a talent different from his own: 'Some quick bright talents can dispense with coals / And burn their boats continually'. Yet, he concludes, it is 'Better still to burn / Upon that gloom where all have felt a chill'.[57] He upholds commonality, here a commonality in misery, against the irresponsible selfhood that flares upon no substance other than its own daring. This is a recognition shared by Yeats in 'In Memory of Major Robert Gregory': 'Some burn damp faggots, others may consume / The entire combustible world in one small room / As though dried straw'. (*CP*, p. 134) Davie would be wary of the Renaissance virtues, the unity of being, and extra-human heroism Yeats proclaimed for Gregory, but he shares with Yeats another wariness about the spectacular appeal of a particular kind of apocalyptic Romantic self-dramatization.[58]

In *Purity of Diction*, Davie takes 'In Memory of Major Robert Gregory' as an example of modern verse which can be 'both lofty and conversational', and these virtues are displayed also, say, in one of his own poems like 'Belfast on a Sunday Afternoon'.[59] This is a conversational voice which shows, as in 1964 Davie claimed Yeats had, a closeness to journalese in some of its verbs and prose-based rhythms: 'first of all we tried to laugh it off... // Pipe bands, flute bands, brass bands and silver bands / ... Came stamping'. The use of abstract words Davie attributes to Yeats's adoption of diction close to 'common speech' is something that he seeks both to explore and to question in his early *ars poetica*, 'With the Grain'. There, the commonality derived from seeing poetry itself as another trade surprisingly comes to seem like a transcendent possibility:

> Why, by an ingrained habit, elevate
>   Into the light of ideas
> The colourful trades, if not like Icarus
>   To climb the beam? High lights
> Are always white, but this ideal sun
>   Dyes only more intensely, and we find
> Enough cross-graining in the most abstract nature.[60]

If there resonates behind this 1961 poem Yeats's injunction in his self-elegy 'Under Ben Bulben' ('Irish poets, learn your trade' (*CP*, p. 327)), there is a correlative sense, which Davie also derived from Yeats, that the mythopoeic can draw upon common experience. The abstract is exposed as sufficiently imbued with a metaphoric life that it can never escape into total whiteness or blankness. A pure diction is always laden with a worldly actuality which comes with the trade, and this is both the weakness and the strong defensiveness within its abstractions.

Whatever symbolic or mythic transcendence it is possible to achieve, then, is predicated upon a fall back into reality. But this should not prevent a looking back down, a civically responsible act, as in 'Among Artisans' Houses', a looking back *from* the poem *upon* how things are. Yeats's role as model for such a mediatory poetic, moving between the personal poeticized voice of 'common speech' and society in developing a responsible 'civic speech' for poetry, is everywhere implicit in Davie's own poems, but stripped of *both* its local and its symbolic resonances. In connection with the former quality and impulse within 'speech', one might cite, for example, the surprising assertion in 'The Seven Sages' that the four great father-figures of Anglo-Irish culture, Burke, Goldsmith, Berkeley and Swift, got their 'schooling' by walking the Irish roads and 'Mimicking what they heard, as children mimic'. (*CP*, p. 242) Yeats's own complex self-struggle around the relation of such intimate listening to cultural and political inheritance has been reduced by Davie, as it had been by Auden, into the singular sign of abstract, 'pure', diction, a token which might stand as trace of (the double-edged concept) 'British' poetry.

Yet Davie's post-war neutral tones do not prevent him, however sceptical he later became of his early model, weighing, as Yeats had, the divisions between the world of art and historical actuality. At the same time, in line with the other 'pull' in Romanticism, he recognized that poetry must be – in a Berkeleyan sense – responsive to the world outside itself. In 'The Hill Field', we find him bemoaning the way in which art can come to interfere between the perceiving eye surveying the field and the actuality of a 'trade':

> It is Breughel or Samuel Palmer,
> Some painter, coming between
> My eye and the truth of the farmer,
> So massively sculpts the scene.

In the manner of late works by Yeats such as, most famously, 'The Circus Animals' Desertion', Davie is aware of the fact that 'Life' cannot be 'encompassed' either poetically or mythically. There is ultimately much that remains 'unexamined'. Or, conversely, 'He never needed to see, / Not with his art to help him' as the split self of the debate-poem 'In the Stopping Train' puts it.[61] Revision and self-revision remained the keys to Davie's responsiveness.

Ultimately, for him, a mark of art's civic responsibility, then, was to recognize its own limits and distance from the world it seeks to describe. So, in the 1981 'The Fountain of Arethusa', the mythic nature of the site is viewed through a historically responsive attention to what is actually there:

> The one in the poem is not
> The one that you will visit.
> Syracuse you may visit,
> The poem also – one
> Casts no light on the other.
>
> Through the one there strays
> One and one only walker.
> The city has its claim
> Upon this one who can
> Meet it in curious ways.
>
> By a brilliant turn of phrase?
> No. For it is the past
> Is brilliant, Pasternak says;
> The debt we owe it, only
> More modest coin repays.

The once-sacred fountain is now 'man-walled', and cigarette-packets float nearby. The 'modest coin' of our historical situation makes for no bold, heroic gesture, but rather the knowledge that 'Warm honesties of makeshift / Transvalue Syracuse'. As de Man and Derrida have recognized within their own contexts, art can but celebrate a past which is irretrievable, however 'brilliant' the medium of celebration. 'Value' is only ever 'transvalue', the partial but non-metonymic recouping of the poem's own imaginings. Davie's poetic abstractions are inherently 'allegorical', temporalized, taking the measure of the temptations they are subject to.[62]

Ultimately the distance between his own work and that of Yeats, along with the other moderns, is generic for Davie. His insistence, as he put it in one of his six 'Epistles' to the Pound scholar Eva Hesse, remained that 'History upon my plan / Is always as comedian', something picked up in the late verse letter to Seamus Heaney, whose own deterministic and tragic view of history is chided as calling 'for Comedy'.[63] Those post-war English securities (however threatened) seem remote from the *tragic* history which Yeats described, and which he wished to *live*. Davie's Yeats has a 'commonality' through 'abstractness' which remains curiously objective and untrammelled, a self-aware system of civic *signs* alert to their own querulous and historically-determined limitation, their *syntax*.

III

The (latterly Anglo-American) Thom Gunn (1929–) has established his own consistent dialogue with Yeats, but taken it off into its own direction. His work shares many of the formal and syntactic preoccupations of Davie and other of the poets who in the 1950s were associated with the so-called Movement, but his relative youth at that time meant that his notion of civic, social and cultural responsibility was very different from theirs.

Gunn's most Yeatsian collection to date would, on the surface of things, seem to have been his second, the 1957 *The Sense of Movement*. The poems there display what he has subsequently called 'a mere Yeatsian wilfulness', a focus upon personal destiny and possibility in contradistinction to more obvious concerns with general society and politics.[64] Most programmatically in 'The Unsettled Motorcyclist's Vision of His Death' (an obvious recollection of Yeats's Irish airman), but throughout the explorations of what Gunn calls 'pose', there seems to be in this collection an intent conversation with Yeats's notion of self-dramatizing heroism and also with antithetical masks. Gunn's notion of 'pose' is dated in an autobiographical essay to a revelation he had during his time as an undergraduate at Cambridge in the Fifties:

> The theory of pose was this: everyone plays a part, whether he knows it or not, so he might as well deliberately design a part, or a series of parts, for himself... one is left in an interesting place somewhere between the starting point – the bare undefined and undirected self, if he ever existed – and the chosen part. This is a place rich in tensions between the achieved and the unachieved.[65]

Gunn's motorcyclist provides an agonizing, literalizing exemplification of such 'tensions', while also seeming to show the poet's sense of the limits of his own theory (what remains 'unachieved'). As he heads across the countryside from the 'firm heath' to the marsh where he will meet his death, he asserts his existential will, as Yeats did in late poems,[66] against that which threatens to engulf him: 'My human will cannot submit / To nature though brought out of it.... / I urge my chosen instrument / Against the mere embodiment.' Yet, contrary to the self-delighting impulse which drives Yeats's airman to his death,[67] or to the wished-for escape from the teeming fertility of the natural world in the Byzantium poems, Gunn's protagonist is destined to be undone in his ambition. The second half of the poem contains the posthumous voice of the motorcyclist as he is 'converted' to earth by the natural forces of decay and plantlife, to which he has come 'by chance'. Where Yeats's airman makes his choice for death from a position of knowledge ('I know that I shall meet my fate... / I balanced all, brought all to mind' (*CP*, p. 135)), Gunn's rider is left to 'multiply in ignorance'.[68]

It is as if Gunn perceives in Yeats's poem, and in the 'pose' which it represents, an unacceptable, wilful refutation of natural process in seeking to control 'fate', and a compensatory, correlative valuing of 'achieved' art. Such a refutation amounts to blindness to the ways in which 'pose' itself is circumscribed by 'chance' and by the organic rhythms of life. 'All unity is from the *Mask*', Yeats had declared in setting out his ideas, 'and the *antithetical mask* is described in the automatic script as a "form created by passion to unite us to ourselves"'. (*AV*, p. 82) Against this, Gunn seems consistently aware of the potential for solipsism within such 'highest' unity, its actual powerlessness before the (non-human) forces amid which the self as Mask must live.

'Where now lies the power to hold the evening back?', as Gunn asks in 'To Yvor Winters, 1955'. However, such questions do not mean that he is despairing of humanity's (limited) powers in this regard. In this poem, he takes up his addressee's primary critical terms (relating them to the traditional between-time of evening) in order to see circumscription as a positive, enhancing quality:

> But sitting in the dusk...
> You keep Rule and Energy in view,
> Much power in each, most in the balanced two:
> Ferocity existing in the fence
> Built by an exercised intelligence.[69]

So Gunn does not relinquish his belief in a fate which randomly brings 'complete negation' at any time, but defends here a balancing, airman-like knowledge within and against that eradication: 'Still it is right to know the force of death'. Elsewhere in *The Sense of Movement*, 'pose' itself takes a role in the 'generation of the very chance / It wars on'. 'Elvis Presley', we are told, may have adopted 'a posture for combat'. It is of the nature of the dramatic interplay that the 'theory of pose' developed in these early poems entails that opposites are forced to co-exist. There would, in Gunn's view, be no 'Rule' without 'Energy', and such powers are all under the aegis of 'intelligence' within traditional verse structures, as though, as in Yeats, the 'Rule' of form heightens the passion or 'Energy' which it contains. (*E&I*, p. 522)

Retrospectively, Gunn has made the technical implications of his view of this rich 'tension' clear:

> Rhythmic form and subject-matter are locked in a permanent embrace: that should be an axiom nowadays. So, in metrical verse, it is the nature of the control being exercised that becomes part of the life being spoken about. It is poetry making great use of the conscious intelligence, but its danger is bombast – the controlling music drowning out everything else. Free verse invites a different style of experience, improvisation. *Its* danger lies in being too relaxed, too lacking in controlling energy.[70]

With Gunn's increasing interest in that 'different style of experience', dating from the LSD-influenced poems of the 1970s, it could be presumed from this simple dichotomy that the concerns with form as a necessary attribute of 'pose' led him to a relaxation of the Yeatsian 'will' which had predominated in the earlier work. Yet, what is striking is the way in which those concerns are transmuted within the 'new' experience, rather than eradicated from it, establishing a different kind of structure and pattern to the original, circumscribing, external one.

With the exploration of Romantic extremes of existential selfhood and its concomitant possibilities for solipsism and nightmarish self-absorption, which began with the 1965 *Misanthropos*, Gunn might be presumed to have transposed the attention to the rhythms of the world beyond the self which so form part of the notion of 'pose' itself. Yet, even at its most extreme, Gunn's writing around these issues never loses its sense of the limits and the boundaries which are being transgressed or overcome. In 'The Geysers', for instance, his poem about a stoned weekend at some hot springs, the opening up to experience which the drugs are reported to have induced is always measured against what was known before:

> A cinderfield that lacks all skin of soil,
> It has no complication, no detail,
> The force too simple and big to comprehend,
> Like a beginning, almost like an end.
> No customs I have learned can make me wise
> To deal with such. And I do recognize
> – For what such recognition may be worth –
> Fire at my centre, burning since my birth....[71]

Gunn's attention to the customary at this point, in terms of poetic form (couplets) and in the retention of a measured, normative syntax and often-abstract diction, as well as in testing the limits of wisdom, is typical of his treatment of such occasions.

The hesitant recognition of a greater Romantic selfdom, the fire at the centre, is managed through a complicated layering and testing of definitions of the self's awareness and experience. The sequence's ending upon a blending of self into others ('my blood is yours the hands that take accept') and Orphic dismemberment ('torn from the self...I am raw meat / I am a god') is shadowed by the sense of the traditional and formal harmoniousness which has gone before. For Gunn, the liberation is palpable, but the escape out of form and 'pose' is potentially also an escape into a violent nightmare and self-estrangement. 'How but in custom and in ceremony / Are innocence and beauty born?' as Yeats asks in 'A Prayer for My Daughter', the poem which immediately follows 'The Second Coming' in *Michael Robartes and the Dancer*, with its vision that 'The blood-dimmed tide is loosed, and everywhere / The ceremony of innocence is drowned'. (*CP*, pp. 190, 189)

Gunn's escape from the accustomed into a 'primal innocence' in this sequence is complicated, and seems to respond to such frighteningly divergent possibilities. It is uncertain and alert to the dangers caused to the self by such new experiences and re-definitions. Merle E. Brown has seen such continuing self-division in Gunn as a marked rebuke to 'the critical maneuvers that have been so popular' since the mid-1960s, strategies which Brown sees most exemplified by Harold Bloom's 'utopian and visionary criticism' of self-motivated self-creation. To Brown, such criticism seems blind to the ways in which 'disgust' lies at the heart of the 'paradisal' and the 'sublime', in Yeats as elsewhere.[72] Yet what I would want to emphasize also is the poetry as a consistent recognition of loss and form of mourning that emerges as a result of such 'recognitions', in Gunn as in Yeats, the perpetual need to weigh present 'experience' against past 'plenitude' and established rhythm within the urge to discover 'new' patterns.

This is further the case in the title sequence of the 1976 *Jack Straw's Castle*, which figures the castle itself as a limit to consciousness in which the protagonist is, like Yeats in his tower in time of civil war but unlike Auden in his modern and neutral Austrian house, 'visited by visions'. The tease of the sequence is in its adoption of a man of straw, of no 'worth' or consideration, as the perceiving consciousness. His lack of any testable, controlling knowledge of many actualities of the world beyond himself leaves him few resources to build upon, so to speak, and he sinks further and further into nightmare as he imagines Charles Manson lurking somewhere in the precincts. It is while on his back in the darkness of his castle's cellar, however, that the walls start to be breached: temporarily, as it turns out, but in ways which signal the final return 'to the world' at the end of the sequence:

> For this is the seat of needs
>
>   so deep, so old
> That even where eye never perceives body
> And where the sharpest ear perceives only
> The light slap and rustle of flesh on stone
> They, the needs, seek ritual and ceremony
> To appease themselves
>   (Oh, the breathing all around me)
> Or they would tear apart the life that feeds them.[73]

At the deepest level of the psyche for Gunn, then, lies that sense of pattern that is also ultimately courtliness and courtesy. Gunn's persona here faces the same choice as he himself had seemed to in 'The Geysers', between the appeasements of a traditionally-sanctioned way of living which is also potentially an openness to community, and a dismemberment in which the self is swept away by 'wider', all-consuming or self-consuming, experience. It is a choice which Yeats was aware of in his 'Pages from a Diary of 1930', and which figured in all of his late meditations on, and wrestling with, the work of the modernist generation following his own. (*E*, p. 373) Yet there, as in the admonitory title of a poem from *In the Seven Woods* of 1904 – 'Never give all the Heart' – Yeats was ever aware of the dangers of yielding all of the self before experience, and so of yielding the possibilities for dramatization and self-dramatization made available through the doctrine of the mask itself. (*CP*, p. 79) For both poets, the flux of experience is present in the syntax of poems and between poems, but it is never to be achieved by an indiscriminate opening of the self to more deeply 'unconscious' or external forces.

In Gunn's work these dual formal possibilities figure in his *equal* interest in the open forms of the Americans William Carlos Williams and Robert Duncan (the latter's Romanticism surely figures at the end of 'The Geysers'), and the traditional formalism of the English tradition from the Renaissance (Fulke Greville, Donne, Jonson) to Hardy and Yeats. A version of the abruptly-shifting, antinomic work of the latter seems, though, to figure prominently amidst the various oppositions which Gunn's poetic successfully holds together: 'The mind / is an impermanent place, isn't it,' as he asks in 'Talbot Road', 'but it looks to permanence.' In 'Iron Landscapes (and the Statue of Liberty)', such a relishing of possibility becomes almost one with the democratic, revolutionary excitements of America. 'Cool seething incompletion that I love', when viewing the 'turbulent' waters of the Hudson, becomes modulated into 'But I'm at peace with the iron landscape too, / Hard because buildings must be hard to last'. 'In the Nixon era', such balanced sympathies are threatened as the political landscape clouds vision, and the Statue of Liberty might be herself now saluting with a clenched fist. But the Yeatsian vision of a strict formalism that contains a Romantic impermanence holds steady beneath the vagaries of the historical moment.[74]

In the much earlier 'Confessions of a Life Artist', a 'poem of the 1960s' which seems to engage once more with the problematics of 'pose', Gunn has dramatized a persona whose choice to perfect his art leads to a similar madness to that suffered by 'Jack Straw':

> Heady,
> to hover above the winds,
> buoyant with a sense of choice.
> Circling above the city,
> to reject the thousand, and
> to select the one. To watch
> the goodly people there, to
> know that their blood circulates,
> that it races as yours does,
> live between extremities.

'Between extremities / Man runs his course', Yeats tells us at the beginning of 'Vacillation', before acknowledging that the existence of large, uncomplicated force ('a brand, or flaming breath') which will destroy 'all antinomies'. (*CP*, p. 249) Gunn's control-freak life artist cannot, however, acknowledge such power. His airman's perspective might lead him 'to select the one', as Yeats does his fisherman, but ultimately he is a life artist unable to consider life: 'Prophecies become fulfilled, though never as expected... // But I am concerned with my/ own knowledge that the design / is everywhere ethical / and harmonious...'. The stiltedness of the voice and the out-of-kilterness of the line-endings (Gunn's clever enjambement 'my/own') reveal the absolute insanity of a choice (one which Yeats himself would never make, of course) of the work over the life.[75]

Again, however, this does not mean that the later Gunn would disavow such a removed perspective, or fail to find his own syntheses of possibility around it. In two poems from the 1982 *The Passages of Joy*, 'Small Plane in Kansas' and 'The Exercise', he thrills to the forming and in-forming extensions of experience to be derived from such conceits. In the first poem, the precariousness of the flight opens upon a familiar dreamscape:

> Out there
> from the height of self-love
> I survey the reduced world.
>
> Mastered by mastering,
> I so much belong to the wind
> I become of it, a gust
> that flows, mindless for ever...
> [where] the world's invisible currents run,
> like symptoms, like remedies.

This allows for the airman's perspective in which (as they are for Gregory in Yeats's poem) worldly possibilities are 'reduced', 'a waste of breath', only within that context of vulnerability which allows the wind to 'master' 'self-love'. The antinomies remain in the last line, presumably motivated by the complication that the wind makes him 'mindless', a word with both positive and negative connotations – but within a context that allows for a continuous, universalizing experience. The tradition of Romantic inspiration, handed on by Yeats in *A Wind Among the Reeds* and elsewhere, is here allowed to assault the centring-upon-the-self which has been a concern of Gunn's writing early and late. But it remains a purely *natural*, secular force in Gunn, freed of, but also limited by, the kinds of mythic possibility offered by Yeats's wind-borne *Sidhe* ('*Away, come away, / Empty your heart of its mortal dream*' (*CP*, p. 55)).

In 'The Exercise' Romanticism is more nakedly to the fore again as a formative presence in a natural incarnation. Gunn recalls his walks by a 'sad little lake' (compare 'The Wild Swans at Coole') in Surrey commuter-land. It is a dismal scene:

> But when the wind took over!
> On the shore I became of it,
> braced and full, or
> it partook of me.

Once again, the mutuality of the interaction with the wind allows Gunn access to a passage of joy which had been unavailable to his earlier solipsistic personae ('What is joy?' asks Yeats in the light of the destructive burning brand at the start of 'Vacillation'): 'I was formed by it, I was formed / by the exercise it gave me. / Exercise in stance, and / in the muscle of feeling.' Unlike Leda in Yeats's poem about sudden violating assault by larger forces, whose fate has clear implications for the violent history of his own country, Gunn, from his more settled context, is certain about the growth in his own power and understanding caused by the wind's feeding: 'The wind blew against me till / I tingled with knowledge.'[76] The wind once again enforces a metamorphosis, a 'change' in the self and its awareness.

It is the openness to the remembrance of such Romantic possibility that ultimately underwrites Gunn's adherence to a version of Yeatsian tradition. 'I am ... a rather derivative poet,' Gunn has admitted, 'I learn from whom I can, mostly consciously. I borrow heavily from my reading because I take my reading seriously.'[77] As he had put it in an earlier poem, 'Back to Life', he recognizes that 'At most', these things are 'a recollection / in the mind only'.[78] But, in his consistent exploration of the 'depths' of Romantic visionary or nightmarish 'self-love', he has also been sensitive to the need for change within an antithetical poetic.

In 'A Sketch of the Great Dejection' from the 1992 *The Man With Night Sweats*, 'The wind was like a punishment to the face and hands. / These were marshes of privation...'. Yet, through an Eliotic 'faring on', the landscape 'came to seem like a place of recuperation'. That sense that, after having to brace himself against assaulting forces, what becomes 'accustomed' becomes healthful, ultimately holds Gunn's personae and Gunn himself open to a naturally-inspired visionary possibility both in the known realms of the self and also in the beyond. In first establishing an aesthetics of 'pose' while simultaneously subjecting that aesthetics to forces internally or externally which challenge 'pose' itself, Gunn redis- covers a ceremoniousness and courtesy within the aggressions and des- titutions of solipsistic modern consciousness.[79]

As such, Gunn's inclusion of Yeats amongst the sources for this pre- occupation, and his consistent exposure of his limitation, remain an inevitable abstraction, ignoring the circumstantial motivations behind the earlier poet's impulsion towards such writing, as they have been argued for by Edna Longley amongst others. Gunn's directly antithetical setting of formal permanence against the experiential excitements of processes of formation partly echo similar vacillations and irresolutions in Yeats, and involve Gunn in a complex interplay between limits, interiorization and externalization. But the interrogations of the solips- ism and misanthropy which might arise within 'pose' from the opera- tion of the forces of 'nature' ultimately lack the emblematic strengths of Yeats's hermetic imagery.

Against such forces, Gunn powerfully and surprisingly laments a lack of permanent rhythm and courtesy. Nature is destructive of 'will', for good or for ill. For the belated Romanticism of Yeats, however, as de Man amongst others has argued, natural forces are in the end an illusion. They provide flesh for the bones of the poetry, but are themselves masks for the esoteric symbolism of the poem's structure.[80] Gunn's poised interrogation of antitheses ultimately therefore is more (*pace* his motor- cyclist) *settled* (always 'either/or', never 'both/and') than the radically dramatic and disjunctive figural life of Yeats's poetry. While it offers a thorough questioning of *some* qualities of pose, and shares much with Yeats in doing so, it finally lacks the fullness and danger of Yeats's anguished, circumscribed and reactive vacillations around similar notions. Gunn's translations of Yeats's ideal ultimately suffer, as do those of Auden and Davie, from that 'overdetermination in *language*' which is an *'underdetermination in meaning'* – the fate of all belated poems, according to Harold Bloom. In the act of translation from one historical and cultural context to another, the 'meaning' of the Yeatsian inheritance has become 'clearer', more abstractly 'readable' and quantifiable, as it was not in the more anxious and self-revising context of later poetry from Ireland.

IV

Ted Hughes (1930–1998), whose own early poetry was often linked with Gunn's, and who, as he said, 'came a bit later' than the Movement poets such as Davie (and so did not accept their idea that they should work to build 'the cosiest arrangement of society'), adopted a different aspect of the Yeatsian poetic as his resolution to 'the position with us'. As he saw it at the time of *Crow* in 1970, Yeats's poem 'The Second Coming' had behind it 'the upsurge that is still producing our modern chaos – the explosion against civilization itself, the oppressive deadness of civilization, the spiritless materialism of it, the stupidity of it'. The 'machinery of religion', the 'rituals and dogma', which used to contain 'the bigger energy, the elemental power circuit of the Universe', had now failed, and it was only by returning to that 'old method' that the chaos could be overcome. Central to Hughes's own attempts to harness that energy into a 'new mythology', such as that in *Crow*, was the influence of Yeats, who 'is the judge' presiding over the putative jury of critics which he felt watched over everything he wrote. Yeats's poetic career offers an ideal which, it is implied, Hughes at the time felt he might follow:

> Every writer if he develops at all develops either outwards into society and history, using wider and more material of that sort, or he develops inwards into imagination and beyond that into spirit, using perhaps no more external material than before and maybe even less, but deepening it and making it operate in the many different inner dimensions until it opens up perhaps the religious or the holy basis of the whole thing. Or he can develop both ways simultaneously. Developing inwardly, of course, means organizing the inner world or at least searching out the patterns there and that is a mythology.... The ideal aspect of Yeats's development is that he managed to develop his poetry both outwardly into history and the common imagery of everyday life at the same time as he developed it inwardly in a sort of close parallel.... His mythology is history, pretty well, and his history is as he said 'the story of my soul'.[81]

Crow itself might therefore be taken as an 'inward development' on Hughes's part. The detailed, grotesque 'theology' that it proposes is an inverted Christianity which mimics some of the blood-mysticism and violence in later Yeats ('power, / Like everything that has the stain of blood, / [is] A property of the living' he asserted in 'Blood and the Moon' (*CP*, p. 239)). At some level, Crow is the Rough Beast from 'The Second Coming', a terrifying apocalyptic entity who is also heralder of a new order:

> When God, disgusted with man,
> Turned towards heaven
> And man, disgusted with God,
> Turned towards Eve,
> Things looked like falling apart.
>
> But Crow　　Crow
> Crow nailed them together....[82]

Crow's nailing even seems to usurp the role of Christ's creator, since it brings about a God who bleeds with man's blood – but then the 'joint' holding heaven and earth together itself becomes infected, to Crow's delight. In this stinking, broken situation, Crow flies the flag of himself, he represents an irredeemably selfish selfhood who seizes upon the chaos caused by the breakdown of 'the machinery of religion' for his own self-delighting purposes.

As such, he represents the third term arising out of the energy deriving from a conflict between antinomies. In a later essay on one poem in the cycle, 'Crow on the Beach', Hughes explains the Trickster cycle from which *Crow* derives its energy as a 'satyr to Tragedy... a series of Tragi-comedies':

> It is a series, and never properly tragic, because Trickster, demon of phallic energy, bearing the spirit of the sperm, is repetitive and indestructible. No matter what fatal mistakes he makes, and what tragic flaws he divulges, he refuses to let sufferings or death detain him, but always circumvents them, and never despairs. Too full of opportunistic ideas for sexual *samadhi*, too unevolved for spiritual ecstasy, too deathless for tragic joy, he rattles along on biological glee.[83]

Crow in his continuous self-creation and sexual energy differs, then, from that quality celebrated in Yeats's 'The Gyres' and 'Lapis Lazuli' from *Last Poems* – a sense of the culminating liberation of style and art in the face of death. Yet that kind of repetitive energy seems to derive also from the fracturing in *English* society which Hughes continually dated to World War I, a fracturing which is allied with the loss of various 'old' machineries in the state. As he wrote early on of Wilfred Owen's poems,

> [t]he real enemy is the Public Monster of Warmongering Insensibility at home. For England, the Great War was, in fact, a kind of civil war (still unfinished – which helps to explain its meaning for modern England, its hold on our feelings...).

Or, as he also put it, the Great War is a 'national ghost...for the first time Adam's descendents found themselves meaningless'.[84]

The historical origins of the fracturing within which Crow exists, then, are clear. Crow's particular Trickster nature offers a new, but unritualized and undogmatic 'theology' to set against that 'civil war'. To that extent, the terms of the mythology remain outside of history, as both Hughes and Yeats similarly recognize that Shakespeare's tragic heroes and heroines are.[85] The hybrid nature of the resulting form, its operation in-between other conflictual forces within a 'modern chaos', is exemplified many times elsewhere in Hughes. Crow is a riddling creature like that described in 'A Riddle' from the 1978 'Alchemical Cave Drama' *Cave Birds*:

> Who am I?...
>
> When you arrived empty
> I gathered up all you had and forsook you
>
> Now as you face your death
> I offer you your life
>
> Just as surely as you are my father
> I shall deliver you....[86]

Within this 'Drama', as within all of Hughes's mythic parables including 'Prometheus on his Crag', there lies the myth of dismemberment of the self and its rebirth which he associates with shamanism and its literary equivalent in the Western tradition, Romanticism. Yeats, following on from Blake, figures for Hughes in his occasional prose writings as the archetypal shamanistic poet, an arduous negotiator with spirits and regular and systematic dealer with the 'supernatural and supersensible realms'.

What is startling, however, in each of the discussions of Yeats in this light, is Hughes's adamant relation of that interiorized methodical inter-action with the spirit world to his historical situation and sense of himself as national poet:

> For him, the methodical work of magic . . . was the path, as he saw it, towards the effective, practical fulfillment of his purpose – a life-work which he dedicated, quite consciously, to the service of his idea of Ireland.

Yeats's nationalism is, therefore, continuous with his shamanism, and both find their origin according to Hughes in Ireland's 'ultimate defeat', the Great Famine in Ireland witnessed by Yeats's parents, the 'bitter culmination' of England's policy towards his country. The spirits Yeats converses with are co-terminous with the spirits of his nation, currently oppressed by 'the ungovernable tides of secular materialism' emanating from England.[87]

Hughes seems to locate in Yeats a particular inter-involvement of mythic method with a political 'conscious' desire, the fulfilled unity of being which Yeats himself felt always to be *vulnerable* to history, not assured by it. Yet such abstracted inter-involvement in its turn plays its part in Hughes's particular establishment of the relation between poem and world. His sympathetic early poem, 'The Thought Fox', would seem to be making elaborate connections between exteriority and interiority, 'world', creative consciousness ('the dark hole of the head') and 'writing',[88] in ways that recall Yeats's creatures such as 'The Hawk', from one voiced perspective an 'observable' reality, from another a 'Yellow-eyed hawk of the mind'. (*CP*, p. 149)

In many ways, then, Yeats looms paradoxically larger than Blake and Shakespeare behind the specifically national poetry that Hughes himself sought to write. Hughes clearly felt the historical parallels between his own strife-haunted situation and Yeats's in the late 1910s and beyond. The violence and blood imagery which marks his work derives from a shared sense of actual and proximate modern war. Hughes's bird 'heroes', from the title-poem of his first book of 1957, *The Hawk in the Rain*, owe more to Yeats's barbarous hawks and owls than to anything in the English tradition. That 'diamond point of will . . . mas-ter- / Fulcrum of all violence where the hawk hangs still' is consonant with the spirit-hawk in *At the Hawk's Well*: 'It flew / As though it would have torn me with its beak, / Or blinded me, smiting with that great wing.'[89]

Hughes's often contrived poems as Poet Laureate gathered in *The Rain-Charm for the Duchy* continued that sense of a century of war and ghostly civil war. In 'A Masque for Three Voices', for example, we are told that 'Tragic drama gives its greatest / Roles to royalty', before Hughes uses the occasion of the Queen Mother's ninetieth birthday to rehearse again the conflicts of the century. Throughout these poems there is a sense that, within his nationalist and mystical sense of England (a hieratic note often enters which is shared with Yeats), Hughes envisions the monarchy as preventing things from falling apart. As the dedicatory poem sees it, souls are wheels, nations are souls, and the Crown is 'at the hub'.[90]

More powerful, however, are his explorations of the destructive energies which threaten the veneer of modern English society, the ways in which an ignorance of the buried mythic energies can allow them to burst through at any moment. Once again, within his most expansive version of this theme, the 1977 *Gaudete*, there are unexplained framing links between the sudden burst of sexual transgression in the peaceful, if voyeur-laden, English village, and Ireland. In the odd shamanistic scene of the Prologue, in which a duplicate of the Reverend Nicholas Lumb is created and filled with 'spirit life', he encounters a Irish cattle-drover who has been seeking him for an unexplained purpose. In the 'Epilogue' we find ourselves 'In a straggly sparse village on the West Coast of Ireland' where Lumb is able to call otters from the lough, and where he hands his poems reflecting upon his experience to some young girls.[91] The whole path of the narrative, in which Lumb establishes a kind of sexual cult amongst the repressed local women, seems a making-explicit of the eroticism which was always present in Yeats's accounts of approaches to the spirit-world. In 'Rosa Alchemica' we are told that 'Eros alone of divinities is altogether a spirit, and hides in passions not of his essence if he would commune with a mortal heart' (*M*, p. 289); similar passions figure in the 'Stories from Michael Robartes and his Friends' which preface *A Vision* itself.

Towards the end of his life, Hughes's quest for the continuing folklore world beneath the surfaces of quotidian English rhythms of life led him towards a consideration of 'Myths, Metres and Rhythms', as he calls it in one essay. Rather than the fixed, artificial patternings of standard English metrics, he was clearly drawn towards the 'flexing, contrapuntal tensions' in a poetic line which to him are tribute to 'natural quantities', the shared mutual understandings of a people which are correlative to the operation of myth. His drawing attention to 'unorthodox rhythms' in Hopkins, to the 'new', ballad-founded metrics of Coleridge, and to the 'natural' unedited metrics of Wyatt, are tributes to the continuation of folk-speech and folk melodies correlative to Yeats's ability to hear folk song, 'a ghostly voice, an unvariable possibility, an unconscious norm' even beneath the opening lines of *Paradise Lost*. (*E&I*, p. 524)

Hughes's own metrics tended, after *Lupercal*, to eschew the formal qualities of that orthodox metre as it had been deployed by his literary ancestors. He said in the 1970 interview about *Crow* that 'the very sound of metre calls up the ghosts of the past and it is difficult to sing one's own tune against that choir. It is easier to speak a language that raises no ghosts'.[92] Yet that parallel urge to capture in poetry the spoken language of English, and to suggest the folk continuities which have been expressed through it across the centuries, is very much of the essence of his exploration of unorthodox metre as it is.[93]

Hughes's poetry, like Yeats's, never strays far from the rhythms of the individual, inflected, speaking voice as the basis for its energy and variety, and to that extent was free of the 'normativizing' or universalizing of Yeats's syntax and diction which continued from Auden's reading of him and which continues at some level in Gunn's. In 'Churn-Milk Joan', originally in *The Remains of Elmet*, Hughes sets mythical and historical possibilities alongside and against each other, only for the story nevertheless to survive:

> Foxes killed her, and her milk spilled.
>
> Or they did not. And it did not.
> Farmers brought their milk this far, and cottagers
> From the top of Luddenden valley left cash
> In the stone's crown . . . .

Here, the historical seems to outweigh the local folkloric temporarily, until 'a word wrenched and the pain came', and the truth of the tale is reasserted, making 'all of us' 'memorials / Of her . . . awful little death'. The inclusiveness of this, its establishment of the poetry at the centre of a tribal and cultural memory, mark Hughes's particular Yeatsian ambition throughout his work, its insistence upon displaced energies which yet form the heart of the nation's life and character.[94]

The difficult relation of that ambition to the 'history' or 'reality' out of which it is purported to derive, an acceptance of fracture in order to achieve a near-mythic but also wished-for historical wholeness, perhaps remains as uncertain in his writing as it does in Yeats (the Devon farm he shared with Sylvia Plath is humorously and fragilely compared with 'The Lake Isle of Innisfree' in *Birthday Letters*, for example).[95] Both early and

late, however, 'Yeats' remained the token by which Hughes could conjure up the suggestion and possibility of that integration of world and
spirit, one steady in its signification. 'He' was indeed the judge by whom
all of Hughes's ambition was to be overlooked.

V

Geoffrey Hill (1932–) is a poet for whom the forces of history and other
circumstances all force the self to revise and return upon its dearest-held
beliefs. Far from being a confessional poet, Hill remains troubled and
fascinated by the means by which 'the dark side' of selfhood, that side
most at the mercy of contemporary circumstance, might be overcome in
works of art. In his early but crucial essay on such matters, 'The Conscious
Mind's Intelligible Structure: A Debate' – an essay in which Yeats seems to
be formally and openly recognized as an influence – the first of Hill's
'epigraphs or texts' refers to a recollection by Mrs. Yeats of Yeats's way of
sorting his papers. Those that were to be kept, Yeats referred to as '*history*'.
As the reteller of the anecdote, Donald R. Pearce, comments, 'all had their
place in an intellectual and personal "history" that was as objective to his
scrutiny as if it were not his own but the life of another man'.

In the 'inconclusive debate' conducted by Hill in the essay, this
version of objectivity in Yeats (one also dear to Davie earlier, in his
citation of Ellmann's phrase) an objectivity which is for Hill 'forensic
rather than domestic', is pitched as both a limitation and a strength.
Yeats was, in Hill's view, unable to attain the kind of 'grammar of assent'
whereby his imagination 'not only leads on to action, but is enriched
and deepened by action'. As a result, Hill identifies a radical disjunction
between two areas of Yeats's life and thought, and indicts Yeats's politics
for their lack of connection with his poetry. It is in his *poetry* that Yeats's
'conscious mind' is most operative. His *politics* are tainted by the drift of
his times: 'the "aristocrat" is conned by a pseudo-aristocracy of the
gutter.' Against such self-deception, it is Yeats's poetic sense of 'near-
perfect pitch', his 'hearing words in depth and . . . therefore hearing, or
sounding, history and morality in depth', which enables him, in Hill's
eyes, to enact the tensions within his mind when confronted by historical actualities. The later mixture of Renaissance courtliness and Anglo-
Irish 'nobility' in Yeats, motivated partly by his sense that his proposed
form of nationalism had been dismissed in the events of 1916, is
excluded by Hill from the poetry's most achieved moments – moments
which display, rather, a poetic mind's proper attention to the resonances
of its own words.

Hill perhaps surprisingly cites 'The Second Coming' and 'Easter 1916' as the works where such enactments can be seen to occur. Of the latter he says that

> One is moved by the artifice of the poem, the mastery of syntactical melody... the tune of the mind mistrustful yet envious, mistrusting the abstraction, mistrusting its own mistrust, drawn half-against its will into the chanting refrain that is both paean and threnos, yet, once drawn, committed utterly to the melody of the refrain.

Hill quotes Yeats's definition in *A Vision*: 'A civilisation is a struggle to keep self-control', before concluding that 'this poem, in its measure and syntax, stands as his more exact imagining of that struggle and that civility'.[96]

What is perhaps most striking here however is Hill's opening acknowledgement that 'artifice' is essentially what 'moves' him, that it is indeed from 'artifice' that the 'conscious mind's intelligible structure' is derived. In a lecture from 1980 on the English poet C. H. Sisson, Hill is alert to the tensions pulling in that word: 'The current ordinary sense of "artifice" is "an ingenious expedient, a manoeuvre, stratagem, device, contrivance, trick"; and yet ' "Artificer" is a slightly antiquated word meaning "one who makes by art or skill... a craftsman" '. In recognition of that 'current' jostling between 'ordinary sense' and the 'slightly antiquated', Hill originates a definition of modern poetic method which seems to balance the two:

> A natural rhythm of thought and sense is inherent [for Sisson] in the language as it is spoken, but subject to 'random agitation'. The poet's struggle, after Flaubert, is concerned with the bringing of random agitation within the domains of formalism by methods more or less Byzantine. That 'more or less' glosses over the crucial struggle which is waged in the mind and heart of every poet between what he strives for in principle and what he finds it possible to achieve in fact.

Hill gives the sources of 'Byzantinism' as Pound's Calvalcanti essay and Canto 98, and Yeats's 'two major poems written in his sixties', but shows how sceptical Sisson himself is of such mandarinism in poetry and in the world of public administration, as well as his own qualified sympathy with that view. Sisson's essay on Yeats, attacking amongst other things that poet's artificial 'celebration of "the artifice of eternity" ', is called 'brilliant, necessary, prejudiced'.[97]

However, the sentences showing that literary history 'after Flaubert' dictates a 'more or less Byzantine' approach to formalism register Hill's mistrust of Sisson's dismissals. Sisson, like every other poet in the century, is Byzantine at least in this sense of formal artifice. The success or failure of the 'method' is more a matter of the poet's own ability than of anything troublesome about the method itself. The attempt to make heard the 'slightly antiquated' but nonetheless telling use of the word 'artifice' against the grain of 'current' usage is to that extent also 'Byzantine'. It requires formal occasion, the technical atonement of 'rhythm and understanding', for such 'deep' resonance within the word to be expressed.

Yet Geoffrey Hill has not, in his promulgation of such antiphonal, highly-wrought artifice, turned a deaf ear to a politically efficacious 'grammar of assent' which connects word to world through action. As a result, he has, throughout his career, displayed a Yeatsian interest in those who have achieved such 'assent' (Yeats noted his own 'envy' for the soldiers involved in the Irish civil war (*CP*, p. 204)) – in Hill's case from Renaissance martyrs to the soldier-poets of the First World War. The phrase about imagination and action in 'The Conscious Mind's Intelligible Structure' he derives from a book on the French writer Charles Péguy. Twelve years after the publication of the 'debate', in his *The Mystery of the Charity of Charles Péguy*, Hill reveals the same admiration. At the same time, however, he alerts us to the trivialization of such enrichings and deepenings as the century has unfolded itself since Péguy's death in the First World War:

> 'Rather the Marne than the *Cahiers*.' True enough
> you took yourself off. Dying, your whole life
> fell into place. ' 'Sieurs-'dames, this is the wall
> where he leaned and rested, this is the well
> from which he drank...'.[98]

Péguy's gruff choice of action and almost certain death at the Battle of the Marne over the writing project, the *Cahiers* which had engaged him for years, is mirrored in the gruffness of Hill's phraseology 'True enough' and the half-rhyme 'nough / life'. These are of a different order to the tinkling parallelism of the tour-guide's 'this is the wall / ... this is the well'. Hill's diction, syntax and rhyme, in other words, are true to that 'embattled hope' out of which Péguy chooses to act (as his prose periods were true in describing Yeats's self-mistrust). Those 'abrupt thoughts and sayings that have the "intricacies of human relations" still clinging to them', which Hill has noted in the work of the First World War poet Ivor Gurney – whereby 'plain speech is wrought from impediment, from inept repetitiousness' – are displayed here as the marks of constrained, fateful choice.[99]

Hill's measure and syntax in this work show both the 'struggle' and the 'civility' which he notices in Yeats's 'Easter 1916', 'mistrustful yet envious'. There is an unflinching steeliness in the acknowledgement and enjambement of lines like 'Dying, your whole life / fell into place' ('you have risen / above all that and fallen flat on your face // among the beetroots'). There is both commendation and hard fact in 'Péguy's cropped skull / dribbles its ichor, its poor thimbleful / A simple lesion of the complex brain'. Taking 'yourself off' can be an act of desertion as well as of martyrdom ('Must men stand by what they write / as by their camp-beds...?'), and might earn a later poet's desperate mockery ('So you just went and took yourself off then'), as well as his admiring sympathetic understanding. Either way, to have your life fall into place is to allow yourself to be picked over by the burial party, and possibly to see your *manoir* opened to crowds of tourists were your writing and act of martyrdom to find some later, debased, currency. Hill's belated tribute to Péguy's 'defeat' shares, then, both the pitch of Yeats's descriptions of his historical circumstances and also the carefully-admiring but sometimes dismissive note of Yeats's elegies for both public and private figures.[100]

In establishing this tone, Hill's elaborate formal method works in ways similar to Yeats's. The dramatic jamming against each other of different materials and styles in his work has nearly always happened within tightly-controlled traditional stanzas (often warranted, it is true, by the historical demands made upon form by his subject-matter) rather than through Poundian experimentalism, however much he has more recently written about Pound rather than Yeats in his own critical prose.[101] What such methods achieve is a metaphysics in which the rhythms and idioms move variously further away from, and closer to, their unreachable but still-desired centre of stability and assent. Such metaphysics seem most predominant in two sequences from the 1979 collection, *Tenebrae*.

In the axiom used as epigraph to 'The Pentecost Castle' from Yeats's letters, the fearfulness of both too great a distance and of too great a proximity are inextricable: 'It is terrible to desire and not possess, and terrible to possess and not desire'. Yet, in the other epigraph from Simone Weil, the dangers of self-love are raised within what seems like a self-transcending objectivity: '...We do not love [in other human beings] their desire. If what we loved in them was their desire, then we should love them as ourself.' By going out to them, we might come close to them, but also we might end where we started. Or, as poem 5 of the sequence has it, 'when I cried out you / made no reply / tonight I shall pass by / without a sound'. Such fastnesses cannot be broken down, such distances cannot be resolved within the passionate paradoxes of the sequence with its sense of dispossession and unanswerable questions: 'how long until this longing / end in unending song' (13). As with Yeats's poems to Maud Gonne and later, more speculative questionings of desire and presence, the dispossession makes here for a richness of dream and poetic life: 'lost in the dream's grasp where / shall I find you everywhere / unmatched in my desire' (12). Hill's lines resonate with and against Yeats's self-question 'Does the imagination dwell the most / Upon the woman won or the woman lost?' (*CP*, p. 197) The inability to 'match' desires, raised by Weil, is both salvific, in that the desire can continue, and a cause for unbreakable suffering, 'this wound / that will not heal' (14).

As with 'Lachrimae Amantis', the last poem of the 'Lachrimae' sequence from this collection, the lover here can only bathe 'for a time' 'in pure tones of promise and remorse', having been fed 'so many nights' the 'urgent comfort' of a dream that ' "your lord is coming, he is close" '.[102] Such 'pure tones' of artifice are, however, constantly open to 'rebuke by life' – that is their promise as well as their remorse. As Hill contends in his lecture 'Poetry As "Menace" and "Atonement" ':

> Romantic art is thoroughly familiar with the reproaches of life. Accusation, self-accusation, are the very life-blood of its most assured rhetoric. As Yeats puts it, in his poem 'The Circus Animals' Desertion' ... [he quotes the poem's last stanza]. But is it possible, though, to revoke 'masterful images' in images that are themselves masterful? Can one renounce 'completion' with epithets and rhyme-patterns that in themselves retain a certain repleteness?[103]

As with rhetorical questions in Yeats, these are questions which Hill might aptly direct towards himself. The 'Byzantine' as potential labyrinth of solipsistic regard lurks within all his attempts at atonement, as 'The Masque of Blackness' from 'Lachrimae' reveals. 'Splendour of life so splendidly contained' seems to be celebrated at the sonnet's beginning, yet we learn that 'Self-love' is 'the slavish master of this trade', and when 'he tires' 'all that he has made / vanishes in the chaos of the dark'.[104] Artifice can soon, through inattention, slide into artificiality; the inattentive master-poet can become worldly 'maestro'. Yet, once again, it is the objectifying, distancing vigour of Yeats's rhythm and cadence in this late poem that Hill chooses to celebrate. He becomes exemplary for the later poet in his irresolvability while becoming also dislocated from his Irish context ('The Circus Animals' Desertion' after all weighs in the balance Yeats's nationalist ambitions) as icon of 'Romantic art'.[105]

When Hill himself uses the epithet 'life-blood', however, in explaining that syntax in 'Poetry as "Menace" and "Atonement"', he is quietly literalizing the actuality which characterizes his poetry early and late, in its passionate attention to those suffering throughout history. Like Yeats in 'Blood and the Moon', Hill acknowledges in the first poem of his first book, 'Genesis', that

> By blood we live, the hot, the cold,
> To ravage and redeem the world:
> There is no bloodless myth will hold.

In Hill, however, such mythological 'bloody, arrogant power' (*CP*, p. 237) is always tempered by the cries of those suffering. 'Among the carnage' of the battlefields in Hill's account of the Wars of the Roses, 'Funeral Music', 'the most delicate souls / Tup in their marriage-blood, gasping "'Jesus'"'. Péguy might 'speak to the blood' in calling for the death of Jean Jaurès but, once 'the metaphors of blood begin to flow', he falls flat on his face 'covered in glory and the blood of beetroots'. Hill's wariness about the deafness of Yeats's later politics, registered in his early essay, is certainly correlative to his own dramatic distancings and *caveats* with the seeming assurance of 'Genesis'. As 'Ovid in the Third Reich' has it, 'Too near the ancient troughs of blood / Innocence is no earthly weapon.'[106] His own historical distance would seem to demand of Hill a greater burden of self-attention than those, including Yeats, whose Romanticism arose from and responded to conflictual circumstance.[107]

With *Canaan* of 1996, Hill took such matters of struggle and civility to the heart of the *urbs*. His castigation of the place-men and the back-handers being passed in the latter days of the Tory Government which fell in 1997 owes much to Blake, Pound, and also to Yeats's disdainful attacks on 'the filthy modern tide'. In 'That Man as a Rational Animal Desires the Knowledge which is His Perfection', Hill dramatizes the voice of one who can 'know / innocence of first inscription' 'with or without assent': 'I imagine singing I imagine // getting it right'. But, everywhere in this land both mythic and real, such imaginings are dogged by, as 'Respublica' calls them, 'The strident high / civic trumpet-ing / of misrule', which we 'stand for'. 'Respublica' itself can only be 'brokenly recalled' in these limping measures. As such, it is again *distance* that might present a solving, resolving perspective, as we are enjoined in 'Concerning Inheritance':

> grant inequity from afar to be in equity's covenant,
> its paradigm drawn on the fiducial stars,
> its aegis anciently a divine shield
>   over the city.

There is undoubtedly something unrepentantly and characteristically mandarin and Byzantine about this, in its diction and its measures. Yet, as Hill asks in 'Cycle', echoing Yeats's rendition of Swift's epitaph (*CP*, p. 245):

> Are we not moved by
>   'savage
> indignation'[108]

The phrase then recurs twice in *The Triumph of Love*, which appeared in America in 1998 and Britain in 1999. The persona adopted by Hill throughout this 150–section poem is close to the Swiftian mask often assumed by Yeats in his later poems, that of an old man raging at the debased values of the times, and at age itself, as a 'reborn ageing child, / privileged to no place of honour'.[109]

Against the drift of contemporary event, Hill dreams once more of the possibility of *'Active virtue'* (his italics) which is implicated with the 'struggle / for a noble vernacular'. Yeats equated that 'virtue' with the 'consciously dramatic...wearing of a mask', and, at some level, it might underwrite Hill's assumption of the Yeatsian and Swiftian persona of railing old man in this poem. (*M*, p. 334) Yet his attention remains very much upon his native poetry. He fears that the exemplars of such virtue in the English tradition, Dryden and Milton, are now 'far back, indistinct':

> Still, I'm convinced that shaping,
> voicing, are types of civic action.[110]

The later work of Geoffrey Hill, like the later work of Yeats, has been stirred by disgust at 'civic matters' into a more exact, explicit (because more immediately threatened), and challenging 'struggle and civility'. The universalized, *poetic*, virtues of ordering syntax which he celebrated in Yeats, despite Yeats's own drift elsewhere, remain, I believe, a model of assent which Hill's poetry continues to aspire towards.

VI

Within the 'inevitable abstractions' involved in the translation of Yeats's writing into the British context from the moment of his death, we find an almost immediate universalization of its poetic, formal and technical characteristics as a means towards establishing the site of poetry as exemplary of certain social and political qualities. The 'true democratic style' that Auden's 'Defence Counsel' praises in his obituary article underpins his own movement towards a more standard syntax after his poetry of the 1930s, as well as towards a generalized and abstract vocabulary. These are qualities which Donald Davie then early discovers in Yeats more than in other possible exemplars from the twentieth-century, a purity of diction and a normative syntax which unquestionably carry 'past civilization' into the present, and which establish the social virtue of poetry itself. That syntax is in its turn sustained with difficulty in Geoffrey Hill's more troubled writing, open to the abrupt shocks of historical violence, yet aspiring to a 'grammar of assent' or '*Active virtue*' which also exemplifies civic equity. For these writers, as for Thom Gunn, Yeats's retention of a *seemingly* conventional and normative form and syntax acts to establish the poem as a coherent entity with universal value. Even where form is absent, it is mourned, and remains a shadowy possibility behind other form-breaking experiences.

Hill's historical distance enables him to dismiss Yeats's own cultural and political perspective, while celebrating particular features of his poetic achievement. For him, as also for Gunn and Hughes, that distance allows them to experiment with 'pose', masks and personae partly inspired by Yeats, while sustaining a sense of the continuities between inner and outer experience, mythic and historical worlds. Even while displaying an unease with the inheritances bequeathed by that traditional form partly mediated to them through the figure of Yeats, they continued to perceive a certain transparency in formal practice. The poetics of existentialism, myth-making, historical imagining, or self-creation are held to be both responsive to cultural and historical circumstance and to be accessible to, and (for Hughes) integrational of, their audience.

In the process of all of these re-readings of Yeats in Britain and (it may be worth noting in passing) especially England, the specific and the local impulses behind his work are resisted or excluded. His own disjunctive style and syntax, with their complex dramatic interplay of presence and absence, symbol and temporality, tradition and selfhood, personal and national history, is rendered into a standardized, regularized and regularizing normativeness. His difficult, rebarbative relation to his culture and times is excluded or reduced, and replaced by a sense of continuity, in which the generality of the experience and the self or selves mediated through the poetry are presumed as an integral and uniting force for social good, whatever historical characteristics force themselves upon the writing. Unlike Irish poets, these are not writers given to dramatic self-remakings across their careers. The methods and procedures are established and continuing; the adherence to coherent syntax and often-abstract vocabulary unassailable.

As such, British poetry since his death partakes of those qualities integral to the formalist criticism which was developed in Cambridge by I.A. Richards, qualities which found fertile ground in America (a point I will take up in my next chapter), and have certain parallels in French theory. The poetry, like the criticism, envisages a 'stable moral climate', and brings 'poetic language [down] to the level of the language of communication'. At some level, it believes in an adequation of the object with the language which names it.[111] That very belatedness and indecipherability which haunts Yeats's sense of his own context have become, in this highly transformative translation, a sense of form as constitutive, as creative and in itself exemplary.

4
Possession and Dispossession: Yeats and American Poetry

John Crowe Ransom, Allen Tate, John Berryman, Robert Lowell, James Merrill, Adrienne Rich, Sylvia Plath, Jorie Graham

From the poems and critical commentaries engaging with his work written in America after Yeats's death, it is clear that he was (and continued to be) central to debates there about the possibilities of poetic meaning and its worth in a hostile contemporary world. In the immediate post-obituary moment, American poets, like the Irish and like Auden, found themselves reassessing the relation of poetic 'value' to their own historical and national situation. In their own elegies for peers and friends, they commenced a process of mourning Yeats through mourning those others which was to characterize American poetry through to the 1970s and beyond. Yeats's formal and modern elegy, 'In Memory of Major Robert Gregory', gains a crucial and immediate afterlife in several poems, and resonates behind many more.

For those poets not immediately wedded to a Poundian poetic, like George Oppen and Louis Zukofsky – or to the Stevens tradition as John Ashbery is – Yeats rather than Eliot seems to have focused much thinking about the relation of poetry to contemporary society and politics, about the place of the poet in society, and about the value of certain kinds of poetic rhetoric. Also, within criticism and literary theory, from the New Critics to Harold Bloom and Paul de Man (as I described in my first chapter), Yeats remained a central influential figure. For the earlier formalist critics, who shared many of the perceptions of the British writer I.A. Richards, but with a particular local cultural inflection, he represented a model of poetic integration and completion through paradox that might be immediately translated to an imagined social realm. For the Yale-based Bloom and de Man, Yeats served a related but ultimately less determining purpose, as embodier of textual undecidability and paradox within a post-Romantic tradition of the sublime, the discussion of which latterly forged links between European and American deconstruction.

As such, as Daniel T. O'Hara has argued, the often valid and theoretically-innovative American discussions of Yeats from the 1970s onwards – discussions which have often informed my own argument in this book – are sometimes blurred by the demands of a specific and local ambition:

> An American critical theorist, in order to know the Sublime, tries to produce it by elaborating his system, with Yeats as the scapegoat muse of the project, his rival theorists as the last incarnations of the Demiurge, and himself, of course, as the Alien God's authentic representative. As such, one could conclude that, thanks to Yeats, critical theory in America, that profession of the sublime, has for nearly half a century been essentially a cult affair or even an occult enterprise . . . .[1]

The danger of this deployment of Yeats as warrant of a certain kind of visionary system within criticism is, as O'Hara points out, that it leads to a collapse into hopeless iteration and obscurity, in which the textual intricacy of the system itself seems to ensure its own value.

'Yeats', as a sign of self-containment emptied of the complexities of origination and attachment that form the ruptured symbolism of his presence in Ireland, comes to stand in America (for poets as well as critics, such have been the entanglements of the two since the New Criticism) for a curiously under-articulated 'meaning' and content. That 'meaning' is, paradoxically, often asserted against an otherwise meaningless post-war culture. The de Manian shift from symbolic presence to sign or allegorical temporality is itself symptomatic of reading at a distance, bringing increased clarity, but also revealing the *absences* and endstoppings which are masked under Yeatsian transliminal plenitude. Harold Bloom's dismissal of the work of Theodore Roethke and John Berryman for its mere reiteration of Yeatsian qualities (something which I will question and in the case of the latter modulate, below), seems to derive from national circumstances, as well as being an abstractable possibility within Yeats's aporias. As if, in these circumstances – to take up the doubt at the heart of 'Ancestral Houses' – *truly* 'some marvellous empty sea-shell . . . were the symbol which shadows the inherited glory . . . '. (*CP*, p. 200)

As Jorie Graham (1951–) wrote in an early poem, 'The Geese', 'at any time, things could fall further apart / and nothing could help them / recover their meaning'. The geese flying overhead seem like 'the passage of time, or a most perfect heading' whose 'relevance' is to be feared by those watching from below, since

> things will not remain connected,
> will not heal,
>
> and the world thickens with texture instead of history,
> texture instead of place.[2]

The 'real' and 'everyday' will, therefore, 'cross' humanity and happen through it, rather than humans controlling those realities. In this revision of 'The Second Coming', the 'texturing' of the world – a 'texturing' of which both this Graham poem and Yeats's are a part – displaces all temporal and spatial continuities. If it is to retain any connection with 'history' and 'place', poetry must, therefore, perpetually overflow its own boundaries. Completion, for Graham, remains something yearned-for but to be denied. It both condemns the world to 'texturing' as text, and yet interrupts the everyday crossing of the world over us by establishing us as subjects. Such subjectivity for Graham, however, can have dangerous political (historical, personal and gender) consequences.

'Imperialism' comes around to remembering the child's first vision of the integrity of her mother's body as

> ... one of the finished things, one of the
> *beauties* (hear it click shut?) a thing
> completely narrowed down to love –[3]

In a letter of September 8 1935, Yeats wrote to Dorothy Wellesley about redrafting his work that 'a poem comes right with a click like a closing box'.[4] Graham shies away from enclosed 'beauty' ('Imperialism' ends with a Dickensonian dash, not a fullstop). Yet, at the same time, as in the lovemaking described in the section of 'Manifest Destiny' set on the founding site of Shiloh battlefield ('They are playing, sort of, at Leda and Swan'), she recognizes the inability of text to capture its own origins, or the origins of life or a nation: 'How can they cross over and the difference between them swell with / existence?' We are ourselves traversed by the everyday in this textured world, but we cannot translate, as Derrida acknowledged, into plenitude.

If this is, for America (as the title of a later poem has it), 'The Phase After History', then questions of possession and dispossession are what abound:

> Is the house empty?
> Is the emptiness housed?
> Where is America here from the landing, my face on

>   My knees, eyes closed to hear
>   Further?[5]

The emptiness at the heart of all rhetorical founding and desire (the need to continually 'hear further') is central to the post-Romantic tropology in Yeats and his afterlife which I have been describing in this book. In both American poetry and critical thought, such anxious questionings, the fear that meaning cannot be recovered and that the nation therefore remain unlocated, even unfounded because unexpressed, was fascinatingly focused almost from the moment of his death upon the significance of Yeats's writing. Since the impact of these questionings echoes across all subsequent poetry through to a contemporary writer such as Graham, I will spend a longer time at the beginning of this chapter discussing the origin of these questionings in writing and thought from the Thirties themselves, before moving on to discuss more recent work.

I

In the years around and immediately after Yeats's death in 1939, the nature of his achievement underwent serious reconsideration in the United States. This was particularly so amongst those poets and critics from the South, including Cleanth Brooks, Robert Penn Warren, Allen Tate and John Crowe Ransom, who had been more recently associated with the Agrarian movement. During the inter-war years, the Agrarians had mounted a critique concerning the failure of modern scientific, technological, and industrialist thought to provide a basis for community, such as that which they felt had ideally existed in the South. In a late published conversation with Warren, Brooks described the significance of Yeats's influence for the thinking of the movement:

> Where Yeats principally differed from his great contemporaries such as Eliot and Pound was in having a base in a backward-looking, traditional society which had hardly yet, as a culture, entered the modern world. Yeats turned that heritage, one that many people would have regarded as a liability, into an immense advantage. The southern writers in the 1920s were very much in Yeats's position: their culture, like Yeats's, had managed to preserve something of the wholeness, spontaneity, and concreteness of an earlier day and thus furnished the necessary other term for the dialectic – that is, passion as against intellection, poetry as against science, tradition as against modernity, an agrarian life as opposed to an industrial life.[6]

The terms in which Brooks describes the 'something' from the past which it is that he feels Yeats has managed to preserve, 'wholeness, spontaneity, and concreteness', were of course freighted with a Coleridgean critical-ideological importance for the movement in criticism of which he, along with Warren, was largely the promulgator – the New Criticism.

In this late conversation, Brooks defended the way in which that movement had prioritized the poem's formal and aesthetic qualities as a verbal artifact, independently of the political and historical pressures upon its making or upon the author's own intentions in making it. He had never, he claims, been interested in a notion of the poem as an empty formality, since 'words open out into the whole world of emotions, ideas, actions'. Nor had he been dismissive of the fact that a knowledge of history could enhance the poem for its readers, since 'what I as a reader must do, with all the help that I can get from history and elsewhere, is to become [an] ideal reader myself'. But, ultimately, Brooks still wanted to defend the notion of poems as 'organic structures', whole in themselves: 'Sometimes, a rich and massive poem seems to possess a life of its own, not merely a life breathed into it by the person who reads it.'[7] Poems can 'possess a life' because they resist possession by any one reader. As such, they are rendered void of any intentionality, *either* on the reader's part *or* on the poet's.[8] In a valueless modern age, poetry offers a vision of unity which both encapsulates both a possibility of seeing beyond circumstance and of looking back or mourning a prelapsarian world.

Across his career, Yeats formed for Brooks the prime exemplar of the ways in which poetry can present 'concrete and meaningful images in terms of which the play of the mind may exhibit itself – that play being, not rigidly conceptual and bare, but enriched with all sorts of associations.' The 1939 book from which this phrase derives, the soon-canonical *Modern Poetry and the Tradition*, crucially confronts the issue of the foundations for the concrete and meaningful within and through Yeats. Brooks discusses particularly the later poetry, and therefore confronts also the issue of the role of the mystical book *A Vision* in underpinning Yeats's symbolic 'system'. He attacks the view, chiefly fostered by Edmund Wilson in *Axel's Castle*, that Yeats is guilty of fleeing from scientific truth and from modern reality, and that his work is therefore irrelevant. Rather, Brooks claims, *A Vision* is 'one of the most remarkable books of the last hundred years'. Yeats's system is seeking to discover a resolution to uncertainties which science has failed to solve,

... to build a system of references which would allow for a unification of sensibility. Yeats wanted to give the authority of the intellect
to attitudes and the intensity of the emotion to judgements.[9]

Yeats emerges from this reading, as from many similar assessments at
the time, as the modern equivalent of metaphysical poets such as
Donne, as they were being re-envisaged for the modern age by T.S.
Eliot. For Eliot's 'a thought to Donne was an experience; it modified
his sensibility', we might read 'Yeats's later poetry, like the poetry of
Donne, reveals the "mind at the finger-tips".'[10]

The terms of Brooks's evaluation of Yeats are repeated again and again
throughout American assessments made of him in the years just after his
death. In contrast with Ireland itself, and (to a lesser extent) with
Britain, America's commemoration highlighted the significance of his
'system' in unifying the impulses of the later work. These writers emphasized the relation of the poetry to the barely modern world of Ireland out
of which it was written, its traditional centredness, and the worth of the
religious and magical in his writing in a barren age of science and
naturalism.

Continuous throughout these assessments is the sense that, despite
the rival claims of T.S. Eliot, Yeats is the greatest poet of the times in his
heroic efforts to go against the grain and to create a vision of wholeness
in spite of lack. His perceived position as a national poet, and as a public
poet able to unite his personal preoccupations with an historical vision,
offered more potential to those continuing to live, work, and write in
America than those of the international, displaced modernists.[11] Yet the
symbolically unifying transparency between poem and world seen to be
figured in Yeats, of course, empties out the *discontinuities*, disjunctions
and liminality which characterize his own poetics of desire. The 'historic-
ally-backward' origins of his vision of Ireland celebrated by Brooks and
others, is, indeed, largely *derived* from his own writings – particularly the
earlier ones, in which the emergent fears about the rise of a mercantile
Catholic middle class from the early 1910s onwards were yet to emerge.
The New Critical reification of the poem based upon a 'reading' of Yeats
is, therefore, marked by a draining out of the radical ruptures within his
symbolic 'unities', and is idealized in the pastoralism it claims to derive
from him.

What emerges in these New Critical debates and subsequently in
American poetry and criticism, therefore, is an anxiety about the
nature of modernity itself, in which *relevance*, the significance of poetry
for its times and its ability to speak beyond itself, is one of the key

preoccupations. The inscription of a Romantic problematics at the very heart of 'modernity', which was a sometime concern of de Man's, emerges in this reading of Yeats and writing after him as a desire to assert the continuities heralded in Brooks's title, *Modern Poetry and the Tradition*, while at the same time revealing despite itself a pressure of locality, temporality and history which questions such seamlessness.[12] What is striking in this is that, within these readings, whether he is located as 'traditionalist' or as 'modern' (or as an eclectic mixture of the two), the vision of 'Yeats' as a fixed, 'known', contained signifier of a set of symbolist values remains constant.

However, sometimes in the critical prose, but more often in the *poetry* of those writers associated with the New Critical movement, anxieties about voiding, disjunction and absence brought about by modernity and a personal sense of time do sometimes surface, revealing the anxiety underlying the integrational readings of Yeats.[13] 'Yeats' has become a dogmatic sign similar to that barren 'lost trace' which Jacques Derrida has identified with writing itself, when, in these instances from America, he seems to fail to offer a salving 'meaning'.[14] Yet there is often also a strong countermovement in these poets' readings, a yearning towards the kind of harmonizations 'Yeats' would seem to proffer.

John Crowe Ransom (1888–1974), who is one of those who in his critical prose had most sought to defend the kinds of unity discovered by Yeats against debasing tendencies in the modern world, shows, even in his poetry published during Yeats's lifetime, something of this ambivalence towards some of Yeats's founding attitudes and symbols. 'The Rose' is a poem which figures the flower crucial to Yeats's early symbolism, where (and particularly in the 1893 collection which takes *The Rose* as its title) it represents an eternal beauty which suffers with humankind across history. Ransom's rose carries none of the communal force of Yeats's, however. Entering a room, forlorn and bereft, the persona of Ransom's poem comes upon 'a most celestial rose' which seems to smile and offer him redemption.

Yet the destruction of the hope visited by the flower upon the persona is curiously modern and ironic in contrast with Yeats's Pre-Raphaelitism:

> . . . I went like one escaping hell
> To drink the fragrance and to touch,
> And stroked, O ludicrous to tell,
> A horrid thing of bric-a-brac,
> A make-believe and mockery
> And nothing that a rose must be.[15]

Ransom's ideal lover, 'beyond all women born', has (like Browning's 'Last Duchess') been spending her smile too easily, hence the sham nature of the flower as symbol. The promiscuity of the loved one, in other words, seems to have debased the integrity of the symbolic potential of the rose itself, and to have broken its traditional associations. Another poem, 'Vaunting Oak', also exposes the 'pitiful error' of humanity's desire to find symbols for its emotions in emblems which are also natural things.[16]

What these mannered poems show, then, is a deep scepticism about the unitary force of symbolism and its religious resonances that Ransom elsewhere sees as having been exemplified by Yeats, and their replacement by an allegorical or exhausted rhetoric of temporality and a mockery of association. 'Necrological' even associates the religious life with death. As the friar in the poem surveys the beautifully arrayed fallen heroes and warriors on a battlefield, he comes to 'liken himself' to them, as though the stasis of the bodies on the field is the equivalent of dutiful compliance to the symbols and rituals of the church.[17]

Such troublings of the symbolic and religious (with correlative uncertainties about the value of the resulting signification) underlie Ransom's transformation of the poem 'Semi-Centennial' into 'Birthday for an Aging Seer (b. June 24, 1865)'. This is a transformation in which the nameless old man of the first poem is unmasked as Yeats in the second. Both poems, like 'Necrological' and much of the earlier work, centre upon the Yeatsian theme of the relationship of art and the artist to the world of action. Both versions keep the pattern of the old man emerging from his house after a long winter to view the changes in nature with the coming of spring, with the narratorial voice assuring us that 'Business better than that had been enacted, / ... within the curled compacted / Grey hemispheres' of the seer. The poem celebrates the life of the mind, and the fact that 'The better part of godhead is design', the ability for the mind to create patterns in contradistinction to nature's cyclical workings – a view of Yeats which anticipates those later discussions of him by the Yale school which we looked at in the opening chapter.

What is startling in Ransom's revision of the poem is that, with the recognition of the old man as Yeats himself in the second version, the elements of Romantic solipsism, and the critical viewpoint presumed in the first fall away. 'Semi-Centennial' has the old man claim 'I am a god', but sets his proclaimed transcendence of the world as potential heresy:

> ' ... For it satisfies
> My royal blood even thus to exercise

> The ancestral arts of my theogony.
> I am a god though none attends to me.'

In the second version, 'Yeats's' claim to godhead contains this potentially fallen resonance, but is shown to be truly performative and empowering:

> 'I am a god transcending things that be,
> And the proper gods have disinherited me...
>
> ...But with my power, and thriving on disrepute,
> I speak and pure souls hear and execute.'

Yeat's ontological heresy towards the normative and proper is countered here by his 'disrepute', his hieratic heresy against the normal accepted behaviour and attitudes of his day. And yet it is this which he claims carries his words' power into actions by later pure-souled acolytes. This becomes clearer in the new final stanza of the second version. 'Semi-Centennial' had ended with a world-weary laconic note which possibly further exposed the old man as a sufferer from *folie de grandeur*: 'He had the magic too, and knew his power, / But was too tired to work it at this hour'. Yet the potential ambiguity of this, its uncertain note of criticism ('He had', as though we are to believe him; '[he] knew' as though it might be merely delusion), is resolved in 'Birthday of an Aging Seer' into certainty, through a surprising establishment of the claim to being a national poet:

> 'My worlds are Irish, and it satisfies
> The Irish folk that I should exercise
> The ancestral arts of their theogony.
> I am their god, and they depend on me.'[18]

The critical note seems to have been dropped totally. 'As to the man's divinity, the Unknown God has implanted in him that special degree of godhood which consists in the freedom of the aesthetic imagination', Ransom's annotations to the poem tell us. The poet's transcendence of the world of being also seems to set him up as the power upon which everything in his nation hangs.

In the retrospective note in *Selected Poems* 'Semi-Centennial' is seen as being 'very much tangled in ambiguities'. The revised 'Birthday of an Aging Seer' falls into line with Ransom's prose statements on Yeats, as when he defends Yeats's 'miraculous' trope-making against the naturalistic 'tidy discourse' and logic of his age:

> To be vivid is to have special and substantial character which is excessive, or goes beyond the general occasion, so that actually we cannot attend to it without suspending the rule. To be vivid importantly, and to a degree that strikes us with an awe of substantial nature, is doubtless to be magnificent . . . and it is the effect in poetry upon which religion capitalizes.[19]

It is as though, in this last stanza that he published, Ransom is answering Yeats's own notorious question in the late 'Man and the Echo', 'Did that play of mine send out / Certain men the English shot?' (*CP*, p. 345), with an emphatic and glorying 'Yes'. In the ontological sphere, he is also complying with Yeats's suggestion in some of his essays that, with the failure of religion, art is taking its place.[20] In this last poem he worked on, Ransom becomes assured that Yeats's Romantic stance came from a true understanding of modernism and a reasoned opposition to it. His prose evaluations of later Yeats at the time of the older poet's death had seemed to acknowledge this, but his own earlier poetic practice, when treating Yeatsian themes, had seemed to deny it. In both cases, however, the reading of Yeats himself remains constant. That value-based integrity and commonality, described frequently from within the critical movement of which Ransom was a part (his *The New Criticism* appeared in 1941), seems a given which can offer either a rebuke, or an alternative, to contemporary debasement. The shift in Ransom's *poetic* stance marks an acceptance of the *relevance* of that vision, one which the temporality of his own poetry and its reading of the times had earlier seemed wary of.

II

Amongst the Agrarians the poet who seems to have immediately felt at ease with a definition of Yeats as a *modern* poet was Allen Tate (1899–1979) – and this perhaps because of his being slightly younger than Ransom. It is Tate's influence, both personal and professional, and the influence of his reading of Yeats, which then had the more vital impact upon the generation of writers first being published just after Yeats's death, Robert Lowell, John Berryman and Theodore Roethke. Tate was convinced, early and surprisingly that, as he said, Yeats's poetry is 'nearer the centre of our main traditions of sensibility and thought than the poetry of Eliot or of Pound' – hence its immediate impact. But Tate went further, in a late essay, when describing the importance of Yeats as an example of what he hoped his own poetry might achieve in the modern world:

> I first began to read the 'Later Yeats' in the early nineteen-twenties. I remember as it were yesterday the impact of 'The Second Coming' and 'In Memory of Major Robert Gregory'. ... At a glance the poems looked quite conventional.... Yet... [they] could not have been written before 1914. I felt at once that here was a poet with whom, by hard labor, I might make myself contemporary.

Intriguingly, in a passage which again emphasizes the immediacy and freshness of the impression, Tate sees the superficially traditional nature of Yeats's outlook and prosody as being paradoxically a mark of his modernity. From the perspective of this late essay, Tate views Yeats's 'system' as a sign of his restlessness and ambition, but also as in itself a mask which allowed him 'to wear the disguise of a pre-modern poet'. Yeats's modernism is, then, 'profound'. *A Vision*, in Tate's eyes, represents a clever guise through which Yeats can speak of his own concerns while seeming to ponder some of the traditional historical and philosophical ideas of the culture.[21] Modernity remains, in a somewhat reactionary but also (to an extent) Yeatsian way, equated with the expression of personality, but is only possible through a retention of the historically-ratified visionary mask which is itself generalized, removed from the tower and the times of its making.

In reviewing his sense of the immediate impact of Yeats upon himself in this late essay, Tate is being consistent with his earlier views of the poet, views which are illuminating about the relation between surface 'traditionalism' and an underlying profound 'modernity' in Yeats's work. When writing of 'the most completely expressed' poem of 'our time', 'In Memory of Major Robert Gregory', in his 1941 essay 'Yeats's Romanticism', Tate saw *A Vision* as Yeats's recognition that necessity and fatedness exists across history. But this recognition leads, paradoxically, to Yeats's liberation as a thinker and poet, since to feel necessity working is also to feel that there are aspects of life in which free will can operate. Tate therefore takes *A Vision* seriously, and attacks those like Edmund Wilson, R.P. Blackmur, T.S. Eliot and Louis MacNeice, who find there only a deluding otherworldliness and 'magic'. For Tate, *A Vision* provides Yeats with a resource of metaphor that pervades the later work, even when it is seemingly absent:

As the system broadens out and merges into the traditional insights of our culture, it tends to disappear in its specific, technical aspects. What disappears is not a philosophy, but only a vast metaphorical structure. In the great elegy, 'In Memory of Major Robert Gregory', we get the couplet:

> But as the outrageous stars incline
> By opposition, square and trine –

which is the only astrological figure in the poem. Yet it must not be assumed that Yeats on this occasion turned off the system; it must be there. Why does it not overtly appear? It has been absorbed into the concrete substance of the poem; the material to be symbolized replaces the symbol, and contains its own meaning.[22]

The 'traditional insights' into which the 'system' merges in its turn leads Yeats into a liberating absorption of those 'insights' into the actual matter of the poem. Symbols are buried there, rather than 'on the surface', in a process by which 'modernity' is rendered as entombing in this particular process of elegizing. The traditionally symbolic loses its 'philosophical' meaning, and becomes metaphorical, only for those metaphors to become subsumed below the 'material to be symbolized'. In the process, the 'truth' or otherwise of the symbolic system – the grounds upon which Yeats had been attacked by such as Wilson – becomes irrelevant. It is the *materiality* of the poetry which, in an argument close to Brooks's on Yeats, assures its 'meaning' and value, independently of the origin of such material.[23]

And indeed this process by which 'the material to be symbolized replaces the symbol' very much informs the substance of Yeats's elegy. Gregory – 'all life's epitome' – as soldier, scholar, horseman and artist, might be taken as the perfect example of the complete beauty and unity of being as it is envisaged in Phase Fifteen in *A Vision*. (pp. 135–7) But these qualities are given concrete expression in the poem itself, in the recounting of specific incidents in Gregory's life and in the naming of the places which he knew. Further, the appearance of Gregory in the poem is as something of a replacement or usurper. The elegy for him replaces the poem in which Yeats 'had thought . . . to have brought to mind / all those that manhood tried, or childhood loved / Or boyish intellect approved, / With some appropriate commentary on each', as the last stanza tells us. 'Imagination' brought about the 'fitter welcome' of Gregory's presence, which usurps the more traditional poem of ritual and hospitality that had been promised in the opening lines:

> Now that we're almost settled in our house
> I'll name the friends that cannot sup with us
> Beside a fire of turf in th'ancient tower....

The 'missing' original poem is cast as a congenial gathering of dead friends on a stormy winter's night by the poet who uses his powers of imagination and memory to summon them. Yeats is 'accustomed to their lack of breath', he tells us, striking a note which in all of the poems written about and around Thoor Ballylee suggests continuity and tradition, often against the antagonistic circumstances of the times (as for example, in 'And may her bridegroom bring to her a house / Where all's accustomed, ceremonious' in 'A Prayer for my Daughter' (*CP*, p. 190)). But Yeats is *not* 'accustomed' to the fact 'that my friend's dear son . . . Could share in that discourtesy of death'. And after this shock of recognition, the tone of the poem shifts from one of assured reminiscence toward the high elegiac. At this point, the 'specific, technical aspect' of the poem would seem to subsume the 'material' and at the same time to modulate it.

Yet this reading might bring some tension into Tate's assertion of a 'modernity' which in essence sublimates the traditional into its 'concrete substance'. The 'unexpected' shift of tone is presumably what signals the elegy's modernity for Tate. The superficially traditional nature of the prosody continues, while the material and tone of the poem change dramatically and gain a new 'meaning' in the process. The 'accustomed' losses are overwhelmed by the irreconcilable loss, which at another level can be read as the destruction of the traditional way of life in the First World War. As Tate says, the poem could not have been written before 1914. However, Yeats's sense of the irreconcilable is more *disjunctive* than Tate's integrational perspective can allow for – as Crazy Jane claims, 'nothing can be sole or whole / That has not been rent'. (*CP*, p. 260) In the elegy's closing lines, he writes that 'a thought / Of that late death took all my heart for speech'. It is as though there is nothing now for the imagination to express but loss, as though 'the material to be symbolized' here represents a *breaking* with symbol and the 'vast metaphorical pattern' of tradition into which it is merged. Tate's generalized quotation of the technical couplet about the 'square and trine' to exemplify his case in fact destroys the concrete substance of the ambiguous syntax of Yeats's stanza. He writes there of his astrologist uncle George Pollexfen's interests as though they were perhaps past before his death, he 'Having grown sluggish and contemplative'.

Rather than presuming sublimation, the complex temporality of the elegy's ending contemplates a silence in which 'speech' is overwhelmed by the writing of *this* poem. Yeats's ability to imaginatively renanimate the dead, 'bringing them to mind', is interrupted by the more immediate need to 'accommodate' Gregory's loss in a model of integration. And yet Yeats is left to reflect upon the *interruption* of the convivial ur-poem by the more clamant *actual* one, as though he cannot get around or over his own writing. The poem's end returns us to the vertiginously slippery syntax of the last line of the opening stanza, and our hair-raising inability to finally establish its subject: 'All, all are in my thoughts to-night being dead.'

Tate's 'concrete materialism' in fact masks, limits and resolves a deeper lack of resolution in the poem: after speech, long silence, not the other way about. This in turn reflects upon the anxiety in integrating within such temporality Gregory as model of unity of being and as embodier of local *cultural* vision, as practising artistic techniques which are *'our* secret discipline / Wherein the gazing heart doubles her might' [my italics]. (*CP*, pp. 132–5)

Tate's view of the traditional as a mask, however, serves further to exacerbate the elegiac nature of his sense of modernity. This is Yeats's profound insight, the feeling that the accustomed might continually be disrupted and usurped by a stronger recognition that, although symbols remain acceptable, they must be so in a different way. They are doomed to be 'metaphorical' rather than philosophical, and in that lies their strength as well as their (illogical) weakness.

Yet, despite this seemingly assured critical sense of the new possibilities of poetic materiality which reading Yeats gave him, the importance of Yeats for Tate's own poetry is a matter of some dispute.[24] Indeed, perhaps because of his emphasis upon materiality, much of the earlier poetry seems preoccupied by recognitions of finality and endstoppedness in death which is even anti-Yeatsian, as in the 1924 poem addressed to Robert Penn Warren, 'To a Romantic':

> . . . You think the dead arise
> Westward and are fabulous:
> The dead are those whose lies
> Were doors to a narrow house.[25]

The past here represents constricting untruth to the young Tate, anxious perhaps to prove his own modernity. Yet other of the early poems are more preoccupied with issues of loss, tradition and inheritance in ways

that are more distinctly similar to Yeats's Coole Park poems. In 'Retroduction to American History' of 1926, the belligerent, debased cityscape
with its spicing of myth and neurotic questioning is obviously derived
from Eliot. But the closing section of the poem shows Tate moving
beyond a bluntly-expressed *Vision*-like 'recognition of necessity' ('Intellect / Connives with heredity, creates fate as Euclid geometry') towards a
more plangent knowledge of lack:

> Heredity
> Proposes love, love exacts language, and we lack
> Language. When shall we speak again? When shall
> The sparrow dusting the gutter sing? When shall
> This drift with silence meet the sun? When shall I wake?[26]

Even with the resonances from T.S. Eliot, the rhetorical questioning
bears a particularly Yeatsian hallmark of uncertainty. The sense that a
language or speech of accustomed relationship is denied by the modern
world, and that 'Vocabulary [has] / Become confusion' seems true to the
ending of 'In Memory of Major Robert Gregory', where, as here, the only
speech to 'take all my heart' is that of unaccustomed loss.

   Heredity as an issue of family and personal inheritance, which burst as
a theme into Yeats's work with the epigraph poem to his 1914 *Responsibilities*, emerges in Tate's 1931 'Emblems'. This poem's final image of
August striking upon the graves of his forefathers like a hawk striking a
crouching hare anticipates the shattering ending of Yeats's 1938 'Man
and the Echo'. But these ideas of the usurpation of the poem and the
present by the lost 'all life's epitome' had surfaced again in Tate's own
great public elegy of 1927/1937, 'Ode to the Confederate Dead'. Again,
when faced with 'the immoderate past' and its heroically fallen, Tate is
forced to question his power to say anything – 'What shall we say of the
bones . . . ?'. The deaths serve to overwhelm the present and the heart's
words:

> What shall we say who have knowledge
> Carried to the heart? Shall we take the act
> To the grave? Shall we, more hopeful, set up the grave
> In the house? The ravenous grave?[27]

Tate, typically, retains that endstoppedness of his earlier work. At the
opening of the poem, the elaborate description of the graveyard with its
decaying monuments brings a deliberately less magnificent sense of the

dead than Yeats's elegy. The grave counts us all, and such is the degree of loss involved in the deaths of these forgotten heroes ('Where are the heroes...?', another poem, 'Causerie', asks), that the only hope is to take the grave into the house.

In its reduction of the heroes to their bones and in its Villonesque relationship to death, Tate's 'Ode' takes on *some* of the qualities of later Yeats. But it does not take on the sense of the complex, variously-successful revivifying power of writing itself. 'What shall we say...?' here picks up the 'when shall we speak...?' of 'Retroduction to American History'. Tate is continually looking for a moment within history in which immediacy can be expressed, only to find it thwarted, lost in writing itself. The Romantic problematic sketched by de Man in 'Intentional Structure of the Image' ('it is in the essence of language to be capable of origination, but of never achieving...absolute identity with itself'[28]), a problematic which is profoundly Yeatsian, is here compounded by what Stanley Cavell has described as a characteristically American figure of 'Finding as Founding'. In discovering the *when* and the *what*, Tate would escape iteration into a 'new' state, breaking from history. Yet, at the same time (to adopt Cavell's term), that state is 'unapproachable'. The wished-for redemptive act succeeds only in bringing death home, stopping the process of founding as it begins and rendering it impossible.[29]

By 1942, when he came to write his actual elegy for Yeats, 'Winter Mask', Tate finds Yeats's own public rhetoric inadequate for answering his questions as to whether there is anything worth living for, politically or otherwise:

> I asked the master Yeats
> Whose great style could not tell
> Why it is man hates
> His own salvation,
> Prefers the way to hell,
> And finds his last safety
> In the self-made curse that bore
> Him towards damnation....[30]

The poem adopts the form of Yeats's own publicly-addressed works like 'The Fisherman' and 'Easter 1916', but only, in this new 'time of war', to run counter to their expressiveness, however specialized or lamenting. This despair, and discovery of lack in the public voice which had earlier provided Tate with one model of how words might be found to express a situation for which language had been rendered inadequate, had been slowly emerging in Tate's poems across the Thirties, in fact. But Yeats's example had seemed also to be providing him with a sense that there were ways of achieving a successful public voice which was not as limiting as he felt the poetry of the American Left to be.

The two poems of 1933, 'Aeneas at Washington' and 'Aeneas at New York' had shown the complications of this poetic. In the former, the founder of Rome has himself been translated, and seems to represent a reminder of the founding ideals of the new republic, America, in whose capital he remembers himself standing 'at nightfall / By the Potomac...'. There is immediately some sense, however, that this new golden age has been superseded. In echo of his own 'Emblems', nature intervenes to render human ambition empty, as the prophetic screech-owl 'whistled his new delight / Consecutively dark'. But this poem serves more as warning, a reflection of the Depression set against the ideals of the Republic's founding, than as an Eliotic or Yeatsian setting of glorious past against debased present which had figured in some of Tate's earlier work.

In 'Aeneas at New York', however, Tate changes tack slightly. The poem is a response to Archibald MacLeish's 'Invocation to the Social Muse', and is freighted with a Yeatsian sense that the poet must stay clear of politics. Rather, Tate affirms that 'First we are priests second we are not whores'. There is a curious blending of the mythic figure of Aeneas with the priest/poet here, as later we are told that 'The poet is he who fights on the passionate / Side and whoever loses he wins'. Tate does not accept, then, the absolute division which MacLeish had made between the poet and social action. Yet his figure of the poet is curiously immune, even here, to the consequences of that action, displaying as he does 'the infallible instinct for the right battle / On the passionate side'.[31] It is just this curiously naive and breezy assurance of poetic victories emerging from historical defeats that Tate loses when seeking consolation in the actual 'time of war' in 1942. The passionate nature of Yeats's poetic, in both private and public spheres, has been rendered uncommunicative by historical circumstance, and Yeats's own retreat into the private mythology of his tower does not answer the most fundamental question which Tate is forced to ask: what is worth living for?

In these circumstances, then, the modern public and elegiac Yeats which Tate was at the same time celebrating in his prose – the way that the 'vast metaphorical pattern' of his 'system' enabled Yeats to make concrete the material which was at the same time raised to symbolic resonance – rings emptily. In 'Winter Mask', the formal prosody that remains from Yeats has finally become detached from anything he might have had to say. Similarly, 'Ode to Our Young Pro-Consuls of the Air' clearly owes something to 'An Irish Airman foresees his Death', but the absurdity of the projected bombing-runs described in the poem with bitter mockery ('Go kill the dying swan') further exacerbates the out-of-jointness with those heroic dead celebrated in the earlier work.

Out of that modern sublimation of tradition into the concrete substance of contemporary poetic actuality, which Tate continued to discover in Yeats, has arisen the sense of actuality itself as sham. A perceived cultural lag in Ireland, which the Agrarians had celebrated earlier and which had made Yeats stand as a model poet for their own development of a Southern consciousness, had perhaps now, in the light of the hellish meaningless of this war, and in the light of Yeats's own actual death, rendered his work redundant. The materialist, integrationist view of him could not account for the new conditions. In accepting Yeats as a sign of such integration, Tate, like others attached to the New Critical project, ultimately rendered this sign inexpressive, a presence that is non-signifying and, curiously, to be held culpable for that.

Yet it is just these uncertainties of immediacy, association and end-stopped, deathly containment which resonate through those poets influenced by Yeats who started to publish in the immediate post-war period – from poets who were personally associated with Tate like Robert Lowell and John Berryman to those, like Theodore Roethke and James Merrill, who were seemingly coming upon many of these issues in-dependently. In all of these poets, the theme of inheritance, and of possession and dispossession is very much to the fore, both in literal and in imaginary or aesthetic ways. Further, taking up the theme of inexpressiveness in Tate's elegy on Yeats, many of these poets are exercised by the unanswerable Yeatsian question of the relation of poetry to life.[32] After the fifteen years of the Depression, which culminated with the end of America's traditional isolationism during World War II following the violation of national boundaries at Pearl Harbor, there existed huge economic and social uncertainty and anxiety over the employability of vast numbers of returning troops. As a result, traditional continuities and roles were being re-examined, and issues of what was to be valued, what should be held onto, were to the fore, in poetry as elsewhere.

III

Where John Berryman (1914–1972) called his first collection (which eventually appeared in 1948) *The Dispossessed*, the poems in the first three books by Robert Lowell (1917–1977) – *Land of Unlikeness* (1944), *Lord Weary's Castle* (1946) and *The Mills of the Kavanaughs* (1951) – were also burdened by a similar sense of a lost inheritance, a loss of power and of meaning in the world. The problem of the relation of fairly elaborate and traditional form to content is also very strong in these early works, since the retention of strong forms often conveys the sense, as Berryman's title poem from the first collection has it, that the poems have become paradoxical 'empty houses where old things take place'.[33]

Berryman's 1942 poem 'Boston Common: A Meditation upon The Hero' represents his first large-scale meditation upon the state of the Republic and its culture, and, as I will show, provides a useful comparison with Lowell's later poems such as 'For the Union Dead' (itself an updating of Tate's 'Ode'), with which it bears many similarities. Berryman's poem, in a looser version of the eight-line stanza favoured by later Yeats for some of his most compelling works, nicely balances its meditation between its two major influences, Yeats and Auden.[34] The instigation for 'Boston Common' is the St. Gaudens statue on the Common commemorating Colonel Shaw and his Negro infantry, many of whom died at Fort Wagner two months after marching through Boston.

Now, at a time of another war, Berryman develops his opening description of a homeless man asleep under the statue into a meditation upon 'The face towards which we hope all history, / Institutions, tears move, the Individual.' The bronze of which the statue is made has become the vital element in modern warfare, and so the kinds of heroism commemorated there seem unavailable to that Individual. The transfiguration of flawed people in Yeats's 'Easter 1916' is rendered unlikely by the fact that we are forced to ask

> Can citizen enact
> His timid will and expectation where . . .
> Tanks and guns, tanks and guns,
> Move and must move their conclusions, where
> The will is mounted and gregarious and bronze?

In this modern world where the Yeatsian will is reduced to violence, the 'official heroes' get interviewed in magazines, 'Man and animal / Sit for their photographs to Fame', the dead heroes who brought about the republic are forgotten by the Individual of the Future, who 'looks another way'

> Watching who labor O that all may see
> And savour the blooming world, flower and sound,
> Tending and tending to peace, – be what their blood,
> Prayer, occupation may – so tend for all:
> A common garden in a private ground.

The celebration of the unity of being at the end of Yeats's ottava rima 'Among School Children' is reduced (however, the *hope* of peace is expressed through this labour) to the making of public gardens where the Individual can fall asleep. The common and the private are at one, and as a result the transcendent hero is an impossible figure.

Berryman's poem is despairing, and ends weakly, in seeking resolution. William James's famous words at the unveiling of the memorial drift to the poet on the breeze and 'poured... /Worship and love irreconcilable / Here to be reconciled' 'Across my hearing and my sight'. Yet the contortedness of the syntax here registers the strain of reconciliation; the impression remains that in this contemporary war the 'Future' in which the bland Individual will reign represents a more desperate Yeatsian loss for Berryman.

Modernity represents a dispossession and an emptiness which leads to a lament over former plenitude, as the democratization seen as necessary in Thirties Auden is regretfully set against a presumed Yeatsian heroic possibility.[35] Berryman's early identification with, and sense of the unrecognized but absolute importance of, Yeats when he was an undergraduate at Cambridge had seen him work himself into such a frenzy that he felt that the spirit of Yeats appeared to him several times in embodied form.[36] In 'Boston Common', when confronted by the violation of American integrity and the technological grimness of modern warfare, however, the symbolic plenitude of this past is rendered a hollow shell of form.

Throughout his career, Berryman looked repeatedly to Yeats to provide those formal models by which he might measure dispossession against possession. He later somewhat arrogantly said of the 1953 *Homage to Mistress Bradstreet*:

> The eight-line stanza I invented here after a lifetime's study, especially of Yeats's, and in particular the one he adopted from Abraham

Cowley for his elegy 'In Memory of Major Robert Gregory'. Mine breaks not at midpoint but after the short third line . . . . I wanted something at once flexible and grave, intense and quiet, able to deal with matter both high and low.[37]

Once more the antithetical qualities of the Yeatsian elegiac are seen as suited to a modern poem of American founding. The variety, the opposing qualities which Berryman derives from Yeats's original, take a surprising turn in his own poem, however. Berryman recasts Yeats's meditative, courteous, even ritualistic, appraisal of Gregory as an active and even intimate dialogue between himself and the pioneering poet, Bradstreet, who arrived in the States soon after the founding fathers.[38] The dangerous version of Romantic 'intensity' described in the elegy, one able to 'consume / The entire combustible world in one small room / As though dried straw'(*CP*, p. 134), exists perhaps most forcefully in Berryman's poem in the imagined dialogue between himself and its subject:

> – Ravishing, ha, what crouches outside ought,
> flamboyant, ill, angelic. Often, now,
> I am afraid of you.
> I am a sobersides; I know.
> I *want* to take you for my lover. – Do.
> – I hear a madness. Harmless I to you
> am not, not I? – No.
> – I cannot but be. Sing a concord of our thought.[39]

Berryman records Yeats telling him during their one meeting at London's Athenaeum Club in 1937 that 'I never revise now except in the interests of a more passionate syntax, a more natural', and it is a lesson which, as this stanza reveals, Berryman himself followed.[40] The effect of this, unlike the varied but stately and honorific pace of the earlier elegy, is to turn that usurpation of the poem's space, which Yeats recognizes the 'late death' of Gregory to effect, into a much more mutual and troubling identification here, but also into love.

The Gregory-like 'life's epitome', which Bradstreet represents in Berryman's version of her, is surely integral to her passionate self-awareness and humanity. That humanity defies the 'chop-logic' of the Puritan founders amongst whom she lives ('Foreswearing it otherwise, they starch their minds'), whereas her self-contained sensuality comes close to denying the Puritan's God ('Silky my breasts not his, mine, mine, to withhold / or tender, tender. ... // torture me, Father, lest I be not thine!').[41] She is much more violently contradictory than the Sydney-like virtues of Gregory in the Yeats, much less idealized. But this seems, paradoxically, to generate the transhistorical identification with her (after the fashion of the Yeatsian mask) registered by Berryman from the beginning. Writing of the attitude Bradstreet's husband, Simon, seems to have taken to her poetry, Berryman acknowledges in the exordium a shared out-of-placeness and awkwardness in regard to the world of their respective days:

> Outside the New World winters in grand dark
> white air lashing high thro' the virgin stands
> foxes down foxholes sigh,
> surely the English heart quails, stunned.
> I doubt if Simon than this blast, that sea,
> spares from his rigour for your poetry
> more. We are on each other's hands
> who care. Both of our worlds unhanded us. Lie stark,
>
> thy eyes look to me mild.[42]

Unlike Gregory, who is described partly through his familiarity and association with the place of his upbringing, Bradstreet's displacement has led her to cower, like the poet-speaker of the exordium, in a foxhole, unhanded by the world. Yet, at another level, ultimately this is something which she, and therefore the epitome she represents, shares with the subject of Yeats's elegy, whose very idealized integrity makes him unsuited for long life: 'What made us dream that he could comb grey hair?'. (*CP*, p. 135)

Berryman appropriates Yeats's form, then, for much more intimate and extreme identificatory purposes than the original, a possibility of course offered for him by the gender of the poem's subject (similar crossings of gender were of course made by Yeats later, in the Crazy Jane poems, the sequence 'A Woman Young and Old', and, more embarrassingly, in the late chambermaid songs[43]). But out of the passionate love and identification comes a similarly regretful and elegiac sense of the impossibility of such all-embracingness within the world – or specifically the New World. Berryman seems to regret the silencing of a potentially founding unity of being within the more masculinist world of Puritan public affairs, of a much more various and sensuous voice than that celebrated in traditional American virtues. *Homage to Mistress*

Bradstreet, then, amounts almost to an attempt to refound American poetry on a much more human and passionate level than that accepted by his contemporary world, a founding also on alternative terms to those deployed by Whitman which had an antithetical appeal for Berryman.[44]

As an act of refounding, the poem bears comparison with Yeats works like 'To Ireland in the Coming Times'; Berryman's transhistorical imagination enables him also to let us know, in this differently-gendered context, that he is 'true brother of a company' that made his country's 'heart begin to beat'. Like Yeats in his poem, Berryman mingles the strains of patriotic song with those of love, casting his 'heart into rhymes' in order to recentre the nation's singing as earlier poets had failed to do. (*CP*, p. 51) The more violently disjunctive syntax than Yeats's reflects the greater strain in that enterprise, but shares with Yeats a sense of the ordering and ceremonious possibilities of the elaborate Gregory-elegy form in a world which, implicitly, is deaf to its different notions of founding 'rigour'. That urge to '*see earliest*' [his italics], which Harold Bloom sees as the primary teaching of 'Emerson's American Gnosis', in Berryman disturbingly undergoes the torments of formal and historical distance.[45]

Yeats's poetry of mourning serves as a model of yearned-for integration and origination once more. The failure to adjust the temporality of the poetry to that of a broader history, to refound history according to the poem's formality, however, registers more apocalyptically in Berryman. Yeats's re-adjusted form remains as a sign of a calmer, quieter loss than that of Berryman's despair at being unable to approach, however he has been possessed by her presence, the image of desired perfection. Berryman's abstraction from the dilemma at the heart of Yeats's inability to incorporate the dead possibility within his poetry, in other words, forces him to try to enter himself into the poem and to possess its central figure, to identify himself with her and as her, at a founding moment for poetry in his nation.

Later in his career, similar complexities of encounter instigate the shift of scene late in *His Toy, His Dream, His Rest* to Dublin, where Berryman's desire to complete *The Dream Songs* is interwoven with his need to 'have it out' with the 'majestic Shade', Yeats. Now, having 'forgotten' Yeats for years, he wonders whether he has read the Yeatsian 'lesson right'. Across the journey of *The Dream Songs*, having suffered the death of friends, Henry (the persona of the sequence who shares some of Berryman's own experiences) has become more death-obsessed. Song 324, the poem for William Carlos Williams, 'An Elegy for W.C.W., the lovely man', for instance, tells how Henry 'would like to lie down / in your sweet silence'.[46] And in Dublin, we hear in Song 312 – where we learn Henry has gone to the city to 'have it out' with Yeats's ghost – he has with him 'your last / strange poems made under the shadow of death'.[47] The next Song acknowledges the suitedness of Yeats's major subjects to his native land, 'The whole place is ghostly: no wonder Yeats believed in fairies / & personal survival'. But the predominant tone of this section of the *Songs* is one of Henry's rootlessness ('It's time to settle down-O // but not yet'), and of the banality of modern Dublin compared with its revolutionary past, something of course lamented by Yeats also in 'September 1913' and elsewhere ('O land of Connolly & Pearse, what have ever you done to deserve these tragic masters?').[48]

Yet this late encounter with the Shade of Yeats on his own soil ends in disillusion for Henry, who finds the Yeatsian resonance gone. He has come to distrust the lack of human understanding in his attitude to life, in ways that echo the endstopping and limitation of Yeats's influence in Tate's elegy for him:

> Yeats knew nothing about life: it was all symbols
> & Wordsworthian egotism: Yeats on Cemetery Ridge
> would not have been scared, like you & me....[49]

This dismissive unmasking of the Yeatsian mask as 'Wordsworthian egotism' prevents the older poet from being associated with that emotion necessary to the fateful, unsettling onward journey upon which *His Toy, His Dream, His Rest* had been predicated. Two of the book's four epigraphs relate to fear as a motivating force.[50] The Songs finally opt for the uncertainties and messiness of life and death over what is perceived as an inexpressive, classical assurance in late Yeats.

Or seemingly so: that mixture of the objective (here the 'symbols') and the egotistical for which Henry dismisses Yeats is, after all, the method of *The Dream Songs* themselves, whose hero is a mask with varying degrees of closeness to Berryman's own face. In a very early comment Berryman made as a student on Yeats, he had acknowledged the danger in overestimating 'the importance of his *life*', while also contrarily maintaining that:

> all obtainable information [on it] may be valuable to me as a critic, and particularly in Yeats's case, for many of the symbols in his poems are personal symbols, to be understood in terms of his history, and only when understood can they be appraised.[51]

Such perceived continuities between the personal and the objective in Yeats render Henry's dismissal of him suspect and *temporary*, if heartfelt – the more so since the primary objectifying element in the Songs, their form, is again indebted to Berryman's 'master'.[52] The dilemma about the relation of the individual's emotional experience to 'masterful images' in poetry had, of course, also preoccupied late Yeats, as 'The Circus Animals' Desertion' amply testifies.

That outfacing of death on 'Cemetry Ridge', which Berryman describes as Yeats's absolute intransigence towards common human feeling, is true of the heroic pose some of the late work, such as that taken in the poem 'Death' itself. But it is also true that, elsewhere in Yeats, a fearful vulnerability before death marks his work, from the sequence 'Upon a Dying Lady' to the lines on ageing in 'Sailing to Byzantium'. Even in Berryman's late dismissal of the importance of Yeats after his second attempt to encounter him, then, we can see something of a ghostly movement towards what Harold Bloom calls the 'apophrades', the return of the repressed, but it is one which gives Berryman little room for manoeuvre.[53]

Sensing the imminence of the end, Berryman can only admit his own inability to grieve. The final song *about* 'my heavy daughter', rather than being a prayer to or for her, recognizes at last an inability to take possession of all habitations: their durability, 'unlike us'. It also recognizes that 'Fall is grievy, brisk. Tears behind the eyes / almost fall'. He has always been 'too late' in his expression, and ends having to 'scold' the daughter rather than, as Yeats had, being anxious about the future on her behalf, since he can find no 'middle ground between things and the soul'.[54] The reduction of Yeats to 'symbols . . . and egotism' necessary to the furtherance of his own journey, in other words, reduces his own grounds for translation and mediation, and establishes his own despairing sense of limitation. Form can no longer guarantee content as it once had; it seems, indeed, divorced from the content it once had. Berryman's passionately various poetic again and again seeks to regain a consonance between the two, but acknowledges its own belatedness in its inevitable failures to do so.

IV

In an interview with Frederick Seidel, Robert Lowell discussed the reasons for his own breaking out from formal prosody (a temporary one as it turned out) in his 1959 collection *Life Studies* in terms which could almost describe Berryman's dilemma:

it seems to me we've gotten into a sort of Alexandrian age. Poets of my generation and particularly younger ones have gotten terribly proficient at these forms. They write a very musical, difficult poem with tremendous skill, perhaps there's never been such skill. Yet the writing seems divorced from the culture. It's become too much something specialized that can't handle much experience. It's become a craft, purely a craft, and there must be some breakthrough back into life. Prose is in many ways better off than poetry.[55]

Lowell himself, in his early works, often showed a *formal* debt (if nothing else) to Yeats, as, more obsessively, did Berryman, and in this they were at one with others of their generation.[56] Yet, leaving aside the fact that Yeats himself took a similar decision to write more prosaically (although in his case of course without breaking out of form) when seeking to remake himself as a modern poet in the years leading to *Responsibilities*,[57] Lowell's anxiety over form and its relation to contemporary culture shows an Agrarian-like dissent from the lack of centre in that culture, a dissent which he shared with others of his generation and perhaps most particularly amongst them with his friend Berryman. In this, Lowell seems to recognize that Yeats's theatrical sense of style and personality are inescapable when considering the stance to be adopted towards history.

'For the Union Dead' takes up the theme of an absolute disjunction between an imaginatively integrated past and a debased present on the same site as Berryman's 'Boston Common, 1942'. The Aquarium at which the young Lowell had marvelled has gone, and now 'giant finned cars nose forward like fish'. The relief on the St. Gaudens' statue is propped up with planks, as diggers mine an underground garage. The lost heroism which has been replaced by a contemporary 'savage servility' shares something of that recognized by Yeats in 'An Irish Airman Foresees his Death'. Colonel Shaw, Lowell writes,

> . . . is out of bounds now. He rejoices in man's lovely,
> peculiar power to choose life and die –
> when he leads his black soldiers to death,
> he cannot bend his back.

The Negro Regiment's commander is an example partly because his rejoicing is consonant with all humanity's extravagance at extreme moments, its 'peculiar power'. It is also partly an aesthetic delight, the 'loveliness' accruing something of that 'traditional sanctity and loveliness' which Yeats heard resonating through Coole Park. (*CP*, p. 245) Yeats's airman embodies and contains 'A lonely impulse of delight...I balanced all, brought all to mind', to whom the future and past seem 'a waste of breath' 'In balance with this life, this death.' (*CP*, p. 135) From the perspective of their imminent deaths, therefore, both Shaw and Gregory attain a literally exorbitant mastery over time. 'This life, this death' in Yeats's elegy are seemingly as eternally present as Shaw's perpetual rejoicing in the face of destiny.

By the end of Lowell's poem, Shaw has been resurrected from the humble trench where his body was flung and has gained something of an airman's exorbitance, 'riding on his bubble'. Both he and Gregory share that 'sudden enlargement of vision' which Yeats felt Shakespeare's heroes and heroines attained at the approach of death. (*E&I*, p. 522) But that exorbitance in Lowell's imagining is itself evanescent, such is the pressure of the loss of centre on his idealism here. Shaw rides ambiguously awaiting his 'blessèd break' – a break out of bounds back into history? or into insignificance?[58] The distracting idioms from advertising and elsewhere which have erupted into this requiem make its defeat of servility through mastering choice unstable. The ideal is clear. The power of it as example is, though, liable to disappear.

A similar uncertainty continues to resonate across Lowell's more public poems, as it had across his Yeatsian preoccupation with dynasty and family. This is particularly true in *Near the Ocean*, the book that followed *For the Union Dead*. The self-consciously and formally (the eight-lined stanza of the Gregory elegy again) Yeatsian opening poems 'Waking Early Sunday Morning' and 'Fourth of July in Maine' carry their vision of a failing American Empire at the time of Vietnam onto an apocalytic scale. At the end of the former, the earth is 'a ghost / orbiting forever lost / in our monotonous sublime'; at the end of 'Fourth of July in Maine', 'We watch the logs fall. Fire once gone, / we're done for', so we must adopt a Horatian *carpe diem* attitude in the current winter of the post-nuclear age.[59]

What is striking, however, is that there seems no alternative in such Lowell poems to the Yeatsian brazen tones of lament that heroism has passed into monotony, or that there are 'no weekends for the gods now'.[60] When, in 'Waking Early Sunday Morning', the poet enjoins himself to seek another strain, to 'Sing softer!', he immediately enters into a Yeatsian dialogue that manifests the qualities it describes:

> But what if new
> diminuendo brings no true
> tenderness, only restlessness,
> excess, the hunger for success,
> sanity of self-deception
> fixed and kicked by reckless caution....[61]

Uncertainty underlies and undermines the potential change of tone to something more personal and intimate. A more Romantic vision of self to set against social contradiction will not necessarily bring escape or freedom. As Lowell's attempt to bring poetry closer to life by adopting free verse in *Life Studies* demonstrates, for him the move to the more explicitly personal is not to escape the dynastic and emotional complications and excess shared by his nation at this point in its imperial history. He writes in 'During a Transatlantic Call', 'I have no faith in my right to will transcendence, / when a house goes, the species is extinct.'[62]

If, after *Near the Ocean* (and despite the seeming attempt to create a distance from the self by reworking some of the poems in *Notebook* as *History*)[63] Lowell would seem to make a retreat into a more personal world, it is one in which the political is continually implicated. In 'Plane-Ticket' from *The Dolphin*, Lowell records a more uneasy sense that 'After fifty so much joy has come / I hardly want to hide my nakedness', in what seems a direct echo of the more-or-less fifty-year-old Yeats's renunciation of his former mythological style in 'A Coat'. But such exposure does not blind Lowell, as it had not Yeats also, to the ways in which (as the epigraph to the collection in which 'A Coat' appears has it), 'In dreams begin responsibilities'.

Lowell does not necessarily seem to have shared Yeats's sense of what 'nakedness' brought, in terms of a closer connection to realities: 'Truth' recalls Auden dismissing Yeats's untruths: '*and for an hour, / I've walked and prayed* – who prays exactly an hour?'. Another sonnet from this collection shows Lowell recognizing that, especially with regard to intense personal emotion, it is sometimes difficult to attain such idealism: 'Sometime I must try to write the truth, / but almost everything has fallen away / lost in passage when we said goodbye to Rome.'[64] Even 'Epilogue' from Lowell's last collection *Day by Day*, which has gained the status of Lowell's *ars poetica*, is freighted by insecurity about its ability to 'say what happened': '*sometimes* everything I write / ... seems a snapshot / ... *Pray for* the grace of accuracy' [my italics].[65] New Critical transparency remains an aspiration, however thwarted. Even at this late stage, Lowell's grasp on the distinction between the 'imagined' and the 'recalled', between art and life, seems as shifting as it does when comparing Yeats's 'The Choice' with his 'The Circus Animals' Desertion'.

This raises further issues about the nature of Lowell's solution to what seems a frequently felt perception in his work of the gap between the art and the life. Yeats had, after all, later on sought to mythologize his own generation and his friends as the bearers of wider history. In the last lines of 'The Municipal Gallery Re-Visited', we are told that 'my glory was I had such friends'. (*CP*, p. 321) In *his* last work, we find that Lowell's anxiety about the relation of his generation's art to the life of the culture is supplemented, as it was in Yeats, by a strong sense of that generation as a tragic one, much as Yeats had earlier denominated the Rhymer poets with whom he was associated in the 1890s in his *Autobiographies*. Like Berryman (who in *The Dream Songs* saw America as 'a country of death')[66], Lowell had a growing sense of the fatedness of his fellow poets and friends. *History* remembers and elegizes Randall Jarrell, Delmore Schwartz, Theodore Roethke and Sylvia Plath, as does Berryman in his *Songs*: towards the end of the book there is an elegy for Berryman himself. In *Day by Day*'s 'For John Berryman', Lowell is ready to recognize the shared destiny of all of his friends, but also to recognize that it shared a false self-aggrandizement:

> I used to want to live
> to avoid your elegy.
> Yet really we had the same life,
> the generic one
> our generation offered
> (*Les Maudits* – the compliment
> each American generation
> pays itself in passing) . . . .[67]

The play on the last word here (compare 'Epilogue', 'We are poor passing facts') carries a Yeatsian burden of repetition in which the way that each generation enters history casts its surviving poet as an unwilling elegist. Yet *Day by Day* as a whole shows a deepening of Lowell's dissatisfaction with such roles and with his own ageing and impending death, which is in its turn reminiscent of those qualities admired by T.S. Eliot in late Yeats.[68]

The wonderful image of a circling through life towards an anonymous and scarred homecoming in the opening sequence 'Ulysses and Circe', has Ulysses uttering a more Yeatsian than Tennysonian complaint,

' "Age is the bilge / we cannot shake from the mop." ' To the end of the sequence, Ulysses is unable to break back into touch with life and Penelope. Arrived back from his odyssey, he 'circles' 'as a shark... / visibly behind the window' of his own palace. As with Berryman, the relation between the adopted mask and the face of the poet himself is an uncertain one, not that 'anti-self or... antithetical self', the *hic* and *ille* of the Yeatsian mask. (*M*, p. 331)

In the poem 'Homecoming' itself, Lowell echoes 'Sailing to Byzantium' as he acknowledges his inability to recapture the past in his native town: '...it's a town for the young, / they break themselves against the surf. // No dog knows my smell.'[69] In place of the Yeatsian countermanding towards a denying, emblematic leap 'out of nature', we find Lowell in these late poems making a rather melancholy acceptance of seasonal repetition and time passing ('Summer to summer, / the poplars sere / in the glare'). At this humanly personal level, then, as in the keynote public works of the Sixties and early Seventies, Lowell seems both conscious of the integrational and challenging Yeatsian 'example' and also aware of its lack of efficacy within his personal and national history. While continuing to press against 'bounds' and divisions, the possibilities offered by his various masks are ultimately unable to 'break loose' into 'life'. Yeats's perceived emblematic antitheticism becomes a more tentative and uncertain wavering between 'experience' (no 'heavenly mansion, raging in the dark' for Lowell, though, as it was in 'The Choice' (*CP*, p. 246)) and bounded art.

V

The post-war American poet in whom the formal artifice of poetry was most to the fore, however, was James Merrill (1926–1995).[70] Merrill shares with Lowell and with early Berryman a need to discover a house or habitation that will hold against the ravages of Time, or 'the sickness of our time' specifically. His 1962 collection *Water Street*, for instance, is framed by the poems, 'An Urban Convalescence' and 'A Tenancy', in which the desire for settlement ('the dull need to make some kind of house / Out of the life lived, out of the love spent' as the former has it), is countered by a sense of impermanence, 'The sickness of our time requires / That these [walls]... be blasted in their prime'.

At the other end of the collection, that aspiration has been transmuted into a recognition that he cannot find a *physical* space of lived reality, however, and that notions of love must take on a metaphorical

life consonant with their poetic setting. Three friends arrive unexpect-
edly with a gift of flowers:

> I put the flowers where I need them most
>
> And then, not asking why they come,
> Invite the visitors to sit.
> If I am host at last
> It is of little more than my own past.
> May others be at home in it.[71]

As Merrill several times reminds us, most explicitly in 'The Broken
Home' from the 1966 *Nights and Days*, his parents divorced when he
was young. Like Berryman, whose poetry is traumatized by his father's
suicide, and Lowell, whose *Life Studies* maps the failure of his parents'
marriage, Merrill's deep unease around such metaphors is dependent
upon his childhood circumstances, as it is upon a sense of failures in
national inheritance. His more elaborate poetic formalism than Lowell's
or Berryman's goes along, however, with a more readily accepted sense
that, as 'A Tenancy' here observes, the structures of poetry might themselves be the place where the isolated individual, alone with the past,
can invite others to 'be at home'.

As in Yeats's paired 'Coole Park, 1929' and 'Coole Park and Ballylee,
1931', the sense of the houses' impermanence allows for a double resonance in which the poem becomes the site of the destroyed but remembered physical structure. As the former Yeats poem has it, 'Here, traveller,
scholar, poet, take your stand / When all those rooms and passages are
gone . . .'. (*CP*, p. 243) The rooms / stanzas of the poems *might* become a
place to take one's stance against the 'sickness of our time', as those of the
tower at Ballylee did most strikingly for Yeats at the time of the civil war.

What is telling, however, is the abstraction of 'my own past' from the
national inheritance in these poems. Yeats's Coole poems render the
house continuous symbolically with both his nationalist ambitions
(however imperfectly fulfilled) and his visionary poetics, in which the
poem itself is made to fill a place once the less durable walls of the house
have been destroyed. In Merrill's poems of habitation, as in Berryman's
and Lowell's, where the subject of possession and dispossession is itself
to the fore, such symbolic vision has become a residue, a trace or mark
within the personal. The lyric voice is set against 'sickness', but can only
querulously counter it. The fear that form might be empty, void of
significance, haunts the poetry and limits its formal consolation.

This sense echoes across Merrill's writing. The end of his own vision-ary epic, *The Changing Light at Sandover*, is situated back at the ballroom of the family home which had figured in 'The Broken Home'. But the room represents 'Empty perfection',

> grave proportions here,
> Here at the heart of the structure, and alone
> Surviving now to tell me where I am:
> In the old ballroom of the Broken Home.[72]

'Grave proportion' is 'alone' expressive and locationary. Like the rooms of Yeats's tower in 'In Memory of Major Robert Gregory', the emptiness is only peopled by the ghosts of those friends and writers who have been conjured across the poem itself. In the last lines of this book, emptiness allows, most importantly, the space (contiguous with the space, the Athens apartment, in which Merrill is 'actually' writing) into which he reads the epic to two of his friends – 'Both rooms are waiting'. The poetry provides the sole content that inhabits the erstwhile perfect and empty structures which pre-exist it.

'The Ballroom at Sandover' is a shockingly elegant place, with 'chan-deliers... / Aclick, their crystal charges one by one / Accenting the donnée sun-beamed through tall / French window, silver leaf and wax-ing bud'. Such wrought elegance is clearly consonant with the stanzaic structures of Merrill's own poetry. He once said in interview that he began writing having recently been 'dazzled' by 'techniques and forms that could be recovered or reinvented from the past without their hav-ing to sound old-fashioned, thanks to any number of stylish "modern" touches like slant rhyme or surrealist imagery'.[73] That formal interest continued down to the last collection of 1995, *A Scattering of Salts* (witness the various divisions of the 15–liners in 'The Ring Cycle', for instance).[74]

In interview, Merrill was also explicit about the way in which adverse circumstances led him to seek escape into artificial counter-realities, although with a strong antithetical sense that such escapes are poten-tially untrue to experience:

Rilke was [early on] five times more poetic to me than Yeats. Yeats seemed by comparison somewhat external to one's situation. ... I must say that I read and admired [Yeats] a lot in my youth. I read 'Sailing to Byzantium' when I was in the army. It got through to me because of the circumstances. I couldn't wait to 'get out of nature'

myself. But what I got from Rilke was more than literary; that emphasis
on the *acceptance* of pain and loneliness. Rilke helps you with suffering, especially in your adolescence....[75]

If this setting of literariness or artifice against a stoical 'more than
literary' acknowledgement seems resolved by Merrill in his discussion
of early influence, however, it is not so readily so in the poetry itself.
'Sailing to Byzantium' and 'Byzantium' particularly, with their yearning
to escape from the ageing of man as a 'dying animal' into the 'artifice of
eternity' (*CP*, p. 193), find repeated echoes in Merrill's work, both playful
and more earnest.

Having once woken in Istanbul with a sudden (and shocking) illness
whereby the right side of his face was entirely paralysed, Merrill, in a
poem recalling the event, has recourse to one of the most telling poems
in the language on mortality:

> It is like a dream,
>
> The 'death-in-life and life-in-death' of Yeats'
> Byzantium; and if so, by the same token,
> Alone in the sleepwalking scene, my flesh has woken
> And sailed for the fixed shore beyond the straits.

'The Thousand and Second Night' then expands into a Manichean
meditation upon 'what I have been, am, and care to be', which is wary
of the kinds of affirmation of artifice or, alternatively, of life itself, which
Yeats's poems vacillate between (it is, after all, only as an old man unable
to share the delights of the young that he sets sail for Byzantium):

> The heart prevails!
> Affirm it! Simple decency rides the blast! –
> Phrases that, quick to smell blood, lurk like sharks
> Within a style's transparent lights and darks.

'The Ballroom at Sandover' had also recognized that 'style' is what we
'are betrayed – or not – by'. 'The Thousand and Second Night' tells of the
recovery of mobility in the poet's face, but also seems itself held rigid by
its inability to escape from 'style' which has been taken over from elsewhere and so might have become inexpressive. The tone of harsh (self-)
mockery increases towards the end with the interruption of a pedago-
gical voice seeking to defend the sequence against an envisaged sceptical

classroom question about the high level of quotation from the 'truly great' in it:

> Fearing to overstate,
> He lets *them* do it – lets their words, I mean,
>
> Enhance his – Yes, what now? Ah. How and when
> Did he 'affirm'? Why, constantly. And how else
> But in the form. Form's what affirms. That's well
> Said, if I do – [*Bells ring.*] Go, gentlemen.[76]

The sequence ends by seeming to acknowledge that the affirmation of the formal qualities of art are something that we all become dependent on: that the Sultan has become enslaved to Scherazade's stories and that the parting of the two causes mutual regret. But the awkward tonalities of the classroom interjection and the attention paid to the duplicities of style leave all questions unanswered. The Sultan wakes 'too late to question what the tale had meant'. 'Form's what affirms', but what does it 'affirm'? Form might be, to recall a term from de Man's essay on criticism that is dependent on it, a 'dead-end'.

Merrill had several times related the fascination he has with remaining 'in two minds about everything' to the fact that to stay in one mind would be to remain 'in reduced circumstances'. The glow fades, as Yeats knew when he chided his own visionary system for its 'harsh geometry'. (*E&I*, p. 518) Merrill has shown a fascination, in fact, for the liberating qualities of Yeatsian dramatization: 'Freedom to be oneself is all very well; the greater freedom is not to be oneself', as he says in a throwaway line in his memoir. That freedom seems to have been most present in Merrill's activities over the ouija board which resulted in the epic *The Changing Light at Sandover*. As he said once again in interview,

> don't you think there comes a time when everyone, not just a poet, wants to get beyond the self? To reach, if you like, the 'god' within you? The board, in however clumsy or absurd a way, allows for precisely that. Or if it's still *yourself* that you're drawing upon, then that self is much stronger and freer and more farseeing than the one you thought you knew.[77]

The epic represents the logical extension of Merrill's preoccupation with the Byzantium poems, poems whose imagery is, after all, also described in *A Vision*. It is, like Yeats's 'system', also dictated through automatic writing. Yeats's enterprise is belittled from the outset – 'POOR OLD YEATS / STILL SIMPLIFYING' is the 'bombshell' dropped by the spirit of Ephraim, JM and DJ's guide to the visionary world of the poem. But Yeats remains the master approached but never revealed in the work ('Oh please, Mr Yeats, you who have always been / such a force in my life!').[78] The huge scope of the poem is unable to throw off the sense that it might be (*contra* notions of influence-as-contest such as Bloom's) 'TEXT TO WBY'S FOOTNOTE; a mere extension of the process of listening to the instructors whose words gave impulse to *A Vision*: 'was our instruction of a piece with yours?'

The question they address to 'WBY' hangs in the air. Yeats, of course, comically 'dictates' his few ouija board answers through the amanuensis DJ's hand, *not* the poet JM's:

> YOU JM
> MIGHT HAVE BEEN DEVOURED BY THE CHIMERA
> LIKE POOR LONGSUFFERING YEATS. MUCH THAT U KNOW
> WAS DICTATED TO HIM BY THE OO
>
> But does Yeats suffer *now*? ANSWER DJ
> YOUR ARE THE HAND
>   DJ, uneasily:
> Well, there's this bump on my palm. It doesn't hurt...
> What else? Often before I know the message
> I feel its beauty, its importance. Tears
> Come to my eyes. Is that Yeats being moved?
> Often it's tiring and obscure. I fumble
> Along, JM finds answers, I feel dumb.
> Is that Yeats too, still making the wrong sense?
> Why can't *he* ever speak?[79]

Yeats remains writing at the end of a tradition (FOOTNOTE); Merrill's epic is caught in a pattern of iteration (TEXT). The remorseless present of the poem, in which mourned friends 'speak' again, cannot govern presence. Bringing back the dead can only make the text live. Prosopopoeia is vulnerable to the rhetoric of temporality, as a 'trace...interiorized *in* mourning *as* that which can no longer be interiorized'.[80] The hourglass which the latter-day instructees draw as a representation of 'ALL HISTORY' bears a 'surprise resemblance' to *A Vision*'s double cones.

Despite the unanswered and unanswerable questions that resonate across Merrill's work in his preoccupations with the twin poles of art and life, he proves surprisingly sympathetic to, and unable to get beyond, the human emotion ('Is that Yeats being moved?') behind Yeats's systematizing. His re-rendering of the Byzantium poems as deriving from a desire for settlement similar to his own finally aligns him once again with the poet he had seemed to ignore in favour of the 'more than literary' Rilke. To that degree, Merrill's remains perhaps the most complex of the engagements which American poetry has made with Yeats since his death. His acceptance of the impulse behind the artifice, from the perspective of a poet most deeply engaged with the difficulties and delights of poetic form, opens up possibilities of intricate exploration alert to antithetical possibility (cornucopia or empty shell) beyond perhaps even that inolved in the possession suffered by Berryman. *In extremis*, Merrill repeats from late Yeats that sense of the shadowing emptiness of form, the lack of a theme, which can lead to an attempt to masterfully outface reality, but also can lead to the heart.

VI

For male American poets, writing after Yeats and haunted or possessed by him, the transplanted, emptied-out formality of his work seems to have become ultimately disappointing. There was a limit to his influence that often revealed the void and dispossession at the heart of American poetry itself, in its public and cultural ambition, but which extended no further. Even more than the British writing in his aftermath, which displayed a greater vacillation in the face of the allure of his writing, Americans seem to have been unable to finally take over and adapt his example to their own concerns. His very *absence*, the untrammelled and scripted nature of his project, for many of these later poets, set an end to its resonance. Within American women's poetry, though, there seems a more uncompleted and undefineable sense of Yeatsian possibility.

The argument made by Sandra M. Gilbert and Susan Gubar about the partial applicability of Harold Bloom's key concepts, which sees concerns with tradition as limited to *male* writers, seems ambiguously borne out by the careers of Adrienne Rich (1929–), Sylvia Plath (1932–1963), and other women poets.[81] Rich's seminal essay of 1971, 'When We Dead Awaken', charts the progress of her writing away from the influence of poets including Auden, MacNeice, Stevens and Yeats, towards a formally freer style truer to her daily experiences. She cites the 1951 poem 'Aunt Jennifer's Tigers', in which the central figure's imaginative work on her tapestry is in sharp contrast to her life, 'ringed with ordeals she was mastered by', as typical of her ambition at the time.[82] Yet the 'imaginary woman' in the poem, seemingly distanced by its formalism and observant tone, of course later reads as exemplary of Rich's own plight. Once again, the process of self-reading across time reveals that the mask is uncertainly distant from the face of the poet and from the formal resurrection of earlier poets through the poem. But in Rich's case here, as with other women poets, that recognition is involved in complex political and personal senses of stance and desired freedoms.

A similar adoption of personae by women writers as a way of allowing them to handle relevant materials which, as Rich says, they 'couldn't pick up barehanded', obviously owes much to the dramatic poetic coming down through Yeats. Anne Sexton has mentioned the significance of his reincarnatory ideas as liberating for the 'truth' of her poetry, enabling her to adopt a series of 'concrete examples' to explore a wide range of female experience: 'I believe I am many people'. That possibility for dramatization clearly then underlies the intimate descriptions of relationship in her 1969 *Love Poems*, and the metamorphic reworkings of fairy tale in the 1971 *Transformations*.[83] Sandra M. Gilbert has herself linked the 'linguistic audacity' of Plath's late poems written after she had moved into one of Yeats's houses in London to the earlier tenant's female vocalizations in 'A Woman Young and Old' and the Crazy Jane poems.[84] At some level, then, the 'anxiety of authorship' which Gilbert and Gubar see as displacing 'anxiety of influence' for women poets, finds a correlation in Yeats's preoccupation with the relationship between 'life' and 'art', particularly with the stylistic and poetic means of giving voice to experience which has been formally excluded from poetry.

Rich's politically-engaged writing from the early 1970s on has continued to be concerned with this theme. 'Diving into the Wreck' of 1972 moves away from 'the book of myths', using words as 'purposes' and 'maps' to discover 'the thing itself'. The speaker recognizes her aloneness, but also the way in which 'threadbare beauty' both derives from and bears evidence of 'damage'. The sea, which is 'not a question of power', instead confers an ambiguous gender upon the diver:

> I am she: I am he
>
> ... whose silver, copper, vermeil cargo lies
> obscurely inside barrels
> half-wedged and left to rot
> we are the half-destroyed instruments
> that once held a course ....[85]

The quest to see 'the treasures that prevail' as a corollary of the escape from given identity shares an impulse with Yeats's Byzantium poems – an impulse which ultimately questions the ability of words to act as maps to thisness or *haeccitas* (witness Yeats's later revisiting of his first poem). The damage which is discovered, the doubt as to whether the questing dive is undertaken through cowardice or courage, inflect Yeats's old man's experience towards an awareness that history has bequeathed women sullied goods and a lack of direction through which to re-establish a 'course'.

Rich's later 'Blue Rock', on a piece of lapis lazuli given to her by a friend, contrasts the vulnerability of her more engaged poetic to time ('Once when I wrote poems they did not change') to the changelessness of the stone itself, as though the value in the gift chides the possible response. Rich recognizes, as she writes in the 'North American Time' sequence earlier in this collection, *Your Native Land Your Life*, that poetry 'never stood a chance / of standing outside history', and that it must be responsible to history's temporality and the sufferings which take place there. But she also understands the costs of that inability, not least in seeking to 'map' the 'native land'.[86]

Such difficult responses to art itself are to the fore also in the work of the displaced American Sylvia Plath. In 'Tale of a Tub' and 'On the Decline of Oracles', Plath adopted variations on the rhymed eight-lined stanza of the Byzantium poems in order to explore the resistance of artifice to individual desire, and the ways in which paternal voices dictate their visions to daughters. The earlier set-piece poem interrogates the entrapment of art ('can our dreams / ever blur the intransigent lines which draw / the shape that shuts us in?'), before acknowledging also its necessity to cover the 'starkness' of the 'constant horror' of human actuality. 'Death ... makes us real', but while alive all we can do is to continue the quest ('in faith / we shall board our imagined ship and wildly sail / among sacred islands of the mad').[87]

In 'On the Decline of Oracles', however, the worth of such Yeatsian wildness is questioned. The visionary 'descrying' of Troy's towers, of 'brazen swan' and 'burning star', is associated with her own now dead father. As such, this activity is of the regretted past rather than of the future, which is 'worth less' as a result. And yet the inescapability of the 'now', the invasion of the 'cloistral eye' by 'gross comic strip', is all that the speaker is left with, whatever the 'voices / Set in my ear'. Such 'decline' then seems to overwrite much of the regret in Plath's later poetry, from the visionary embodiment in 'Sculptor' ('his chisel bequeaths / Them life livelier than ours'), to 'Candles' ('They are the last romantics').[88]

In one of the last poems, 'Child', where 'Your clear eye is the one absolutely beautiful thing', the failure to find images 'grand and classical' for this 'pool' seems wholly a self-diagnosed weakness on the poet's part, and to leave her only the starless 'dark / ceiling' of death. Plath, while having acknowledged the inadequacy of visions such as those of her 'beloved Yeats', whose spirit she felt blessing her in her last lodging, is left to wring her own hands in awareness that she cannot find images to match her own experience to compare with those of Yeats's prayers for his children.[89] With the vision gone, itself rendered illegitimate, Plath's own voice seems open to that which will extinguish it.[90]

Hélène Cixous has argued that a distinguishing feature of all women's writing is that it shows them bearing their pain rather than allowing death to work, rather than seeking to rid themselves of pain through mourning, as men have traditionally done. The whole of the language and literature is remembered as each additional memory is inscribed, and will continue to be so. As such, women are better able to see their own deaths.[91]

For these American women poets (as for the Irish Eavan Boland), poets who have sought to negotiate with Yeats's inheritance amongst that of other constraining voices, their different position with regard to tradition as held by male writers, and by Yeats himself, opens up a further range of possibility which goes beyond this book's limits. Male poets' quest for canonical dominance found a reflection, at however great a remove, in the cultural and historical situational struggles and difficulties amidst which Yeats found himself. Yet women's writing, sometimes happening from within his shadow but more often striking back against him, offers a possibility in which antitheses of presence and absence, possession and dispossession are both subsumed and continually in play, resisting the (however temporarily successful) work of mourning which is done in each poem, resisting all finality and endstopping.

Notes

1 Yeats: Influence, Tradition and the Problematics of Reading

1 In 'The Epistemology of Metaphor', de Man argues that 'Rhetoric . . . is not in itself a historical but an epistemological discipline. This may well account for the fact that patterns of historical periodization are at the same time so productive as heuristic devices yet so demonstrably aberrant.' (*Aesthetic Ideology*, edited with an introduction by Andrzei Warminski (Minneapolis: University of Minnesota Press, 1996), p. 50.

2 *Lady Gregory's Diaries 1892–1902*, edited by James Pethica (Gerrard's Cross: Colin Smythe, 1996), p. 214. Pethica makes the same link to 'Magic' I make below, but does not follow through the implications of Yeats's words for notions of literary influence.

3 *Uncollected Prose by W.B. Yeats*, Collected and Edited by John P. Frayne and Colton Johnson, Volume II (Basingstoke: Macmillan, 1975), p. 56. In an earlier lecture, on 'Nationality and Literature' of 1893, Yeats had seemed to imply that his Irishness might open his work to a body of epic tradition which would save him from the 'subtlety and obscurity' of the modern English lyric, where it was only possible to 'judge of ideas and feelings apart from action'. In a move which heralds much of his later thinking and sense of cultural unease, however, he argues in the end here for a different type of poetry which lies somewhere between the ancient and the modern, the native and the cosmopolitan, i.e. the dramatic (*Uncollected Prose by W.B. Yeats*, Collected and Edited by John P. Frayne, Volume I (London: Macmillan, 1970), pp. 267–75).

4 Yeats had discussed the religious potential of the arts once institutionalized religion had failed in his 1897 essay 'William Blake and the Imagination' and in his 1898 'The Autumn of the Body': 'The arts are, I believe, about to take upon their shoulders the burdens that have fallen from the shoulders of the priests, and to lead us back upon our journey by filling our thoughts with the essences of things, and not with things.' (*E&I*, p. 193). 'Magic', too, recognizes the greater ability of 'barbaric people' to receive influences from other minds (ibid., p. 41).

5 In his *Mémoires for Paul de Man*, Jacques Derrida argues that it is such anachronism which underlies all use of memory, or 'traces of a past that has never been present': 'Resurrection, which is always the formal element of 'truth', a recurrent difference between a present and its presence, does not resuscitate a past which had been present; it engages the future.' (New York: Columbia University Press, 1986, p. 58). Such recognition makes us ironically or allegorically aware of our (lack of) presence in the present.

6 In the 'Anima Hominis' part of *Per Amica Silentia Lunae* of 1917, Yeats takes a stronger view than this, suggesting that even the 'modification' which an individual might make in tradition is an inevitable one: 'It is not permitted to

a man who takes up pen or chisel, to seek originality, for passion is his only business, and he cannot but mould or sing after a new fashion because no disaster is like another.' (*M*, p. 339).

7   Paul de Man has argued that such dilemmas are central to all post-Hegelian visions of art, which is necessarily 'of the past' in that it 'materially inscribes, and thus ever forgets, its ideal content' while at the same time, 'since the synthesis of memory is the only activity of the intellect to occur as sensory manifestation of an idea, memory is a truth of which the aesthetic is the defensive, ideological, and censored translation'. As a result of this, in terms which might describe what I have been saying here about Yeats's relation to the past, 'Memory effects remembrance (or recollection) just as the I effaces itself.' ('Sign and Symbol in Hegel's *Aesthetics*', *Critical Inquiry* Volume 8, No. 4, Summer 1982, pp. 773–4. The essay was subsequently collected in *Aesthetic Ideology*, pp. 91–104.) Yeats's misreading of Hegel as arguing that 'the two ends of the see-saw are one another's negation' in contrast to the Blakean knowledge that 'a negation is not a contrary' only serves to emphasize the importance to him of sustaining a continuity within and between seemingly opposed ideas (*AV*, pp. 72–3).

8   'Tradition and the Individual Talent', *Selected Prose of T.S. Eliot* edited with an Introduction by Frank Kermode (London: Faber 1975), p. 38.

9   *Ruin the Sacred Truths: Poetry and Belief from the Bible to the Present* (Cambridge, Mass.: Harvard University Press, 1989), pp. 7–8. In *Kabbalah and Criticism*, Bloom has described the Freudian notion of tradition as 'repressed material in the mind of the individual' as proving that tradition has no referential aspect, 'like the Romantic imagination or like God' (New York: The Seabury Press, 1975, p. 97).

Bloom's more recent attention to 'facticity' and those transferences, often without a conscious origin, which occur through a history of reading, returns to a preoccupation he had at the beginning of his discussions of literary influence. In *The Anxiety of Influence: a Theory of Poetry* of 16 years earlier, Bloom had established literary meaning as only operative through literary history. 'The meaning of a poem can only be a poem', he claimed, and not, as the New Critics had argued, 'itself': 'And not a poem chosen with total arbitrariness, but any central poem by an indubitable precursor, even if the ephebe *never read* that poem ... We are dealing with primal words, but antithetical meanings, and an ephebe's best misinterpretation may well be of poems he has never read' (Oxford: Oxford University Press, 1973, p. 70). Earlier in the book, though, Bloom had argued that the initial swerve away in the belated poem from the precursor text 'must be considered as though it were simultaneously intentional and involuntary ...' (pp. 44–5).

Peter de Bolla has argued that around such central assertions, Bloom slightly confuses his own case (as he does here) by using terms such as 'ephebe, precursor, anxiety and influence', all of which imply that literary history is 'a psychic drama between individuals and not a textual production which results from the interaction of poet, precursor, poem and the act of misreading.' (*Harold Bloom: Towards Historical Rhetorics*, London: Routledge, 1988, p. 22). While it is true, however, that Bloom has frequently asserted that, as he puts it in *A Map of Misreading*, 'Influence, as I conceive it, means that there are *no* texts, but only relationships between texts' (New York:

Oxford University Press, 1975, p. 3), Bloom's own practice has consistently defined the relationships between ephebe and 'indubitable precursors': Wordsworth and Milton or Whitman and Emerson, for example. This suggests that the critical acts of interpretation, misreading and misprision which Bloom argues make up literary history *do* (*pace* de Bolla, p. 35), have 'origins as such': in *Yeats*, for example, Bloom claims that 'It is perhaps inevitable that Yeats, the conscious heir of the Romantics, compels us to a new kind of critical study of Romantic influence.' (New York: Oxford University Press, 1970, p. 7). This kind of 'origination' will feature strongly in my own selection of poets to be discussed within the shadow of Yeatsian influence.

10   *A Map of Misreading*, pp. 3, 77; cp. *Kabbalah and Criticism*'s 'How does one accommodate a fresh and vital new religious impulse . . . when one inherits a religious tradition already so rich and coherent that it allows very little room for fresh revelations or even speculations?' (p. 33). Bloom's notion of belatedness here is close to that developed by Walter Jackson Bate in his *The Burden of the Past and the English Poet*, a belatedness or 'burden' which Bate agrees has 'become far more pressing in the modern world' (*Influx: Essays on Literary Influence*, edited by Ronald Primeau, New York: Kennikat Press, 1977), p. 100).

11   Op. cit., p. 4.

12   Graham Allen has argued that 'Bloom's refusal to historicize the *history* of transumptive allusion leads him into an interpretative impasse. Not only do his various theories appear to predetermine the entropic history of language and meaning . . . without an ability to historicize such a process . . . Bloom is forced back upon a certain literalization of his terms.' (*Harold Bloom: A Poetics of Conflict*, Hemel Hempstead: Harvester Wheatsheaf 1994, p. 116). Bloom is himself dismissive of movements in criticism towards social history and 'neo-Marxism', telling Imre Salusinszky that 'the experience of literature is the experience of isolate and solipsizing glory' (*Criticism in Society*, London: Methuen, 1987, p. 65).

13   In Part Two of his book, de Bolla seems to be partly responding to the dilemmas caused by Bloom's repeated use of slightly confusing key terms by making stronger a Bloomian definition of the diachronic movement of history as both productive of and responsive to rhetorical tropes: 'For the tropes that determine [for example] Coleridge's verse are not uniquely the pure product of Coleridge's 'genius'; they are also culturally, politically, and ideologically determined . . . they are, to some extent, productive of history itself.' (p. 125).

14   Marjorie Howes provides an illuminating discussion of this dilemma in her *Yeats's Nations: Gender, Class, and Irishness* (Cambridge: Cambridge University Press, 1996), especially Chapters 1–3.

15   *Uncollected Prose*, Volume I, p. 162.

16   '*Ulysses*, Order and Myth', *Selected Prose of T.S. Eliot*, p. 177.

17   *The Collected Letters of W.B. Yeats*, Volume I, 1865–1895, edited by John Kelly and Eric Domville (Oxford: Oxford University Press, 1986), p. 409.

18   *Uncollected Prose*, Volume I, p. 224.

19   See *The Works of William Blake: Poetic, Symbolical and Critical*, edited by Yeats and Edwin John Ellis (London: Bernard Quaritch, 1893), pp. 2–3, and also Yeats's introduction to his selection *The Poems of William Blake* (London: Lawrence & Bullen, 1893).

20 *W.B. Yeats and T. Sturge Moore: Their Correspondance 1901–1937*, edited by Ursula Bridge (London: Routledge & Kegan Paul, 1953), p. 154. Seamus Deane has discussed the defeated sense of Yeats's view of history and the self in 'Yeats and the Idea of Revolution', *Celtic Revivals: Essays in Modern Irish Literature* (London: Faber, 1985), pp. 38–50. Harold Bloom, reading Emerson and Whitman, finds defeat at the heart of poetry and criticism: 'In this agon, this struggle [between adverting subject and language], neither the fiction of the subject nor the trope of language is strong enough to win final victory' (*Agon: Towards a Theory of Revisionism* (New York: Oxford University Press, 1983), p. 29).

21 *Uncollected Prose by W.B. Yeats*, Volume II, pp. 195–6. Only a couple of years earlier, though, Yeats had been sanguine about the virtues of belonging to a defeated people: 'It is hardly an exaggeration to say that the spiritual history of the world has been the history of the conquered races.' (ibid., p. 70). Marjorie Howes, however, argues that in such figurations of Irish defeat, Yeats was partly reinscribing Arnoldian ideas of the Celt (op. cit., pp. 35–6).

22 'Yeats and the English', *The Internationalism of Irish Literature and Drama*, edited by Joseph McMinn (Gerrard's Cross: Colin Smythe, 1992), p. 234.

23 Edward W. Said has approached a similar issue from a different angle to Bhabha's in his 'Yeats and Decolonization' (*Nationalism, Colonialism and Literature*, edited by Seamus Deane (Minneapolis: University of Minnesota Press, 1979). Yet Said's retention of a teleological version of history, in which it is possible to describe stages of progressive decolonization, would seem to be at odds with the indecipherability characteristic of Yeats's own sense of his situation.

24 Homi K. Bhabha, *The Location of Culture* (London: Routledge, 1994), pp. 114, 224, 86. Derrida has argued that it is not 'the lexical richness, the semantic infiniteness of a word or a concept which counts'. In writing of his favoured word 'hymen' as a signifier of the in-between and contradictory, he discusses the possibility of becoming trapped within the implications of its 'irreplaceable character': 'It produces its effect first and foremost through . . . syntax. . . . If we replaced 'hymen' by 'marriage' or 'crime', 'identity' or 'difference', etc., the effect would be the same . . . . it is possible to recognize a certain serial law through these points of indefinite pivoting . . .'. (*Dissemination*, translated with an introduction by Barbara Johnson (London: The Athlone Press, 1993), pp. 220–1). Earlier, Derrida had defined deconstructive reading as countering 'static' earlier concentration upon 'concepts or words' as demanding that 'One must constitute a chain in motion, the effects of a network and the play of a syntax.' (p. 194). Such emphases make even Edward Larrissy's insightful discussion of Yeatsian undecidability in terms of the 'hymen' seem somewhat mannered (*Yeats the Poet: the measures of difference* (Hemel Hempstead: Harvester Wheatsheaf, 1994), pp. 3–4, 179–85). Yeats's increasing emphasis upon syntax over content, as in his 1937 comment to the young John Berryman discussed in Chapter 4, suggests an increasingly dynamic notion of its possibilities across his career.

25 *The Gift of Death*, translated by David Wills (Chicago: University of Chicago Press, 1995), pp. 14–15. This does not mean, however, that the self 'assembled' or 'awakened' in this way is for Derrida 'sayable'. (p. 20) Rather, it is at this point that the self is most threatened and vulnerable to death's

gift. It is true that it is impossible to die and so prevent someone else from having to do so, and that such impossibility might seem a warrant of identity. Yet, as Yeats's constant stylistic rehearsals of death exemplify, it is in the face of death that the undermining mixture of feelings and thought occurs. Derrida sees such tropes of undecidability, paradoxes and aporias, as 'the revelation of conceptual thinking at its limit, at its death and finitude' (p. 68). Elsewhere, Derrida takes death itself as an aporia: 'Who will guarantee that the name, the ability to name death (like that of naming the other, and it is the same) does not participate as much in the dissimulation of the 'as such' of death as in its revelation, and that language is not precisely the origin of the nontruth of death, and of the other?' (*Aporias*, translated by Thomas Dutoit (Stanford: University of Stanford Press, 1993), p. 76).

26 As Balachandra Rajan has pointed out, even the late poems questing fixity are unsettled and unsettling. 'Byzantium' concludes with a vision of a 'gong-tormented sea' in which 'the ocean's inherent fluidity must be further torn' ('Its Own Executioner: Yeats and the Fragment', *Yeats: An Annual of Critical and Textual Studies*, Volume III, 1985, edited by George Bornstein and Richard J. Finneran (Ithaca: Cornell University Press), p. 85). Lee Zimmerman has argued, in 'Singing Amid Uncertainty: Yeats's Closing Questions', that another sign of irresolvability in the poems (beyond that contradictoriness recognized as early as Richard Ellmann's *The Identity of Yeats*), is his frequent use of questions as 'endings' (*Yeats Annual* No. 2, edited by Richard J. Finneran (Basingstoke: Macmillan, 1983), p. 37).

27 Tuesday (?July 1915), *Letters*, edited by Alan Wade (London: Rupert Hart-Davis, 1954), p. 598.

28 In *Yeats*, Harold Bloom sees the poet's continual undergoing of ' "new bitterness, new disappointment" for the finding of the true mask' as 'Yeats's highly individual contribution to the Romantic sublime', but also a sign of his creative misinterpretation of his precursors Blake and Shelley, who would dismiss such worldliness as 'natural religion' and not the basis of Imagination (p. 184). In *Agon*, Bloom argues that it is this which makes Yeats the 'major Gnostic poet in the language' because of 'the powerful trope that he calls "breaks" ', as in 'Byzantium''s 'Marbles of the dancing floor / Break bitter furies of complexity'. Yeats's Gnostic knowledge resides in the fact that he knows 'Break' to be a lie, since in his art ' "breaks" also means "makes" or the creation by and in catastrophe' (p. 46).

29 In *Louis MacNeice: a Study*, Edna Longley has related such extravagance to Yeats's and MacNeice's Anglo-Irish inheritance (London: Faber, 1988, p. xii).

30 Jacques Derrida, in his recent discussions of gifts and giving, has identified writing itself as a form of surplus which challenges other economies: 'As an identifiable, bordered, posed subject, the one who writes and his or her writing never give anything without calculating, consciously or unconsciously, its reappropriation, its exchange, or its circular return – and by definition this means reappropriation with surplus-value, a certain capitalization'. Earlier, he had asserted that gifts, through their refusal of a normative economics, share a certain rhythm with the alternative economies of writing. Yet such expectation of return within writing (which might be taken as both a figure of reading and of literary influence) enters it into a realm of the impossible and indecipherability, since 'there is no more gift once the

other *receives'* – even if the gift is refused. The surplus, the excess in giving, is rendered meaningless if the receiver acknowledges the gift as gift and so enters it into a normative economics of exchange. (*Given Time: I. Counterfeit Money*, translated by Peggy Kamuf (Chicago: The University of Chicago Press, 1992), pp. 101, 40–4, 14–15.) Yeats's appreciation of the gratuitousness of the gift is exemplified in the campaign around the Lane pictures, as in the exorbitantly-titled 'To a Wealthy Man who promised a second Subscription to the Dublin Municipal Gallery if it were proved the People wanted Pictures' ('Let Paudeens play at pitch and toss, / Look up in the sun's eye and give / What the exultant heart calls good / That some new day may breed the best') (*CP*, pp. 107–8). The fact that the campaign had to be fought at all, however, reveals frustration at what happens when gifts are not reciprocated. Later, when in 'The Tower' Yeats was seeking to align himself with a particular version of Anglo-Irish inheritance, his sense of the innate generosity of such forebears is again predominant. He celebrates 'The people of Burke and Grattan / That gave, though free to refuse...'. (*CP*, p. 198)

31　Such anxiety surfaces again in the introductory rhymes to *Responsibilities*, with their pleas for pardon from his (male) forebears: 'Pardon that for barren passion's sake, / Although I have come close on forty-nine, / I have no child, I have nothing but a book, / Nothing but that to prove your blood and mine' (*CP*, p. 101). In the 1902 essay 'Speaking to the Psaltery', Yeats had written of his natural dislike of print and paper (*E&I*, p. 13).

32　'Image and Emblem in Yeats', *The Rhetoric of Romanticism* (New York: Columbia University Press, 1984), pp. 193–4. De Man himself, however, favours a reading of the sequences according to the 'stylistic patterns' formed by their emblems, an allegorical network which denies the seeming naturalism of Yeatsian imagery. De Man sees Yeats, in other words, as subject to that tension between symbol and allegory which he traced in Romanticism across his career. He makes the same point in his reading of 'Among School Children' in *Allegories of Reading* (New Haven: Yale University Press, 1979), pp. 11–12. De Man's colleague at Yale, J. Hillis Miller, followed him in this reading of Yeats in *The Linguistic Moment: From Wordsworth to Stevens* (Princeton: Princeton University Press, 1985), pp. 342–3.

33　De Man sees this as a dilemma which Romantic poetry throughout was concerned to dramatize, since language can never achieve 'the absolute identity with itself which exists in the natural object' ('The Intentional Structure of the Image', op. cit., p. 6). 'My Table', from 'Meditations in Time of Civil War', shows Yeats's awareness of the need in each generation to forge anew 'changeless' works of art (*CP*, pp. 202–3).

34　See also my article ' "Passionate Improvisations": Grierson, Eliot and the Byronic Integrations of Yeats's Later Poetry' forthcoming in *English*, which suggests that the discovery of formal and idiomatic possibilities in Byron's work also played a large part in enabling Yeats to play his form off against his content from the mid-1920s onwards.

35　David Lloyd has discussed similar syntactic ambiguities elsewhere in Yeats's later work, and seen them as symptomatic of his increasing feelings of political marginalization after the Rising of 1916 (*Anomalous States: Irish Writing and the Post-Colonial Moment*, Dublin: The Lilliput Press, 1993, pp. 63ff). Yet I would argue that such uncertainties are present throughout Yeats's work, an element of its indecipherability, as in the emblematic 'The Rose of the World': 'For those red lips, with all their mournful pride, / Mournful that no new wonder may betide, / Troy...'. See also Joseph Adams, *Yeats and the Masks of Syntax* (Basingstoke: Macmillan, 1984, p. 82), for this sense of the syntax of the poetry as the site of undecidability from the earliest poems onward.

36 Op. cit., pp. 152–6. Where Bhabha's key terms are useful in such instances is in establishing that in colonial contexts the recognitions that tradition bestows are only partial forms of identification, and as such are a 'measure of the liminality of cultural modernity' whereby the colonized countries experience the hybridity which characterizes modernity before the metropolitan colonizing ones do. As Bhabha argues in his essay 'Dissemination': 'The problematic boundaries of modernity are enacted in [the] ambivalent temporalities of the nation-space. The language of culture and community is poised on the fissure of the present becoming the rhetorical figures of a national past.' A nation's modernity exists, then, in a 'disjunctive time', a time which might describe both Yeats's appropriation of foreign narratives alongside native ones in the undecidable tropes of perpetual emergence during his Celtic Twilight and Abbey Theatre involvements, as well as the oddly posthumous assertion of national history against modernity in 'The Municipal Gallery Revisited' (ibid., pp. 142, 186).

37 *Blindness and Insight: Essays in the Rhetoric of Contemporary Criticism* (2nd edn., London: Methuen, 1983), pp. 187–228. Harold Bloom argues in *Kabbalah and Criticism* that 'Even as the language of modern or post-Miltonic poetry becomes more over-determined . . . so signification tends to wander, which means that a loss of meaning accompanies a tradition's temporal passage' (p. 88).

38 *Revolution in Poetic Language*, translated by Margaret Waller (New York: Columbia University Press, 1984), pp. 24, 27.

39 Such variousness in Yeats and in his potential influence makes the focus upon a single aspect of the work, such as that of Terence Diggory in his *Yeats and American Poetry: the Tradition of the Self*, seem wrongheaded. As Marjorie Perloff complained in her review of Diggory's book, 'the narrow focus on the self and mask makes it impossible to assess Yeats's influence on later poets, poets who might well be influenced by Yeats's rhetoric or his imagery, his renewal of genre or his treatment of history – areas that inevitably fall outside Diggory's parameters'. (*Yeats Annual*, No. 3, edited by Warwick Gould (Basingstoke: Macmillan, 1985), p. 272)

40 *Of Grammatology*, translated by Gayatri Chakravorty Spivak (Baltimore: Johns Hopkins University Press, 1976), pp. 143, 155. The troubling masturbatory implications of a desire which can only express itself fully in the absence of the loved one (p. 151) are mirrored in Yeats's description of such activity in his *Memoirs*, the torture of 'sexual desire and disappointed love' in the mid 1890s leading to masturbation which, 'no matter how moderate I was, would make me ill' (edited by Denis Donoghue, London, Macmillan, 1972, pp. 71–2, 125).

41 Daniel T. O'Hara has discussed this centrality of Yeats in both deconstructive and New Critical thought in 'Yeats in Theory', *Post-Structuralist Readings of English Poetry*, edited by Richard Machin and Christopher Norris (Cambridge: Cambridge University Press, 1987), pp. 349–68.

42 *A Map of Misreading*, p. 13.
43 *W.B. Yeats: Interviews and Recollections*, Volume II, edited by E.H. Mikhail (Basingstoke: Macmillan, 1977), p. 203.
44 *Agon*, pp. 124, 107.
45 *The Anxiety of Influence*, p. 130. A similar sense of the need to resist the notion that the later text might simply repeat or mimic an earlier drives Tilottama Rajan's arguments against Kristevan intertextuality as a model for literary influence. Kristeva fails to account for the 'problem of intention', Rajan argues, and therefore sees texts as mere mirrors of each other, rather than as sites in which the 'metaphorical construction' of an authorial consciousness is 'foregrounded' ('Intertextuality and the Subject of Reading / Writing', *Influence and Intertextuality in Literary History*, edited by Jay Clayton and Eric Rothstein (Madison: The University of Wisconsin Press, 1991), pp. 67–71).
46 Op. cit., p. 126.
47 'Shelley Disfigured', *The Rhetoric of Romanticism*, p. 96. In *Yeats and the Poetry of Death: Elegy, Self-Elegy and the Sublime*, Jahan Ramanazani notes the explicitness of Yeats's preoccupation with, and struggle against, death, in his public and private elegies, and also the significance of this for Bloom's founding work on influence in *Yeats*. But Ramanazani concludes from close readings of the poems that Yeats does not fit the compensatory model very clearly, since his later self-elegizing serves ultimately to eradicate the whole notion of death (New Haven: Yale University Press, 1990, see pp. 45, 158, 186). In *Poetry of Mourning: The Modern Elegy from Hardy to Heaney*, Ramanazani goes further, to propose that, for the twentieth-century elegist, the models of compensation within elegy which had held hitherto were redundant: 'the modern elegist tends not to achieve but to resist compensation, not to override but to sustain anger, not to heal but to reopen the wounds of loss' (Chicago: Chicago University Press, 1994, p. xi). In both books, Yeats figures as the significant figure in renewing the genre of elegy for the century, and for also, in his poems' honesty and frequent aggression towards the lamented dead, establishing a tone which has lasted through those elegists he has influenced, including Auden, Plath, Berryman and Lowell.
48 Op. cit., p. 236. In 'The Breaking of Form', Bloom insists that there is no way for experience to enter a poem as it were extra-poetically, ' . . . another aspect of a limitation of poetry which defines poetry: a poem can be about experience or emotion or whatever only by initially encountering another poem, which is to say a poem must handle experience and emotion as if they already were rival poems' (*Deconstruction and Criticism*, New York: The Seabury Press, 1979, p. 15).
49 *A Map of Misreading*, p. 10.
50 *Agon*, p. 238.
51 *Poetry and Repression: Revisionism from Blake to Stevens* (New Haven: Yale University Press, 1976), p. 134.
52 *Kabbalah and Criticism*, p. 114.
53 De Man discussed and distanced himself from New Critical thinking in 'Form and Intent in the American New Criticism' and 'The Dead-End of Formalist Criticism', both collected in *Blindness and Insight*.
54 Bloom also concludes, however, that Yeats is himself weaker in his assertion than his own precursors, Blake and Shelley, through his insistence upon

systematizing his vision and appealing to 'communal voices' in Ireland rather than to the solitary voice of Gnosticism: 'That so great and unique a poet abdicated the idea of man to a conception of destiny, however Homeric, is not less than tragic...' (p. 471). In the 1970s and 80s, Bloom tended to be dismissive of those twentieth-century poets who wrote consciously in the field of influence of major precursors, finding the work of John Berryman and Theodore Roethke, for instance, 'too near' that of their masters and therefore unindividuated (*The Anxiety of Influence*, p. 28), and seeming to favour only the English poet Geoffrey Hill. More latterly, with the Chelsea House series of edited critical books and *The Western Canon* (Basingstoke: Macmillan, 1995), Bloom has, albeit controversially, accepted recent writers into his purview. Daniel T. O'Hara has claimed that, by the end of the 1970s, Bloom himself was tainted by that historical determinism which he had found a damning weakness in Yeats at their outset: 'For Bloom's theory calls for the growing solipsism of the poet and so, in the final analysis, for the "death" of poetry in the birth of "poetic" criticism.... the final danger of the irony of revisionism is, of course, that one will become the antithetical image of all that one originally held dear.' (*The Yale Critics: Deconstruction in America*, edited by Jonathan Arac, Wlad Godzich, Wallace Martin (Minneapolis: University of Minnesota Press, 1983), p. 124).

55 Op. cit., p. 30. Cp. 'The American critic here and now, in my judgement, needs to keep faith both with American poetry and with the American Negative, which means one must not yield either to the school of Deconstruction or to the perpetual British school of Common Sense.' (p. 335).

56 Bloom acknowledges the central significance of his reading of Emerson over his writings on influence in *A Recent Imagining: Interviews with Harold Bloom, Geoffrey Hartman, J. Hillis Miller, Paul de Man*, by Robert Moynihan (Connecticut: Archon Books, 1986), p. 27.

57 Op. cit., pp. 32, 60. See also *Kabbalah and Criticism*, which directly argues against Derrida's favouring of the endless play of writing over speech by offering its own cabbalistic possibility: 'Kabbalah stops the movement of Derrida's "trace", since it has a *point* of the primordial, where presence and absence co-exist in continuous interplay.' (p. 53) Derrida does not however himself rule orality out of texts as Bloom claims he does. Rather, he sees the split between the oral and writing as historically-conditioned from Plato onwards, while wanting to see the family scene as the scene of writing much as Bloom does (*Dissemination*, pp. 149ff.).

58 See the 'Coda: Poetic Crossing' (Bloom's most sustained answer to de Man) in *Wallace Stevens: The Poems of Our Climate* (Ithaca: Cornell University Press, 1977). Peter de Bolla has written a lucid and engaged account of Bloom's debates with and partial appropriation of de Man's arguments in his *Harold Bloom: Towards Historical Rhetorics* – see especially pp. 67–80 and 93–101. The drive behind such debates might be gauged from de Man's review of *The Anxiety of Influence*, in which he accused Bloom of wanting ultimately to hold on to a (for de Man unacceptable) notion that language 'is a tool manipulated by extralinguistic impulses rooted in a subject' (*Blindness and Insight*, p. 276).

59 *Kabbalah and Criticism*, pp. 104, 108.

60 See e.g. *Agon*, p. 29.

61   Op. cit., p. 270.
62   *The Madwoman in the Attic: The Woman Writer and the Nineteenth-Century Literary Imagination* (New Haven: Yale University Press, 1979), pp. 48–9; *The Hélène Cixous Reader*, edited by Susan Sellers (London: Routledge, 1994), p. 39. Elizabeth Butler Cullingford has offered an insightful reading of Yeats from a woman's perspective in her *Gender and History in Yeats's Love Poetry* (Cambridge: Cambridge University Press, 1993).
63   'Limited Inc. a b c . . .', *Limited Inc* (Evanston, Illinois: Northwestern University Press, 1988), pp. 56, 130.
64   Ibid., p. 5.
65   Op.cit., pp. 50, 56, 58.
66   See de Man's 'Kant and Schiller', *Aesthetic Ideology*, pp. 132–4.
67   *On the Name*, edited by Thomas Dutoit, Stanford: Stanford University Press, 1995, pp. 119, 143, 144; Kristeva, *Revolution in Poetic Language*, p. 130.
68   J. Hillis Miller, who is otherwise one of the most moving and accomplished appliers of recent theoretical ideas to what he calls the 'other' which we negotiate with when reading texts from the past and write on them, is not innocent of such manoeuvres: 'Every poem has other poems anterior to it to which it refers in one way or another. It also contains linguistic elements which are self-referential or "metapoetical". Some language in the poem is about the poem itself. . . . Critical discourse is language about language which is already about its own language. The language of the poem in its turn is about other poems which precede it and to which it is "allegorically" related. These earlier poems also have anterior texts to which they refer in an endless sequence, each item referring back to earlier ones or ahead to the ones not yet written in a movement of meaning without origin or end. . . . The interpreter of a given text can only in one way or another enter into [a text's] play of language. . . . Beginning and end are exposed for the first time as shadows generated by language itself.' ('Williams' "Spring and All"' in *Tropes, Parables, Performatives: Essays on Twentieth Century Literature*, Hemel Hempstead: Harvester Wheatsheaf, 1990, pp. 89, 102.)
69   *Revolution in Poetic Language*, pp. 25–30. The book appeared in France in 1974.
70   Op. cit., pp. 67, 99.
71   *The Resistance to Theory* (Manchester: Manchester University Press, 1986), pp. 49–50.
72   *The Rhetoric of Romanticism*, pp. 76, 80–1; op. cit., p. 26. Yet see also Derrida's subsequent discussion, pp. 33–40, on the painful inadequacy of our ability to internalize such voices, an inadequacy which underlies mourning and the work of language as mourning.
73   Op. cit., pp. x, 74.
74   *Blindness and Insight*, p. 92.
75   *Recognitions: a Study in Poetics* (Oxford: Clarendon Press, 1990), pp. 33, 46, 489.
76   *The Anxiety of Influence*, p. 11.
77   *The Resistance to Theory*, p. 30. Derrida, while acknowledging that rhyme is 'one of the most remarkable instances of . . . production of a new sign' ultimately emphasizes its contingency and haphazardness (*Dissemination*, p. 256).
78   Daniel T. O'Hara locates the failure of Bloom's reading of Yeats, with its final dismissal on the grounds of historical determinism, precisely in this blind-

ness to formal possibility: '...he fails to understand that from the first...
Yeats is experimenting with the Romantic form of internalized quest, as he
experiments with all inherited literary forms, in order to play out the impulse
behind such forms in his work rather than live them out painfully to the
bitter end'. The varying proximity of such forms to the lived experience they
purport to describe establishes Yeats's 'tragic knowledge', the focus of
O'Hara's study (*Tragic Knowledge: Yeats's 'Autobiography' and Hermeneutics*,
New York: Columbia University Press, 1981, pp. 50–1).

79 O'Hara, in his discussion of the centrality of Yeats to American critical
thinking from New Criticism through to de Man, has pointed to the
limitation of the sublime as a key concept in writing from R.P. Blackmur
through Northrop Frye to Bloom: 'the sublime exceeds and at the same
time conventionalizes its own formulations, authorizes and trangresses
all authority structures including those of the sublime experience itself.
The sublime, in short, cannot finally be distinguished from the principle
of change itself, however vainly one attempts to conceptualize the latter.
Consequently, the sublime discloses the essential nature of all literary ideas –
their fundamental groundlessness that makes every effort to theorize on
their basis in the manner of academic philosophy a ridiculous enterprise
at worst and at best a diverting work of literary art' ('Yeats in Theory',
p. 359).

80 In *Modernist Poetics of History: Pound, Eliot and the Sense of the Past*, Longenbach suggests that it is the sense of history as 'existential' – i.e. as an active
interchange between the perceiving mind in the present and the ghosts of
the past – which Yeats derived from Pater and which in turn he handed on to
Pound and Eliot after him. While Eliot was the more sceptical about the
magical and spiritual basis of this version of history as it is encouraged by
Yeats, Pound derived much of his method in *The Cantos* from the ritual
revivification of the dead, as figured in the case of Tiresias in *Canto* I (Princeton: Princeton University Press, 1987, pp. 1–44).

81 The Australian poet A.D. Hope would seem an exception, but as he admits in
his essay 'Coming to Grips with Proteus', 'the nature of [the] haunting has
never been clear to me' (*Yeats Annual* No. 4, edited by Warwick Gould
(Basingstoke: Macmillan, 1986), p. 161). During the apprenticeship of the
West Indian Derek Walcott, as Stewart Brown has argued, Yeats clearly served
as a 'model of purpose' in creating a specifically native and national literature, as well as in translating that tradition through Classical models (a
strain in Walcott's writing which culminated in the 1990 *Omeros*). Yeats's
sense of inheritance and decay also unspecifically figures in works such as
'Ruins of a Great House' (*The Art of Derek Walcott*, edited by Brown, Bridgend:
Seren, 1991, p. 24). More recently, having himself been a beneficiary of
what Yeats called 'the bounty of Sweden', the Nobel Prize, Walcott has
registered again the earlier poet's work of national founding (the copper-
beech in Coole park has roots, he writes, which 'are Ireland's'). But, he
reflects from the house built with the prize-money, there is 'nothing beyond
those waves I care to remember, / but a few friends gone, and that is a
different care / in this headland without distinction' (*The Bounty*, London:
Faber, 1997, p. 61).

82 *Given Time*, p. 4.

2 'The Terror of his Vision': Yeats and Irish Poetry Louis MacNeice, Austin Clarke, Patrick Kavanagh, Brian Coffey, Padraic Fallon, Thomas Kinsella, Seamus Heaney, Derek Mahon, Eavan Boland, Paul Muldoon

1 *Agon: Towards A Theory of Revisionism* (New York: Oxford University Press, 1983), p. 236.
2 'In the Irish Grain', *The Figure in the Cave and Other Essays* (Dublin: The Lilliput Press, 1989), p. 122.
3 *Revolution in Poetic Language*, translated by Peggy Waller (New York: Columbia University Press, 1984), p. 43.
4 *The Rhetoric of Romanticism* (New York: Columbia University Press, 1984), pp. 65, 122. De Man's comments on the necessary fragmentariness of his project and writing on Romanticism are given in the Preface; having recognized that other critics including Auerbach and Adorno have made the 'fragmentary nature of post-romantic literature a stylistic principle of their own', de Man argues that the fragmentariness of his own style is not so willed, but rather a 'repeated frustration in a persistent attempt to write as if a dialectical summation were possible beyond the breaks and interruptions that the readings disclose'. He is attempting instead 'to recuperate on the level of style what is lost on the level of history'. Yet even this might be to fall back upon a problematic which results upon our particular place in the history of writing: 'By stating the inevitability of fragmentation in a mode that is itself fragmented, one restores the aesthetic unity of manner and substance that may well be what is in question in the historical study of romanticism' (p. ix). Within Irish literature from this century, written under pressures of fragmentation which Yeats had himself seen as the result of historical deprivation, the dangers of repetition and the concomitant inevitabilities are, as will become clear, the key concern.
5 *W.B. Yeats and T. Sturge Moore: Their Correspondance 1901–1937*, edited by Ursula Bridge (London: Routledge & Kegan Paul, 1953), p. 114.
6 Jon Stallworthy, *Louis MacNeice* (London: Faber, 1995), pp. 253, 294.
7 London: Faber, 1967 edition, p. 17.
8 In his 1940 review, MacNeice saw The Irish 'Troubles' of 1916–22 as focusing the dialectical qualities of Yeats's thought in which 'he began to conceive of life as a developing whole, a whole which depends upon the conflict of the parts'. (*Selected Literary Criticism of Louis MacNeice*, edited by Alan Heuser, Oxford: Clarendon Press, 1987, p. 118).
9 *Modern Poetry: a Personal Essay*, Second Edition, Oxford: Clarendon Press, 1968, 'Preface'.
10 Op. cit., pp. 16, 44. In *Modern Poetry*, MacNeice had also suggested that Yeats's Irish subject-matter, in his adaptation of legends, and his identification with Irish nationalism, meant that he had 'to recognize the palpable realities of living people and contemporary problems'. (p. 10.) In his essay 'Poetry To-Day' of 1935, MacNeice had suggested that even the Celtic Twilight had a value not only for Yeats himself, in establishing his connection with his times, but that it might stand as an example for more contemporary writing

because in the Irish movement 'poetry was heathily mixed up with politics'. Later, in a review of Yeats's *Letters* of 1954, MacNeice attacked the Orwellian view of Yeats as a Fascist by condemning that view's ignorance of the 'simple peculiarities of Ireland as a whole or the more complex peculiarities of that Protestant minority to which Yeats, like many another ardent nationalist, belonged.' (*Selected Literary Criticism of Louis MacNeice*, pp. 15, 118, 190). John Montague makes a similar point about the way in which Yeats's nationalism saved him from aestheticism in 'In the Irish Grain', op. cit., p. 122. Thomas Whitaker has argued, in more existential terms, that 'Yeats's dialogue with history' 'saved him, by and large, from romantic self-deification' (*Swan and Shadow*, Chapel Hill: University of North Carolina Press, 1964, p. 8).

11 Op. cit., pp. 156, 191.

12 *Louis MacNeice: A Study* (London: Faber, 1988), p. 27.

13 *Collected Poems of Louis MacNeice* (London: Faber, 1979 edition), p. 164. In *Louis MacNeice: The Poet in his Contexts*, Peter McDonald has compared the form of 'Dublin' to that of its model 'Easter 1916' in order to reveal the 'dangerous otherness' of the city which, unlike the transcendent aspiration Yeats displayed at a similar moment of historical upheaval, left MacNeice questioning notions of the self and identity. Later in the book, however, McDonald sees such uncertainty as deriving from MacNeice's time in England during the 1930s, rather than being endemic in the various strains and remakings which he had traced in the work of Yeats itself. McDonald's claim in this context that 'Yeats used Ireland to create a dominant myth of the self' seems counter to the saving and salving 'impurity' of Irish reality which MacNeice finds in the older poet (pp. 100, 227).

14 Op. cit., pp. 278, 131.

15 Ibid., pp. 133, 136, 137.

16 Ibid., pp. 233–4.

17 Op. cit., p. 140. See also p. 197, on his conclusion that, given this zestfulness, Yeats's cyclical determinist philosophy is perhaps a 'bluff'. The Belfast poet James Simmons, who has clearly been influenced in his own song- and poetry-making by Yeats's use of another popular form, the ballad, shows a similar gaiety in defiance of painful experience throughout his work. In 'Meditations in Time of Divorce', for example, he writes of feeling 'potential / not loss... / in good faith embracing / necessity, constantly singing...' (*Poems 1956–1986* Dublin: Gallery Press, 1986, p. 146). In 'Death of a King', his reminiscence of the night George VI died, he directly echoes 'Lapis Lazuli': 'My heart was warm. I thought, In the same way / as Hamlet and Lear, King George is gay'. As a result of such happiness, those around him tell him to 'show some respect' (*Elegies*, Maynooth: Sotto Voce Press, 1995, p. 30). Such untrammelled trangressiveness has marked the social daring of Simmons's poetry throughout. In his elegies (as he remarks in the Preface to this collection), this note is attained by his reliance on the four beat couplet which he says he learnt from Auden's 'Elegy for W.B. Yeats', a form which Auden in his turn derived from 'Under Ben Bulben'.

18 *Romanticism and Contemporary Criticism: The Gauss Seminar and Other Papers*, edited by E.S. Burt, Kevin Newmark and Andrej Warminski, Baltimore: Johns Hopkins University Press, 1993, p. 129.

19 Op. cit., pp. 523–4.

20   *Selected Criticism*, p. 118.
21   Paul de Man, 'The Rhetoric of Temporality', *Blindness & Insight: Essays in the Rhetoric of Contemporary Criticism* (London: Methuen, 1983 2nd edn) pp. 207–9.
22   *Reviews and Essays of Austin Clarke*, edited by Gregory A. Schirmer (Gerrard's Cross: Colin Smythe, 1995), pp. 18, 16. In dismissing MacNeice's *The Poetry of W.B. Yeats* in *The Dublin Magazine*, Clarke claimed that MacNeice's study shows little acquaintance with Irish letters as a whole, and as a result seeks to identify the nature of Yeats's work by discussing both the influence upon it of English Romanticism and also its associations with modernism. An 'arbitrary and tiresome exercise', Clarke concludes, since Yeats remained 'strategically on the edge of tradition in the 'nineties as well as in the 'thirties'. Here as elsewhere, Clarke seems to be anxious to recover as valuable the very Celtic Twilight writing which MacNeice had tended to overlook as an aestheticism only tenuously related to Irish 'reality' (ibid., pp. 10–12). More recent Anglo-Irish poets have dramatized the difficulty of defining a relation to Ireland in more uncertain terms than those of Yeats. In 'Cloncha', James Simmons lists the various 'adorations' of the 'Anglo-Irish boy' within the country, before seeing the growth towards adulthood as further destabilizing that relation: 'Today he searched for anecdotes / to establish his rights there...'. As a result he remains 'a stranger / in the present moment / happily'. (*Poems 1956–1986*, p. 158–9). Richard Murphy's sequence *The Price of Stone*, centring each sonnet as it does on a different habitation, suggests the uprootedness of his culture with the failure of the Big House tradition in the country. These two poets have been discussed in this light by Terence Brown in his essay 'Poets and Patrimony: Richard Murphy and James Simmons' in *Ireland's Literature: Selected Essays* (Mullingar: The Lilliput Press, 1988).
23   *Collected Poems*, edited by Liam Miller (Dublin: Dolmen Press/Oxford: Oxford University Press, 1974), pp. 207, 249.
24   Ibid., p. 398.
25   *The Complete Poems of Patrick Kavanagh*, with commentary by Peter Kavanagh (New York: Kavanagh Head Press, 1996), p. 366.
26   Ibid., p. 66.
27   See Chapter 3 of Marjorie Howes's *Yeats's Nations: Gender, Class and Irishness* (Cambridge: Cambridge University Press, 1996), for a full discussion of Yeats's attitudes in this area.
28   *Collected Pruse* (London, MacGibbon and Kee, 1967), pp. 15, 255.
29   Ibid., pp. 28, 251.
30   Ibid., pp. 268, 254, 154.
31   Op. cit., pp. 253, 124, 40.
32   In a review of 1897, 'The Tribes of Danu', Yeats wrote 'The Poet is happy, as Homer was happy, who can see from his door mountains.... If the poet cannot find immortal and mysterious things in his own country, he must write of far-off countries...' (*Uncollected Prose by W.B. Yeats*, Volume II, collected and edited by John P. Frayne and Colton Johnson, London: Macmillan, 1975, p. 55).
33   *The Rhetoric of Romanticism*, p. 6.
34   *Patrick Kavanagh: Born-Again Romantic* (Dublin: Gill and Macmillan, 1991), pp. 414–16.

35 Edna Longley has argued that Yeats's adoption of masks was impelled by the hostility which his writing generated in Ireland, and was therefore 'essential to [his] artistic survival' ('Introductory Reflections', *That Accusing Eye: Yeats and his Irish Readers*, *Yeats Annual* No. 12, edited by Warwick Gould and Edna Longley, Basingstoke: Macmillan, 1996, p. 14).

36 *Complete Poems*, p. 349; *Collected Prose*, p. 255.

37 Op. cit., p. 308.

38 Jacques Derrida sees in this gesture the defining particularity of literature: 'No doubt literature... seems to aim toward the filling of a lack (whole) in a whole that should not itself in its essence be missing (to) itself. But literature is also the *exception to everything*: at once the exception in the whole, the want-of-wholeness in the whole, and... that which exists by itself... (*Dissemination*, translated by Barbara Johnson, London: The Athlone Press, 1993, p. 56).

39 Quoted by Alex Davis, ' "Poetry is Ontology" ': Brian Coffey's Poetics', *Modernism and Ireland: The Poetry of the 1930s*, edited by Patricia Coughlan and Alex Davis (Cork: Cork University Press, 1995), p. 157.

40 'The Contemporary Criticism of Romanticism', *Romanticism and Contemporary Criticism*, pp. 3–23.

41 *Poems and Versions 1929–1990* (Dublin, The Dedalus Press, 1991), pp. 72–3.

42 Ibid., pp. 76–7.

43 See, for example, 'Est Prodest', *Collected Poems*, edited by J.C.C. Mays (Dublin: Dedalus Press, 1989), p. 85. Elsewhere, Devlin was capable of mocking the apocalyptic afflatus of Yeats, as in the derisory allusion to 'The Second Coming' in 'Liffey Bridge' (p. 58).

44 Op. cit., pp. 80, 81, 84, 86, 87.

45 *Mémoires: for Paul de Man* (New York: Columbia University Press, 1986), p. 138. See also *Given Time: I. Counterfeit Money*, translated by Peggy Kamuf (Chicago: University of Chicago Press, 1992), pp. 40–1, on the rhythm and excess of gifts.

46 *The Poems of Matthew Arnold*, edited by Kenneth Allott (London: Longman, 1965), p. 242.

47 *The Rhetoric of Romanticism*, p. 143; *Letters of W.B. Yeats*, edited by Allen Wade (London: Rupert Hart-Davis, 1954), p. 607.

48 Op. cit., pp. 121–2, 156.

49 Homer here seems to exemplify ideally that 'crossing' between 'voicing and writing' which Harold Bloom wants to defend as the worth of poetry against the textual deconstructionists: 'the *places* of poetry are images of voice, even as the *figures* of poetry are images of writing' (*Wallace Stevens: The Poems of Our Climate* (Ithaca: Cornell University Press, 1977), p. 401. This reading of deconstruction itself seems partial, however. Derrida has claimed that 'Without the possibility of differance, the desire of presence as such would not find its breathing-space', as though for him writing and orality are interwoven in an aporetic undecidability (*Of Grammatology*, translated by Gayatri Chakravorty Spivak, Baltimore: Johns Hopkins University Press, 1976, p. 143).

50 See, for example, the discussion of his work in Dillon Johnston's *Irish Poetry After Joyce* (Notre Dame: University of Notre Dame Press, 1985).

51 *Collected Poems* (Dublin/Manchester: Gallery/Carcanet, 1990), p. 44.

52 Derrida seems to want to keep the moment of this absence itself undecided, allowing that it might occur both with the publication of the text and with the actual physical death of the author (*Given Time*, pp. 4, 100).

53 Op. cit., p. 85.

54 *The Gift of Death*, translated by David Wills (Chicago: University of Chicago Press, 1995), pp. 14–15.

55 Op. cit., p. 114.

56 Ibid., pp. 15, 12.

57 *Nightwalker and Other Poems* (Dublin: The Dolmen Press, 1968), p. 50. The poem is one of few earlier works which Kinsella has chosen not to include in his *Collected Poems 1956–1994* (Oxford: Oxford University Press, 1996), perhaps indicating an increased feeling of proximity latterly between his own work and Yeats's. Brian John, in his *Reading the Ground: the Poetry of Thomas Kinsella* (Washington: The Catholic University of America Press, 1996), traces such a movement as one of the plots behind his close readings of the individual poems.

58 Edited by Thomas Dutoit (Stanford: Stanford University Press, 1995), p. 119.

59 *The Dual Tradition: An Essay on Poetry and Politics in Ireland* (Manchester: Carcanet, 1995), p. 89.

60 *Mémoires*, pp. 38, 66.

61 *Collected Poems*, p. 240.

62 Ibid., pp. 169–71.

63 Ibid., p. 253.

64 *The Dual Tradition*, p. 76.

65 See, for example, Seamus Deane's 'Heroic Styles: the tradition of an idea', and Richard Kearney's 'Myth and Motherland', in *Ireland's Field Day*, Field Day Theatre Company (London: Hutchinson, 1985).

66 I discuss this relationship in more detail in the chapter on Heaney in my *Irish Poetry: Politics, History, Negotiation* (Basingstoke: Macmillan, 1997). The native modernism which I trace in various contemporary poets there (in their responses to a violent history and partly as a negotiation with certain aspects of Yeatsian influence), is, I would now argue, a productive categorization, but also itself entangled in the kinds of Romantic undecidability which are integral to Yeats's own work and inheritance.

67 *The Redress of Poetry: Oxford Lectures* (London: Faber, 1995), p. 163, 158.

68 London: Faber, 1991, p. 50.

69 Ibid., p. 78.

70 The phrase from Yeats is quoted from *Letters on Poetry from W.B. Yeats to Dorothy Wellesley* (London: Oxford University Press, 1964 edition), p. 176.

71 'The Art of Poetry LXXV', *The Paris Review* 144, Fall 1997, p. 104. Paul de Man, *Romanticism and Contemporary Criticism*, p. 58. See also Derrida's commentary on this aspect of de Man's writing, especially *Mémoires*, p. 58.

72 Op. cit., pp. 199, 202.

73 *Dissemination*, pp. 173–285.

74 No. 271, March '89, unnumbered page. In this article, as well, Heaney dates the new assurance within Yeats's work from his fiftieth year; the piece appeared a month before Heaney's own fiftieth birthday.

75 *The Letters of W.B. Yeats*, p. 798.

76 Heaney discusses 'Long-legged Fly' at the end of his 1978 lecture 'The Makings of a Music' as the 'transcendent realization' of Yeats's central preoccupation with the question 'what is the relationship between the creative moment in the life of the individual and the effect of that moment's conception throughout history?' (*Preoccupations: Selected Prose 1968–1978*, London: Faber, 1980, p. 77).

77 *North* (London: Faber, 1992 reset edition), p. x.

78 'Funeral Rites', ibid., p. 7.

79 *Seamus Heaney* (London: Faber, 1986), p. 109.

80 *Preoccupations*, p. 33.

81 Op. cit., p. 52.

82 Ibid., p. 11.

83 Op. cit., p. 31. Such political issues play around the question mark of Heaney's 1978 lecture 'Yeats As An Example?' collected in *Preoccupations*, where the earlier poet's cold vision of things is set to his detriment, in Heaney's view, against the human warmth of Lowell's work. (pp. 98–100) Yeats's ability to remake himself across his career, which Heaney clearly finds admirable and which he dramatizes to the full here, is what remains exemplary – a similar notion of that self-remaking informs my own comments on Heaney.

84 Corcoran notes that Heaney had himself commented that *North* was divided into two halves: a Yeatsian 'heaven' in the first, a Kavanagh-like 'home' in the second (op. cit., p. 98). And yet, as I hope to have shown, those absolute divisions impact upon each other throughout.

85 See 'Yeats As An Example?', pp. 109–10 and 'Yeats's Nobility', the *Fortnight* commemorative piece, in which Heaney claims that 'it is possible that we have insufficiently pondered his hard-won insight that all reality comes to us as the reward of labour. There is surely good political meaning in his sense of life as an abounding conflict of opposites, and in his vision of reality as a process in which opposites die each others' life, live each others' death'.

86 *The Spirit Level* (London: Faber, 1996), pp. 29–30.

87 Ibid., p. 18.

88 Ibid., pp. 34, 37.

89 *Crediting Poetry* (Loughcrew: The Gallery Press, 1995), p. 28.

90 Op. cit., 69, 46, 65, 70.

91 Ibid., p. 47.

92 *Irish Poetry After Joyce*, p. 24.

93 'Landscape (after Baudelaire)' (Loughcrew: The Gallery Press, 1997), p. 11.

94 Ibid., p. 29.

95 Ibid., p. 15.

96 'Yeats, Form and Northern Irish Poetry', *Yeats Annual* No. 12, pp. 229–34.

97 *Selected Poems* (Harmondsworth/Loughcrew: Penguin/Gallery, 1993), p. 170.

98 Ibid., pp. 115–16, 49. In his 1989 review 'An Irascible Patient', Mahon had claimed that 'There are certain figures in the history of literature before whom one falls silent. Shakespeare, of course; Yeats maybe; certainly Baudelaire. In the cases of Shakespeare and Yeats, the silence is not a disagreeable one; we know that, despite the storms and rages, everything will be all right in the end, and so it is. Anglophone literature is, on the whole, ultimately consolatory' (*Journalism* (Loughcrew: The Gallery Press, 1996), p. 129).

99 Ibid., p. 57.

100 'Young Eavan and Early Boland', *Journalism*, p. 107.
101 *Collected Poems* (Manchester: Carcanet, 1995), p. 8.
102 *Object Lessons: The Life of the Woman and the Poet in Our Time* (Manchester: Carcanet, 1995), p. 134.
103 Op.cit, pp. 3–4.
104 Ibid., p. xii.
105 Ibid., p. 52.
106 For example, James Simmons's sequence of dramatic monologues on the breakdown of a mixed Catholic/Protestant marriage, *Sex, Rectitude & Loneliness*, which is set in 1988 at the time of a notorious incident in which some British soldiers were dragged from their car and killed during a Catholic funeral, includes a section called 'Maeve Remembers': 'the soldier's pain / was part of us. It felt to me / as if the people's pain drove them to kill. / . . . I wasn't scared when he hit me, / just surprised.' (Belfast: Lapwing Publications, 1993, pp. 41–2).
107 *Object Lessons*, p. 189.
108 'Whose?' the poem which concludes *The Lost Land*, for instance, dramatizes in the contrast between its two stanzas, the ambiguous achievements of a self-sacrificing patriot, who rinses the land with his blood, and the poet, whose achievement is self-involved whilst also potentially personally affecting: '*Beautiful land* I whispered. . . . / . . . Nothing moved. / Except my hands across the page. And these words'. (Manchester: Carcanet, 1998, p. 58).
109 Ibid., pp. 56–7.
110 *Object Lessons*, p. 166.
111 *Collected Poems*, p. 198, 208.
112 Ibid., p. 151.
113 Ibid., p. 58.
114 See William A. Wilson, 'Yeats, Muldoon, and Heroic History', *Learning their Trade: Essays on W.B. Yeats and Contemporary Poetry*, edited by Deborah Fleming (West Cornwall, Connecticut: Locust Hill Press, 1993), p. 30.
115 ' "The Half-Said Thing to Them is Dearest": Paul Muldoon', *Poetry in Contemporary Irish Literature*, edited by Michael Kenneally (Gerrard's Cross: Colin Smythe, 1995), p. 415.
116 London: Faber, 1998, p. 10.
117 'Squarings' viii, *Seeing Things*, p. 62.
118 Ibid, p. 27. Such skewings are taken up again in poem xxiv of the concluding sequence, 'Bangle (Slight Return)' (p. 134), and harmonize jarringly with the swerves of Heaney's recent work, discussed above.
119 Ibid., p. 93.
120 O'Donoghue has noted that 'disconcerting uses of tenses' are frequent in Irish poetry also (op. cit., p. 412). Yeats figures alongside Robert Frost as an example of the complex interplay between poetry and history in Muldoon's 'Getting Around: Notes Towards an *Ars Poetica*', *Essays in Criticism*, Vol. XLVIII No. 2, April 1998, pp. 107–28.
121 Clair Wills, in *Reading Paul Muldoon* (Newcastle upon Tyne, 1998), pp. 207–8, discusses this obsessive rhyming in recent Muldoon.
122 *The Annals of Chile* (London: Faber, 1994), p. 25.
123 'Timothy', *Hay*, p. 102.

124 *Aporias*, translated by Thomas Dutoit (Stanford: Stanford University Press, 1993), pp. 60–2; see also *Mémoires*, pp. 34–9.

125 *Variorum Edition of the Poems of W.B. Yeats*, edited by Peter Allt and Russell K. Alspach (New York: Macmillan, 1977 edition), p. 778.

126 'The Books Interview', *The Observer Review*, 15 November 1998, p. 14.

127 *Inventing Ireland: The Literature of the Modern Nation* (London: Jonathan Cape, 1995), p. 124.

3   Inevitable Abstractions: Yeats and British Poetry W.H. Auden, Donald Davie, Thom Gunn, Ted Hughes, Geoffrey Hill

1 'The Rhetoric of Temporality', *Blindness & Insight: Essays in the Rhetoric of Contemporary Criticism* (London: Methuen, 1983 2nd edn), pp. 188–9.

2 George Barker (who had an Irish Catholic mother, but was exiled from Ireland for much of his life), would seem to be the only English poet to have had a similarly complex and self-revising relationship to Yeats, which was also bound up with his complex relationship to Ireland itself. 'No matter how close to the ground I bend, his breath / Is not for me, and all divisions widen', Barker concluded in an elegy for Yeats. Yet he later became more reconciled, offering a kind of benediction in 'Ben Bulben Revisited' from his last book, *Street Ballads*: 'Sleep on, old man, among / The ruins and the echoes, / The small lies and the great rimes, / The stones and the rocky poems, / For they at least belong / By the Ben Bulben of dreams.' (London: Faber, 1992, pp. 2–3). See Robert Fraser, ' "The Pilgrimage Along the Drogheda Road": W.B. Yeats, George Barker, and the Idea of Ireland', *Yeats Annual* No. 3, edited by Warwick Gould (Basingstoke: Macmillan, 1985), pp. 133–44.

3 See especially Kristeva's *Revolution in Poetic Language*, translated by Margaret Waller (New York: Columbia University Press, 1984), p. 24, for a full discussion of the possibilities for this reinscription in modern poetry.

4 *After Babel: Aspects of Language and Translation* (Oxford: Oxford University Press, 1975), p. 28.

5 *Positions*, translated by Alan Bass (Chicago: University of Chicago Press, 1981), p. 20. In reflecting upon his own translations of Yeats, the French poet Yves Bonnefoy illustrates this difficulty by quoting the opening of the last stanza of 'Among School Children', and comments: 'c'est là, à mon sens, un des ces points où la pensée – puisque, à l'évidence, il y en a une – passe par l'ellipse ou l'ambiguïté sans pour autant être détrônée au profit de la masse de signfiants qui certes l'entoure et l'assaille; d'où la nécessité pour le traducteur d'intervenir, sinon il laisserait se défaire les équilibres du texte. De quoi s'agit-il, dans ce cas? D'une ambiguïté qui est dans le mot "labour" . . .' (*Quarante-cinq poèmes* (Paris: Gallimard, 1993), p. 29).

6 *The Letters of W.B. Yeats*, edited by Allan Wade (Rupert Hart-Davis, London, 1954), p. 608.

7 'W.B. Yeats', *The Avoidance of Literature: Collected Essays* (Manchester: Carcanet, 1978), p. 259. As early as the 1930s, English critics had been distilling away the Irish element in Yeats's work. F.R. Leavis, writing in 1932, argued that 'Mr. Yeats starts in the English tradition, but he is from the outset an

Irish poet.... [His] Irishness is more than a matter of using Irish themes and an Irish atmosphere.' While recognizing that these interests give Yeats's poetry 'as it were, an external validation', they seem also curiously bound up in Leavis's mind with Yeats's hermeticism. Yeats is ultimately dismissed therefore as unable to become truly modern (*New Bearings in English Poetry: A Study of the Contemporary Situation* (London: Chatto & Windus), pp. 34–8). Leavis increasingly found Yeats's work empty. In his reviews of both *The Winding Stair* and *Last Poems*, he lamented their lack of 'the world of sense, the pride and beauty of life' or 'the fullness of life' (*A Selection from Scrutiny*, Volume I (Cambridge: Cambridge University Press, 1968), pp. 93–6.

8   *On the Name*, edited by Thomas Dutoit (Stanford: Stanford University Press, 1995), p. 119.

9   'Persuasions to Rejoice', *Auden Studies 2: W.H. Auden, 'The Language of Learning and the Language of Love'*, edited by Katherine Bucknell and Nicholas Jenkins (Oxford: Oxford University Press, 1994), pp. 155–63.

10   See Richard Ellmann, *Yeats: The Man and the Masks* (Harmondsworth: Penguin, 1987 edition), pp. 19–21, for discussion of this shared belief between father and son.

11   *The English Auden: Poems, Essays and Dramatic Writings 1927–1939*, edited by Edward Mendelson (London: Faber, 1977), p. 393.

12   Auden's biographer, Humphrey Carpenter, has related the inclusion of section II of the poem in the *London Mercury* version of April (it had been absent on first publication in *The New Republic* of 8 March) to Auden's having spoken at a dinner to raise money for refugees of the Spanish Civil War. Auden's supreme success as a public orator at this event made him feel 'just covered with dirt afterwards', as he wrote in a letter at the time, and he vowed 'never, *never*' to speak again at a public meeting. Carpenter concludes 'This decision was reflected in the lines he now added to his poem about Yeats.... In these lines, all Auden's attempts during the previous ten years to involve his poetry in politics and society were categorically rejected.' (*W.H. Auden: A Biography*, London: George Allen & Unwin, 1981, p. 256).

13   '... it is safe to say, I think, that the political events which took place in Ireland from 1916 to 1922 were a contributing cause' to the 'astonishing' and continuing 'increase in power' in Yeats's later work. 'Yeats is probably the only poet in this century who has written great poetry on political subjects.' Further, and in some contradiction to his conclusions on diction in the 1939 elegiac essay, Auden seeks to excuse Yeats's anti-democratic views by saying that, as a poet, Yeats's primary concern was with aesthetics. 'Democracy has many virtues, but aesthetic appeal is hardly one of them.' A poet might convince himself that it is 'the least vicious form of government, but his heart will not exactly glow at the idea'. '"I Am of Ireland"', review of Allen Wade's *Letters of W.B. Yeats*, *The New Yorker*, Vol. XXXI, No. 5, March 19, 1955, pp. 134, 137.

14   *The English Auden*, p. 242.

15   Simon Dentith has argued that Auden's style and generic choices have much in common with suburban poetry of the Thirties ('Thirties Poetry and the Landscape of Suburbia', *Rewriting the Thirties: Modernism and After*, edited by Keith Williams and Steven Matthews (Harlow: Longman, 1997), p. 116). Yeats himself associated Irish (and all) towns with the mechanistic gen-

eralizing urge in modern life which he despised. 'Life is never the same twice and cannot be generalized,' as he wrote to his father in 1909 (*The Letters of W.B. Yeats*, p. 534).

16 *The Dyer's Hand and other essays* (London: Faber, 1963), p. 71. The 'Defence Counsel''s choice of *The Winding Stair* as exemplar of these virtues is surprising. Its opening elegy for Eva Gore-Booth and Con Markievicz describes 'All the folly of a fight / With a common wrong or right'. In 'Blood and the Moon', Yeats wrote one of his most politically extremist poems – even called by Donald Davie 'A Fascist Poem' (*Trying to Explain*, Manchester: Carcanet, 1980). In 'Coole Park, 1929' and 'Coole Park and Ballylee, 1931', he wrote some of his most 'feudal' works, to adopt a word from the 'Public Prosecutor''s vocabulary. But the collection also includes 'Remorse for Intemperate Speech', which offers as an excuse for such 'folly' Yeats's Irish provenance; 'Vacillation', which shows his constant state of uncertainty around his principal concerns; and 'The Choice', whose recognition of the need to decide between 'perfection of the life, or of the work' is, as I will show in this chapter, integral to Auden's own hesitations around, and fascinations with, these matters across his career (*CP*, pp. 233, 237, 242–5, 254, 249, 246).

17 Quoted by Carpenter, op. cit., p. 416, from a 1964 letter to Stephen Spender. Carpenter sees the rejection by Auden of his poem 'September 1, 1939' from his 1966 edition of *Collected Shorter Poems* as validation of this dismissal of an important early influence. In 'On "A Change of Air" ', Auden himself noted that 'It was not the fault of Yeats or Rilke that I allowed myself to be seduced by them into writing poems which were false to my personal and poetic nature.' (*The Contemporary Poet as Artist and Critic*, edited by Anthony Ostroff, Boston: Little, Brown and Company, 1964, p. 185). John Fuller, in *W.H. Auden: a Commentary* (London: Faber 1998) and Anthony Hecht in *The Hidden Law: the Poetry of W.H. Auden* (Cambridge, Massachusetts: Harvard University Press, 1993) make little of Yeats's influence in the later work of Auden. Fuller only gives a couple of references to him in Auden's work post-1939. Edward Callan goes so far as to claim that 'In the second half of his life Auden developed an almost obsessive fear of the danger of Yeats's kind of outlook... [with] the hardening of his conviction that the greatest threats to individual freedom in the modern world – the Utopias of left and right – were a direct legacy of the Romantic outlook on which Yeats prided himself' (*Auden: A Carnival of Intellect*, New York: Oxford University Press, 1983, pp. 145–6).

18 Harold Bloom, *A Map of Misreading* (New York: Oxford University Press, 1975), p. 3; *The Anxiety of Influence: A Theory of Poetry* (Oxford: Oxford University Press, 1973), p. 68.

19 Seamus Deane, amongst many others, has explored the notion of the Irish as an alluring yet threatening 'other' for the English in his 'Civilians and Barbarians', *Ireland's Field Day* (London: Hutchinson, 1985), pp. 33–42.

20 The Eliotic nature of Auden's vocabulary here, leaning as it does in its notion of integration and dissociation upon the vocabulary of Eliot's 'The Metaphysical Poets' essay, is not alien to Yeats's own sense of traditional possibility. He had discovered similar qualities of integration to those Eliot later famously advertised in Donne, when reading that poet in 1912 (see Roy Foster *W.B. Yeats A Life. I The Apprentice Mage* (Oxford: Oxford University Press, 1997), p. 468).

21 *The Kenyon Review*, 10, Spring 1948, pp. 187–92 *passim*. In *New Year Letter*, written soon after Auden's arrival in the States, literary forebears are imagined in a context similar to that of the 'debate' in 'The Public v. the Late Mr. W.B. Yeats'; they are a 'summary tribunal which / In a perpetual session sits'. The belated poet is forced before that court to answer the Lear-like rhetorical question 'as he faces them alone, / O who can show convincing proof / That he is worthy of their love?' Yeats was not, however, sitting on the bench on 1 January 1940, although the poem rehearses the yearning for an alternative society where (in the terms of this poem) 'form is truth... content love, / Its pluralist interstices / The homes of happiness and peace' which harmonize with the invocation to Yeats in the elegy (*Collected Poems*, edited by Edward Mendelson (London: Faber, 1991 edition), pp. 202–3, 240). Auden's views in 'Yeats As An Example' are consonant with the role that Yeats played for Auden, MacNeice, and the other Thirties poets during the '30s itself. In 'Yeats and the Poets of the Thirties', Samuel Hynes has stressed the importance of his work as a model for later poets writing 'political poetry', i.e. in Spender's phrase 'poetry concerned with the individual faced with historical crisis'. Hynes also insightfully considers the relation of these poets to history in comparison to Yeats's, and concludes that theirs is also a 'politics of tragedy', an 'elegiac' history which 'expresses personal feelings of present loss' (*Modern Irish Literature: Essays in Honor of William York Tindall*, edited by Raymond J. Porter and James D. Brophy (New York: Iona College Press), 1972, pp. 5, 15).

22 *Recognitions: a Study in Poetics* (Oxford: Clarendon Press, 1990), p. 33.

23 In *Auden*, Richard Davenport-Hines dates his subject's reconversion to Christianity to a visit to a German-speaking movie house in the Yorkville district of Manhattan in November 1939; whenever a Pole appeared on the screen the audience shouted 'Kill them!' After this, Auden was 'filled with a sense of evil that was irresistible to any secular power' (London: Minerva, 1996, pp. 200–1).

24 *Collected Poems*, p. 242.

25 *The English Auden*, pp. 243, 206.

26 Samuel Hynes (op. cit., p. 7) has suggested that Auden's use of the term parable to describe 'what art really is' in his Thirties essays like 'Psychology and Art Today' itself derives from the example of Yeats poems like 'The Second Coming' – called a parable by MacNeice in his book *Yeats*. In his Sixties talk 'On "A Change of Air"', Auden described a parable-poem as one to which 'the answer to the question "Who is the *You* of the poem?" is... whoever happens to be reading the poem' (op. cit., p. 183).

27 'The relationship between sign and symbol... is one of mutual obliteration; hence the temptation to confuse and forget the distinction between them.... The art, the *techné*, of writing... can only be preserved in the figural mode of the symbol, the very mode it has to do away with if it is to occur at all. ('Sign and Symbol in Hegel's *Aesthetics*', *Critical Inquiry*, Volume 8 No. 4, Summer 1982, pp. 770–73).

28 *Modernist Poetics of History: Pound, Eliot and the Sense of the Past* (Princeton: Princeton University Press, 1987), pp. 1–44.

29 *Collected Poems*, pp. 641, 622, 657.

30 Ibid., pp. 598, 611–12, 597.

31 *Secondary Worlds* (London: Faber, 1968), pp. 74, 113, 118. Interestingly, early in the lectures, Auden considers again the undeniable appeal for the isolated artist of playing a role in the public world. (p. 31) In the 'Caliban to His Audience' section of *The Sea and the Mirror*, the speaker wittily dismisses art's 'higher' claims, and indicts its neglect of the personal quotidian life (*Collected Poems*, pp. 433–5). This does not, however, prevent Caliban from being susceptible to a vision of 'Wholly Other Life' and 'rejoice in the perfected Work that is not ours' at the end of his speech (ibid., p. 444).

32 Ibid., p. 603.

33 *Eminent Domain: Yeats among Wilde, Joyce, Pound, Eliot & Auden* (New York: Oxford University Press, 1967), p. 112. The Auden quotation is from *The Dyer's Hand*, p. 19. This divorce between art and life is, for Auden, what makes poetry's religious witness 'indirect and negative': 'if the Word was indeed made flesh, then it is demanded of men that their words and their lives be in concord. . . . The poet is not there to convert the world.' (*Secondary Worlds*, pp. 118–19) This, and other statements about the 'secondary world' of poetry (such as that it 'resists the question of sincerity: the words mean neither more nor less than they say' (p. 42)), enter important caveats into Auden's notion earlier in the 1960s that Yeats's example, amongst others, seduced him into falsehoods about his 'personal and poetic nature'. As he himself admits here, what might be *personally* untrue is not necessarily *poetically* so, if the poet is not aware of the untruth at the time of writing.

34 W.H. Auden and Chester Kallmann, *Libretti*, edited by Edward Mendelson (London: Faber, 1993), p. 246. In his Introduction to the volume, Mendelson argues that *some* of the details of the artist-genius Mittenhofer's life indicate that the collaborators were also thinking of Auden himself as a model for him. The relation of poet to his patroness carries echoes of Auden's with Caroline Newton; the love triangle echoes his situation with Kallmann himself (p. xxvii).

35 Ibid., p. 218. Auden, of course, valued the retention of traditional poetic form, number and rhyme across his life, as did Yeats, whose deployment of it we have seen Auden admire in 'Yeats As An Example'. In his talk 'On "A Change of Air"', Auden argued using another model that 'I want to write poetry as Robert Frost defines it, namely, untranslatable speech.' Poetry makes us aware of 'the rhythmical value of the syllables or of each word as a unique entity with unique overtones' (op. cit., p. 185).

36 Op. cit., p. 242.

37 Auden's later rebuke to that element within Yeats's Romantic mythology which the 'Defence Counsel' in 'The Public v. Mr. W.B. Yeats' had sought to argue away, the hero, is everywhere evident and undeniable. Simeon gives the Christian basis for the rebuke in *For the Time Being*, the 'Christmas Oratorio' of 1941–2: 'Because in him the Flesh is united to the Word without magical transformation, Imagination is redeemed from promiscuous fornication with her own images. The tragic conflict of Virtue with Necessity is no longer confined to the Exceptional Hero; for disaster is not the impact of a curse upon a few great families, but issues continually from the hubris of every tainted will.' (*Collected Poems*, pp. 388–9).

38 *Secondary Worlds*, p. 102.

39 Earlier in his poetry, Auden had not totally ruled out the attraction of those things which form part of symbolist (and Yeatsian) stage machineries. In 'Nocturne', for example, a poem probably from 1951, 'my heart' immediately responds to a sudden appearance of the moon with the self-injunction '"Adore Her, Mother, Virgin, Muse"', while the split-self's 'mind' dismisses such afflatus, calling the moon instead 'That bunch of barren craters'. In a dialectical resolution, however, the moon is prosopopeiacally 'supposed' as assuming a very human face with 'Features I've actually seen', which might serve as – in very inflected Yeatsian terms – an anti-type, 'A counter-image, anyway, / To balance with its lack of weight / My world, the private motor-car / And all the engines of the State.' (*Collected Poems*, pp. 586–7)

40 Ibid, pp. 541–2.

41 *The Hidden Law*, p. 304.

42 *Dissemination*, translated with an introduction by Barbara Johnson (London: The Athlone Press, 1993), p. 181.

43 *Collected Poems*, pp. 618–715.

44 *The English Auden*, p. 370.

45 From the publication of these two books in one volume (Harmondsworth: Penguin, 1992), p. 318.

46 Ellmann, 'Joyce and Yeats' *Kenyon Review*, Volume VII, No. 4, Winter 1945, p. 636, and *Eminent Domain*, p. 52. In an early essay, 'Professor Heller and the Boots', Davie had argued – much as Auden had – that Yeats was a 'great occasional poet'. But Davie's sense of the occasional poet was different from Auden's use of the term to cover great public and personal events: 'even his mythopoeic poems are drawing continually upon common experience, on whims, on quirks and oddities like the girl doing a tinker's shuffle picked up upon the street, or on things he merely *happened* to see or to remember, like Lois Fuller's Chinese dancers' (*The Poet in the Imaginary Museum: essays of two decades*, edited by Barry Alpert (Manchester: Carcanet, 1977), p. 23).

47 *Purity of Diction in English Verse*, op. cit., p. 10.

48 *The Poet in the Imaginary Museum*, pp. 128–31.

49 London: Routledge & Kegan Paul, pp. 178–81.

50 'Landscape As Poetic Focus', *The Poet in the Imaginary Museum*, p. 169; *Thomas Hardy and British Poetry* (London: Routledge & Kegan Paul, 1973), p. 103. In this latter book, Davie discusses the British intelligensia on pp. 91–3 in terms that resonate also through his argument in the essay 'A Fascist Poem: Yeats's "Blood and the Moon"'. The essay seeks to maintain that Yeats's extremist tendencies date from at least ten years before *Last Poems*: 'the poem surely is an extreme formulation of the anguish felt by the intellectual under the repressive tolerance (as we used to call it some years ago) which is wished upon him by modern societies such as the British and American'. Yeats's wish, early and late, to 'be *held responsible*' for the consequences of his own utterances, as in 'Man and the Echo', is a mark of the real detachment of the intellectual from the life of his or her times, as Davie sees it (*Trying to Explain*, Manchester: Carcanet, 1980, p. 172).

51 Op. cit., pp. 71, 64. Philip Larkin had of course renounced the influence of a Vernon Watkins-mediated Yeatsian poetics upon himself in his 'Introduction to *The North Ship*' (*Required Writing: Miscellaneous Pieces 1955–1982* (London:

Faber, 1983), pp. 29–30). Strikingly, two Irish poets, Seamus Heaney and Tom Paulin, have argued that Yeatsian characteristics *are* present in even the late work. See Heaney's 'The Main of Light', *The Government of the Tongue* (London: Faber, 1988), pp. 15–22 and Paulin's 'She did Not Change: Philip Larkin', *Minotaur: Poetry and the Nation State* (London: Faber, 1992), pp. 233–51.

52 *Collected Poems* (Manchester: Carcanet, 1990), p. 19.

53 Ibid., pp. 27, 41, 26.

54 In 'Yeats, Berkeley and Romanticism', Davie argues that it was the older Yeats, affected by the Irish philosopher's writings, who came to reject the younger Yeats's Romanticism, which had revealed itself in his perpetual arguments with himself and origination of the compensatory notion of the mask. The later Yeats could not, however, ultimately subdue the earlier. A poem like 'Among School Children', Davie argues, recognizes that such Romanticism is an inevitable part of humanity (*Older Masters*, Manchester: Carcanet, 1992, pp. 133–9).

55 Op. cit., p. 32.

56 *Yeats and English Renaissance Literature*, by Wayne K. Chapman (Basingstoke: Macmillan, 1991), p. 127.

57 Op.cit., p. 71.

58 Davie's 'Remembering the Thirties' contains his most explicit statement of a grudging and historically-compromised dismissal of that heroism Yeats held to: 'yet it may be better, if we must, / To praise a stance impressive and absurd / Than not to see the hero for the dust.' (ibid., p. 35).

59 Op. cit., p. 52.

60 Ibid., pp. 85–6.

61 Ibid., pp. 111, 286.

62 Ibid., p. 318. Davie's frequent abstracting, surveying perspective across his career, from several of the poems I have quoted here to the later 'Ox-bow', might show the influence of that source which he identifies behind Auden's frequent use of the same perspective – Hardy, with his 'hawk's vision' (*Thomas Hardy and British Poetry*, p. 122). Yet this is a perspective shared by Yeats also, from 'An Irish Airman Foresees His Death' to his poem 'The Hawk'.

63 Op. cit., pp. 216, 376.

64 'My Life Up To Now', *The Occasions of Poetry: Essays in Criticism and Autobiography* (London: Faber, 1982), p. 177. Gunn is commenting on the frequent use of the word 'will' in the collection.

65 'Cambridge in the Fifties', ibid., p. 162. The influences behind the theory of pose are mixed in Gunn's memory of them: 'the dramatics of John Donne, somewhat . . . Yeats's theory of masks, and most strongly . . . the behaviour of Stendhal's heroes' (pp. 161–2). More recently in interview, though, Gunn has described the importance of discovering Yeats's work during his undergraduate years: 'It was extraordinary because we'd always understood that Eliot was the king of the world, that Eliot was *the* modern poet. There was no possible rival, and suddenly here was somebody as good or better, it seemed to us, someone with a lot more rigor, a bigger range, and more exciting.' ('An Anglo-American Poet: Interview with Jim Powell', *Shelf Life: Essays, Memoirs and an Interview*, London: Faber, 1994, p. 223).

66 See *Yeats and the Poetry of Death: Elegy, Self-Elegy and the Sublime*, by Jahan Ramanazani (New Haven: Yale University Press, 1990), pp. 6, 15, 46, 186.

67   Patrick J. Keane has linked the self-delight of the airman to the 'tragic joy' of the later poems, and sets it in a line of Romantic heroism from Byron's 'Manfred' to Shelley's 'Alastor' and Tennyson's 'Ulysses' (*Yeats's Interactions With Tradition* (Columbia: University of Missouri Press, 1987), pp. 243–82).

68   *Collected Poems* (London: Faber, 1994), pp. 54–5. The resolution to this poem seems to consolidate the opening poem of the collection, 'On the Move', in which the bikers' presumption that 'Much that is natural, to the will must yield' is seen as 'a part solution' before, in another turn, acknowledging that in their situation, 'At worst, one is in motion; and at best, / Reaching no absolute, in which to rest, / One is always nearer by not keeping still' (ibid., p. 40). The elaborately-rhymed eight-line stanzas of this setpiece poem echo the use of similar forms in late Yeats; it is a form which Gunn himself has several times taken up again. 'The Inherited Estate' in this collection makes most obvious use of the form Yeats deployed in his Coole Park poems, even enjoining its addressee to carve in a tree 'names / That swell with time', much as Yeats and others did at Lady Gregory's estate. See also 'In Santa Maria del Popolo' (p. 93), 'Venetian Blind' (p. 392) and 'The Differences' (p. 413).

69   Ibid., p. 70. The rich tension of Gunn's ambivalent feelings towards Winters initially centred upon his mentor's systematic demolition of Yeats's work in class, since 'I adored Yeats and was grateful to a career which had seemed exemplary to me in showing how a spirit of romanticism could survive, self-correcting and self-nourishing, into the twentieth century.' Gunn equates 'romanticism' here with an 'immersion in the life of the senses', and a Keatsian sense that 'nothing ever becomes real until it is experienced' – a temperamental difference to Winters, who felt that sensory experience 'destroy[s] the power of discrimination' ('On A Drying Hill: Yvor Winters', *Shelf Life*, pp. 200, 210). Yeats, as my opening chapter shows, would himself have balked at Gunn's equation, but it is one that he has continued with. In reviewing the last collection by Robert Duncan, Gunn sees Yeats as a vital 'link in the long chain' which carries a notion of Romantic impulse from Coleridge through to the 'open form' poetics which Duncan, following Charles Olsen, found in the work of Pound and Williams. In discussing a poem like 'In Memory of Major Robert Gregory', however, Gunn typically enters the note of 'pose' or Winterian 'Rule' against such a suggestion of pure energy, saying that Yeats's submission to impulse there, as elsewhere, is, 'characteristically, a calculated dramatic effect' ('The High Road: A Last Collection', ibid., p. 131).

70   'My Life Up to Now, op. cit., p. 179. In his essay 'Hardy and the Ballads', Gunn had seemed to find the quality of bombast (which he there calls 'rhetoric') particularly in the 'minor works' of Yeats: Hardy 'is never rhetorical' (ibid., p. 104).

71   'The Geyser', op. cit., p. 241.

72   *Double Lyric: Divisiveness and Communal Creativity in Recent English Poetry* (London: Routledge & Kegan Paul, 1980), p. 144.

73   Op. cit., p. 274.

74   Ibid., pp. 384, 231–2.

75   Ibid., pp. 160, 163. Such a wariness at the excesses involved in being 'out of nature' presumably grants him 'Uncle Willie' Yeats's ticket to the rumbunc-

tiously and outrageously gay phallic party in 'Punch Rubicundus': 'The surprises of age are no surprise. I am / like one who lurks at a urinal all afternoon. ... / But this *can't* be Byzantium' (p. 398).

76 Ibid., pp. 330–1.

77 *The Occasions of Poetry*, p. 186.

78 Op. cit., p. 176.

79 Ibid., pp. 423–4. Gunn's poems of empathy for derelicts in the city have always been marked by the way they allow several planes of diction and understanding to knock against each other in ways that discover a grace and beauty, however restricted, however hampered. In the group of such poems gathered in part 3 of *The Man With Night Sweats*, we find Tow Head in 'Skateboard' 'Wearing dirty white/in dishevelment as delicate / as the falling draperies / on a dandyish / Renaissance saint.' (p. 433); in 'Outside the Diner' we see an alcoholic sleeping it off in the back of a wrecked auto, 'beard blinded by sleep / turned toward the light.' (p. 435).

80 'Landscape in Wordsworth and Yeats', *The Rhetoric of Romanticism* (New York: Columbia University Press, pp. 133–43).

81 'Ted Hughes and *Crow*' an interview with Ekbert Faas in Faas's *Ted Hughes: the Unaccommodated Universe* (Santa Barbara: Black Sparrow Press, 1980), pp. 200–204 *passim*. In expanding upon his comments on 'The Second Coming' later, Hughes again linked the Rough Beast in the poem to Blake's 'Tyger', while bringing out the political complexities of the piece as harbinger of an Irish nationalist revolution. Hughes is, however, concerned to assert the Rough Beast's place within a 'larger "sacred" mythos based largely on occultism', and also to defend his own mythological poetry in this vein from any charge of 'propaganda-like explicit political and philosophical exhortations' (*Winter Pollen: Occasional Prose*, edited by William Scammell (London: Faber, 1994), pp. 264–6).

82 'Crow Blacker Than Ever' (London: Faber, 1974 edition), p. 69.

83 *Winter Pollen*, p. 241. The Trickster shares something of the quality of The Hanged Man in Leonard Baskin's designs as Hughes sees them, 'the gallows joke to end all gallows jokes' (ibid., p. 98).

84 Ibid., pp. 43, 70–2. Hughes's poems on the War are largely gathered in *Wolfwatching* (London: Faber, 1989), which includes tributes to both his father and his Uncle Walt who were wounded in the conflict as well as a sense of the continuity of its aftermath: in 'Dust As We Are', Hughes combs the hair of his 'post-war father'; 'I divined / ...The fragility of skull. And I filled / With his knowledge.' (p. 11).

85 See Yeats, *E&I*, pp. 255, 523. Hughes's identification of 'the great theme' in Shakespeare's collected works as that between a dying, medieval Catholicism and an emergent puritanism meant, he claims, that each individual at the time felt a Civil War raging inside them: 'They could create a provisional *persona*, an emergency self, to deal with the crisis....And this is where Shakespeare's hero comes staggering in. Mother-wet, weak-legged, horrified at the task, boggling – Hamlet.' (*Winter Pollen*, pp. 110–1). The appeal for Hughes of such literature of conflictual historical crises was more recently extended in his *Tales from Ovid*, written at a time, he says in his Introduction, when 'The obsolete paraphernalia of the old official religion were lying in heaps.... The mythic plane, so to speak, had been defrocked. At the same

time, perhaps one could say as a result, the Empire was flooded with ecstatic cults. For all its Augustan stability, it was at sea in hysteria and despair.... The tension between these extremes, and occasionally their collision, can be felt in these tales.' (London: Faber, 1997, pp. x–xi).

86 New York: The Viking Press, p. 44.

87 *Winter Pollen*, pp. 58, 270–1. The latter passages come in an essay on 'The Poetic Self' in Eliot, but, since Eliot's tribe has no national basis, but is 'all Western man', Hughes seems to be arguing, his shamanism is less straightforward than that of the firmly centred Yeats's.

88 *The Hawk in the Rain* (London: Faber, 1957), p. 14.

89 Yeats, *Collected Plays* (Basingstoke: Macmillan, 1977), p. 214; Hughes, op. cit., p. 11. Other poems in this first collection of Hughes's seem directly related to Yeats's manner and themes. 'The Conversion of the Reverend Skinner' is a reworking of the Crazy Jane poems; 'The Ancient Heroes and the Bomber Pilot' seems to bring together the Irish Airman with the heroes of the Cuchulain cycle, suggesting that the remote killing of modern warfare is 'cold and small' compared with their epic feats (p. 57).

90 London: Faber, pp. 29 and unnumbered. Hughes uses his lengthy prose note to the masque to re-explore his sense of England's century as shadowed by the First World War (pp. 58–60).

91 London: Faber, 1977, pp. 13, 173.

92 Op. cit., p. 208. Earlier in the interview he had in this vein questioned the 'mysterious business' of literary influence: 'Sometimes it's just a few words that open up a whole prospect.... Then again the influences that really count are most likely not literary at all. Maybe it would be best of all to have no influences.' (p. 203)

93 In interview, Hughes has suggested that, having initially been preoccupied by Kipling's metrics, 'I met Yeats via the third part of his poem "The Wanderings of Oisin", which was in the kind of meter I was looking for. Yeats sucked me in through the Irish folklore and myth and the occult business' ('The Art of Poetry LXXI', *Paris Review* 134, Spring 1995, p. 61). From the outset, Hughes deployed lines extended beyond the length of the English pentameter in his poetry, such as those in that section of Yeats's early epic. The possibilities of variously stressing such lines, as well as of variously breaking and dividing the line itself, might also play a part in the frequent interchange of long and short lines later in his career: see, for one instance, 'It was a screeching woman and he had her by the throat – / He held it // A gone steering wheel bouncing towards a cliff edge – / He held it // A trunk of jewels dragging into a black depth – he held it', from 'Truth Kills Everybody' in *Crow* (p. 83).

94 London: Faber, 1979, p. 56. In his essay 'Laureate of the Free Market? Ted Hughes', Tom Paulin notes several times the relationship between Hughes's outlook and Yeats's, before seeking to describe the Hughes reading voice: 'This is shaman-chant, tribal music, but wildly eclectic and displaced.... Hughes's reading voice absorbs and dominates, gathers his readers into himself and won't let them escape.... His poems are meant to happen in the moment; they are one-off oral events, speech acts which distrust the fixity of print.' (*Minotaur*, p. 268). Nicholas Bishop has sought to map Hughes's remarks in the Faas interview about the inner and outer movements of the imagination and about Yeats onto Hughes's own career, seeing *Crow, Gaudete*

and *Cave Birds* as moves into the self and *Remains of Elmet* a move into an outer history (*Re-Making Poetry: Ted Hughes and a New Critical Psychology*, Hemel Hempstead: Harvester Wheatsheaf, 1991, p. 204). As I have hoped to show, however, Hughes is a poet who starts where later Yeats left off, with these elements all interchangeable, though with one perhaps more to the fore at any time.

95 London: Faber, 1998, p. 126.

96 *Agenda*, Vol. 9 No. 4–Vol. 10 No. 1, Autumn–Winter 1971–2, p. 14, 19, 21, 22–3. More recently, Hill has doubted the value of the later work of T.S. Eliot by taking up the issue of 'pitch' once more and setting it against 'tone', 'the style . . . of address to his audience.' 'Pitch' involves us in the 'sensuous interest' of words, whereby we discover their 'centre of gravity' and we can see again the conscious mind enacting its operations. Eliot, according to Hill, declines in *Four Quartets* into 'tone'; the style of his address to an audience has lost its centre and direction, and run with the drift of expectation and the times rather than redeeming them ('Dividing Legacies', *Agenda*, Vol. 34 No. 2, Summer 1996, pp. 19, 21–2).

97 'C.H. Sisson', *PN Review*, No. 39, Vol. 11 No. 1, March 1984, p. 13, 12.

98 *Collected Poems* (Harmondsworth: Penguin, 1985), pp. 184–5.

99 'Gurney's "Hobby" ', *Essays in Criticism*, Vol. XXXIV No. 2, April 1984, pp. 99, 120.

100 Op. cit., 184, 187, 195, 183. In his essay on Péguy which appears with the poem, Hill says his work is 'my homage to the triumph of his "defeat"'. (p. 207) Jahan Ramanazani has traced a twentieth-century transformation in the genre of elegy back to Yeats, who was first to point out the 'personal limitations' of the person being elegized – as in his comments on the dead political martyrs in 'Easter 1916', for example. This innovation was picked up by Auden throughout his career, but is prominent from his early elegy on Yeats himself, Ramanazani argues, where the dead poet is, as we have seen, described as 'silly' (*Poetry of Mourning: The Modern Elegy from Hardy to Heaney*, Chicago: The University of Chicago Press, 1994, p. 183).

101 See the concluding essay, 'Our Word is Our Bond' in *The Lords of Limit: Essays on Literature and Ideas* (London: André Deutsch, 1984), and *The Enemy's Country: Words, Contexture and Other Circumstances of Language* (Oxford: Clarendon Press, 1991). Henry Hart's conclusion, derived from his reading of Hill's 1971 Yeats essay, that 'In the heyday of the Movement, Hill wanted to write poems somewhere between the traditional syntax of Yeats and the dislocated syntax of Pound, the purified diction of Wordsworth and the linguistic density of Joyce', seems both historically tendentious and also highly questionable with regard to the poetry itself. Hill's 'dislocations' have never been as extreme as Pound's, which after all emerged in a poetics of juxtaposition, of 'setting planes in relation'. Moreover, Yeats's syntax was itself capable of 'dislocation', or of sudden changes in direction, as Hill seems to be acknowledging with his citation of the last two lines of 'The Second Coming' in the essay itself.

102 Op. cit., pp. 139, 143–4, 151.

103 *The Lords of Limit*, p. 3.

104 Op. cit., p. 146.

105   Hill's selection of epigraph for 'The Pentecost Castle' sequence also makes it remote from its original place in Yeats's cultural and historical ambition. The original phrase about the intractable double-bind of desire and possession is followed by a concluding sentence: 'Because of this we long for an age which has the unity which Plato somewhere defined as sorrowing and rejoicing over the same things.' (*The Letters of W.B. Yeats*, pp. 810–11).
106   Op. cit., pp. 15, 72, 187, 191, 185, 61.
107   In Hill's version of Ibsen's *Brand*, the protagonist diagnoses the nature of what he perceives as the sickness of his society: 'this hideous age / ordains blood and iron . . . / The best go. The worst wring their hands, / groaning, "The age, the age demands!"' (Harmondsworth: Penguin, 1996, p. 160). While not being out of sympathy with at least the latter part of Brand's assertion (he titled a dismissive review of a biography of Pound 'The Age Demanded (Again)', *Agenda* Vol. 26, No. 3, Autumn 1988), Hill's version is alert to the callousness and potential farcicality of the unyielding wilfulness of Brand in the play, as in the final moments when an avalanche is about to bury him and he cries out desperately, aggressively and childishly, 'Why is man's own proud will his curse? / Answer!' (p. 161).
108   Harmondsworth: Penguin, 1996, pp. 2, 29, 70, 39.
109   Yeats, as exemplary poet of ageing, figures in the work of the Welsh poet Dylan Thomas and of his friend Vernon Watkins (the introducer of Larkin to Yeats's work). Thomas's famous lament 'Do Not Go Gentle Into That Good Night' deploys a late-Yeatsian idiom ('Grave men, near death, who see with blinding sight / Blind eyes could blaze like meteors and be gay, / Rage, rage against the dying of the light' (*The Poems*, edited by Daniel Jones, London: Dent, 1971, p. 208)). Watkins claimed in a 1966 lecture that Yeats was more important to him than any other poet because 'he had shown me . . . how a lyric poet should grow old' (*Poetry Wales*, Volume 12, No. 4, Spring 1977, p. 64). Watkins's poem 'Yeats in Dublin: in memory of W.B. Yeats', recalling a visit paid to the poet in his old age, reveals the dearth that he felt was all he could offer before the resurrectionary power of his host: 'To that broken vision / What could we bring, / blinded by the shadow / Of the mounting wing? / Had he not loosed the tongue of dust / And made the dead lips sing?' (*Collected Poems* (Ipswich: Golgonooza Press, 1986), p. 67).
110   Harmondsworth: Penguin, 1999, pp. 62, 36.
111   As Paul de Man has phrased it in 'The Dead-End of Formalist Criticism', *Blindness & Insight*, pp. 232–4, 244.

4   Possession and Dispossession: Yeats and American Poetry John Crowe Ransom, Allen Tate, John Berryman, Robert Lowell, James Merrill, Adrienne Rich, Sylvia Plath, Jorie Graham

1   'Yeats in Theory', *Post-Structuralist Readings of English Poetry*, edited by Richard Machin and Christopher Norris (Cambridge: Cambridge University Press, 1987), p. 366.
2   *The Dream of the Unified Field: Selected Poems* (Manchester: Carcanet, 1996), p. 12.

3   Ibid., p. 94. See also p. 106.
4   *Letters on Poetry from W.B. Yeats to Dorothy Wellesley* (London: Oxford University Press, 1964 edition), p. 22.
5   Op. cit., pp. 186–8, 155.
6   *The Possibilities of Order: Cleanth Brooks and his Work*, edited by Lewis P. Simpson (Baton Rouge: Louisiana State University Press, 1976), p. 118–19.
7   Ibid., pp. 22, 31, 43–4. Brooks and Warren promulgated their notion of the poem as an organism in their 1939 book *Understanding Poetry: An Anthology for College Students* (New York: Holt), which subsequently went through numerous editions. The book uses four poems by Yeats as examples of how to read, with only two from T.S. Eliot, and cites in its introduction Yeats's essay, 'The Symbolism of Poetry', as the source for its doctrine of the organic relation between the different parts of the poem.
8   Paul de Man has offered a critique of the failure of the New Critics to include intentionality in their thinking in two essays reprinted in *Blindness & Insight: Essays in the Rhetoric of Contemporary Criticism* (London: Methuen, 1986 2nd edn) – 'Form and Intent in the American New Criticism' and 'The Dead-End of Formalist Criticism'. See especially pp. 28–31, where de Man points out the totalizing intent of such criticism, its resistance to the *temporality* of literature.
9   Chapel Hill: The University of North Carolina Press, 1939, pp. 173, 176.
10 'The Metaphysical Poets', *Selected Prose of T.S. Eliot*, edited by Frank Kermode (London: Faber, 1975), p. 64; op. cit., p. 62. Wayne K. Chapman, in his *Yeats and English Renaissance Literature* (Basingstoke: Macmillan, 1991), discusses the significance of Donne for Yeats, and sees his views on him as in many ways premonitory of Eliot's more famous statements. Brooks's discussion of Yeats continued in similar terms through *The Well Wrought Urn: Studies in the Structure of Poetry* (1947), *The Hidden God: Studies in Hemingway, Faulkner, Yeats, Eliot and Warren* (1963) and *A Shaping Joy: Studies in the Writer's Craft* (1971), which takes its title from Yeats's essay 'Poetry and Tradition'.(*E&I*, p. 255) For a discussion of Brooks's views on Yeats, see Mark Royden Winchell, *Cleanth Brooks and the Rise of Modern Criticism* (Charlottesville: University of Virginia Press, 1996).
11 These themes are discussed in essays in the Yeats Special Issue of the Brooks and Warren edited *The Southern Review* (Volume VII, Number 3, Winter 1941). The essay by F.O. Matthiessen, 'The Crooked Road', claims that 'One of the themes [in Yeats] which must possess absorption for Americans is what it means to be a national poet' (p. 456), and traces the emergence in Yeats – especially in poems like 'I am of Ireland' – of a concrete realization of a public poetry which is at one with his personal concerns. Donald Davidson's 'Yeats and the Centaur' discovers a more complex relation between the poet's work and the 'popular lore' of Ireland. John Crowe Ransom's piece, 'The Irish, the Gaelic, the Byzantine', defends the ambition of Yeats in an age where a predominating naturalism is antagonistic to his particular 'unlogical' way of packing together heterogeneous materials (p. 543). (Ransom's argument here is a development of his earlier 'Yeats and his Symbols' in *The Kenyon Review*, Volume I, No. 3, Summer 1939.) Allen Tate's 'Yeats's Romanticism: Notes and Suggestions' again urges us to recognize, despite the arguments of Wilson and Louis MacNeice, that Yeats strove to reunite sensibility and

intellect and that *A Vision* underlies the concrete substance of the later poems. What is interesting is that these key themes are also developed in the essays by younger poet-critics contributing to the Special Issue. Randall Jarrell, in 'The Development of Yeats's Sense of Reality', claims that the cyclic version of history which came to Yeats through *A Vision* enabled him to resolve a split in himself between the city he hated and yet where he was forced to live, and the Sligo of his childhood. Delmore Schwartz, in 'An Unwritten Book', claims that it was the proximity to the people and their speech which Yeats gained through his work at the Abbey Theatre which gave him the idiom and also the fascinating complexity of his later style. 'As expression, Yeats's later poetry suggests the possibility of endless study. ... The metrical mastery which accomplishes so much works through varia- tions of the iambic structure of a complexity which is such that the proper names for such devices do not, so far as I know, exist.' (This essay is reprinted in *Selected Essays of Delmore Schwartz*, edited by Donald A. Dike and David H. Zucker, Chicago: University of Chicago Press, 1970. This passage appears on p. 96). Only R.P. Blackmur, in 'Between Myth and Philosophy: Fragments of W.B. Yeats', counters this unanimous sense of unification, by claiming that Yeats was too ambitious in his 'system', and that he kept coming on things which the system could not explain, so that he could not believe in its power. Yeats was destined to remain an 'ad-libber', a fragmentary master, whom Blackmur sees as, in an Eliotic way, reflecting in his oeuvre the 'intolerable disorder' of the times (p. 424–5). The view expressed by Blackmur in this essay does, however, directly counter that in his 1936 'The Later Poetry of W.B. Yeats', which had spoken in recognizable ways of the 'organic unity' of the best poetry and which also defended the 'major tool of the imagination' represented by Yeats's 'magical' interests within a 'rational, but deliberately incomplete, because progressive, society' (*Language as Gesture: Essays in Poetry* (New York: Harcourt, Brace and Company, 1952, pp. 83, 95).

12 See Paul de Man, 'The Contemporary Criticism of Romanticism', *Romanticism and Contemporary Criticism: The Gauss Seminar and Other Papers*, edited by E.S. Burt, Kevin Newmark and Andrej Warminski (Baltimore: Johns Hopkins University Press, 1993).

13 In an overview of 'The Present State of Poetry', 'In the United States', which Robert Penn Warren contributed to a symposium in *The Kenyon Review* of Autumn 1939, however, he had seemed to doubt the significance of Yeats's influence. 'Because the solution achieved by Yeats is so personal and precar- ious, his effect on contemporary American poetry, though very great, has been less central than that of Eliot; as an immediate effect it has been primarily technical, an effect relating to ideals of style... (Vol. I, No. 4, p. 396). In terms of its potential influence upon subsequent writing in America, then, Warren seems to feel that Yeats's work might prove to manifest an empty formality, and that his actual words and the synthesis offered might not open up to the world in which people were living.

Terence Diggory has argued that Yeats's influence can be seen in the 'Ver- sions of Pastoral' in the poetry of the Agrarians, Tate, Ransom and Warren, as also in their religious affiliations (*Yeats & American Poetry: the Tradition of the Self*, Princeton, New Jersey: Princeton University Press, 1983, pp. 135–56). Diggory's book contains much pioneering work in the field of discussion of

Yeats's influence upon American poetry, to which all subsequent work in the field must be indebted. This chapter, however, takes a different tack to the 'tradition of the self' centred argument of Diggory's book, and also focuses upon poems and some poets who are not considered in his debates.

14 *Dissemination*, translated by Barbara Johnson (London: The Athlone Press, 1993), p. 152.

15 *Selected Poems*, New York: The Ecco Press, 1973, p. 6.

16 Ibid., p. 16.

17 Ibid, p. 42. This seeming ambivalence towards religious compliance does perhaps suggest the reasons why Ransom later discovered more appeal in Yeats's eclectic religious sensibility, as he describes it in 'Yeats and his Symbols', than in Eliot's remaking of Christianity for the modern age. In the 'Preface' to the 'Sixteen Poems in Eight Pairings' section of the 1973 final edition of his *Selected Poems*, Ransom remarks: 'I must have observed several times in print that the man who limits himself, aspiring to true goodliness or saintliness, seems to us very far from possessing that entire vitality which Providence has meant for him. He has not elected the whole joy of life' (p. 110). Yeats's example might have enabled Ransom's poetic both early and late to challenge a monotheistic version of religion which denied that 'joy'. Certainly the most moving elegies by Ransom in his early output set that 'joy' against stasis – 'There was such speed in her little body, / And such lightness in her footfall, / It is no wonder her brown study / Astonishes us all.' ('Elegy for John Whiteside's Daughter', p. 7).

18 'Semi-Centennial' appears on pp. 136–7 of the 1973 *Selected Poems*; 'Birthday of an Aging Seer' on pp. 138–9.

19 'The Irish, the Gaelic, the Byzantine', p. 545.

20 See, for example, 'The arts, I believe, are about to take upon their shoulders the burdens that have fallen from the shoulders of priests...', 'The Autumn of the Body' (1898), *E&I*, p. 193.

21 'Yeats's Romanticism', originally in *The Southern Review* Yeats Special Issue, reprinted in *The Man of Letters in the Modern World: Selected Essays 1928–1955* (Cleveland and New York: The World Publishing Company, 1964 edition), p. 236; 'Poetry Modern and Unmodern' (1968), *Essays of Four Decades* (London: Oxford University Press, 1970), pp. 224, 235.

22 Op. cit., p. 233–4.

23 In resisting Michael Riffaterre's sense of poetry as non-referential in its descriptiveness, de Man turns to the one thing that is certain in the process of reading: 'The materiality (as distinct from the phenomenality)...the unseen...whose existence thus becomes a certain *there* and a certain *then* which can become a *here* and a *now* in the reading "now" taking place, is not the materiality of the mind...but the materiality of an inscription.' ('Hypogram and Inscription', *The Resistance to Theory*, Manchester: Manchester University Press, 1986, p. 51).

24 Diggory, although he does discuss some early poems by Tate, takes the line that Tate only came to value Yeats's work in the Thirties, when Yeats's pastoralism became important for the Agrarian movement, and also at around the time of his elegy for Yeats, 'Winter Mask'. Eliot had been the primary influence upon the young Tate; he was to be replaced by Yeats for the 'generalized pastoral' of poems like the 1936 'Cold Pastoral' (op. cit., p. 146).

Others though have disputed this kind of chronology. R.K. Meiners has written that, although this is not a part of his subject, 'it should be pointed out that Tate's interest in and usage of Yeats does not by any means enter his poetry [as many have claimed] only with the poems in *The Winter Sea*. Howard Nemerov was correct in saying Tate's themes resemble those of Yeats more than any other poet, and even the language of his earlier poetry shows a good deal of affinity with Yeats' (*The Last Alternatives: A Study of the Works of Allen Tate*, New York: Haskell House Publishers, 1973, p. 124).

25   *Collected Poems 1919–1976* (New York: Farrar, Straus, Giroux), 1977, p. 7.

26   Ibid., p. 12.

27   Ibid., p. 22.

28   *The Rhetoric of Romanticism* (New York: Columbia University Press, 1984), p. 6.

29   *This New Yet Unapproachable America: Lectures After Emerson After Wittgenstein* (Albuquerque: Living Batch Press, 1989), pp. 77–118.

30   Ibid., p. 113. Tate had written a curious 'elegy' for a Tennessee version of Yeats much earlier, in his 1923 'Reflections in an Old House', which nativizes the Irish poet's themes (Helen, rebuilding, etc.) in ways concurrent with Brooks's later vision of Yeats as traditionalist.

31   Ibid., p. 70. MacLeish's own changing relationship to Yeats's influence in discussed by Diggory on pp. 166–80.

32   Marjorie Perloff, in seeking to describe what she sees as the 'peculiar malaise' of the generation of poets who began to be published just after the Second World War, sees the work as being pulled in two irreconcilable directions. On the one hand, these poets 'inherited the doctrine, codified by the New Criticism, of the rigid separation of *art* from *life*'. On the other hand, 'the doctrine of art versus life . . . now came to blows with the more deep-seated belief, inherited from the Romantics, who stand, of course, squarely behind the so-called confessional mode of Lowell even as they stand behind Roethke's vegetal animism, a belief in the artist as hero, exempt from ordinary rules and ordinary morality, and its corollary that genius and madness are but near allied'. ('*Poetes Maudits* of the Genteel Tradition', *Robert Lowell: Essays on the Poetry*, edited by Steven Gould Axelrod and Helen Deese, Cambridge: Cambridge University Press, 1986, p. 106).

33   *Collected Poems 1937–1971*, edited and introduced by Charles Thornbury (London: Faber, 1990), p. 67. Such anxieties were of course not absent from Yeats's Big House poems, reflecting the uncertainties of his historical and political inheritance, as Marjorie Howes has argued (*Yeats's Nations: Gender, Class, and Irishness*, Cambridge: Cambridge University Press, 1996, pp. 102–30).

34   Berryman felt that by 1935 America had had an 'Auden climate set in strongly. Poetry became ominous, flat and social'. This, he claimed, meant that Yeats's influence was less strong amongst his contemporaries. Many of the young poets, because of the predominance of Auden (and also of Stevens) simply had not read later Yeats at all, and, 'In the second place, Yeats's personality is so distinct and powerful that few writers have cared to submit to it in the hope of coming out themselves.' ('Poetry Chronicle, 1948: Waiting for the End, Boys', *The Freedom of the Poet*, New York, Farrar, Straus & Giroux, 1976, pp. 297, 299). But elsewhere Berryman did not hesitate to

acknowledge the importance of his own choice to brave that powerful influence. In his 1965 'One Answer to a Question' he mapped the history of influences upon his own writing from an apprenticeship when he did not imitate anyone until 'Then came Yeats, whom I didn't so much wish to resemble as to *be*, and for several fumbling years I wrote in what it is convenient to call "period style", the Anglo-American style of the 1930s, with no voice of my own, learning chiefly from middle and later Yeats and from the brilliant young Englishman W.H. Auden. Yeats somehow saved me from the then-crushing influences of Ezra Pound and T.S. Eliot – luckily as I now feel – but he could not teach me to sound like myself (whatever that was) or tell me what to write about.' (Ibid., p. 323).

35   'Boston Common' appears in *Collected Poems* pp. 41–6.

36   *We Dream of Honour: John Berryman's Letters to His Mother*, edited by Richard J. Kelly (New York and London: W.W. Norton, 1988), p. 91. At the time of writing 'The Dance' in 1952, Theodore Roethke (1908–1963) worked himself into a similar frenzy, in which he had 'the actual sense of a Presence – as if Yeats himself were *in* that room'. The apparition is confirmatory for Roethke, since it appears as benediction for his renewal as a poet after a long period being blocked: 'I wept for joy. At last I was somebody again' (On *the Poet and His Craft: Selected Prose of Theodore Roethke*, edited with an introduction by Ralph J. Mills, Jr., Seattle and London: University of Washington Press, 1965, p. 24).

37   'One Answer to a Question: Changes', *The Freedom of the Poet*, p. 328. Some critics have, however, claimed that Ben Jonson's Carey-Morrison Ode lies behind Yeats's form in his Elegy (see Wayne K. Chapman, *Yeats and English Renaissance Literature*, Basingstoke: Macmillan, 1991, p. 138).

38   In an early essay, 'The Ritual of W.B. Yeats', Berryman had defined that ritual as 'a code or form of ceremonies, the formal character imposed on any experience as it is given objective existence by the imagination working in craft. The experience attains independent aesthetic vitality precisely through and by its limitation. Coming nearer to Yeats, we can say that this effective form will be meditative and single . . . ' (*The Freedom of the Poet*, pp. 248–9). Galway Kinnell has recorded that the sense of poetry as a form of dialogue, ending in singleness or reconciliation, is what he has learnt most usefully from Yeats. 'I think my interest in the poem made of sections, of elements that don't come together until the end, probably derives from Yeats, from poems like "Among Schoolchildren"[*sic*]. I've always loved how all the materials of that poem come back woven together and transformed. In this way Yeats's more complicated poems resemble the Platonic dialogue'. (An Interview with Wayne Dodd and Stanley Plumly, 1972, *Walking Down the Stairs: Selections From Interviews*, Ann Arbor: The University of Michigan Press, 1978, p. 43).

39   *Collected Poems*, p. 140.

40   *We Dream of Honour*, p. 99. Yeats was, at the time of the meeting, perhaps preoccupied by this passionate syntax since it is central to his project of making the language of poetry coincide with 'passionate, normal speech', as it is described in his 'A General Introduction to My Work' of the same year. (*E&I*, p. 521) Berryman several times in his poetry recounted the story of his meeting with Yeats, in *Sonnets to Chris* 5 (*Collected Poems*, p. 73), and in poem 215 of *The Dream Songs* (London: Faber, 1990, p. 234).

41 Ibid., pp. 138, 142. Bradstreet epitomizes, therefore, something of that meta-physical heterogeneity between thought and feeling which T.S. Eliot praised in Donne and which Wayne K. Chapman has described as being important to Yeats in the early 1910s. It is this metaphysically heterogeneous Yeats who was clearly important for Theodore Roethke in his mature work. The sequence 'Four for Sir John Davies' and the love poems section of *Words for the Wind* (1958) show more of the toughness of Yeats's love poetry from the 1910s onward than the symbolic suggestiveness of the sequence in *The Rose*. At the end of 'The Vigil', the concluding poem to 'Four for Sir John Davies', the Yeatsian cadence modulates towards a metaphysical continuity which Roethke in his prose associated with 'the divine' (see, for instance, 'On "Identity"', *On the Poet and His Craft*, p. 27):

> The world is for the living. Who are they?
> We dared the dark to reach the white and warm.
> She was the wind when the wind was in my way;
> Alive at noon, I perished in her form.
> Who rise from flesh to spirit know the fall:
> The word outleaps the world and light is all.
> (*Collected Poems*, London: Faber, 1985, p. 103)

The combination of the influence of Yeats and Donne in these poems has been discussed by Jenijoy La Belle, *The Echoing Wood of Theodore Roethke* (Princeton New Jersey: Princeton University Press, 1976), pp. 114, 123–5.

42 Ibid., p. 133. Berryman's own wife at the time of the poem's composition, Eileen Simpson, has recorded the extent of the identification he felt with the subject of his poem: 'Mistress Bradstreet was vividly present at all hours of the day and night (John's working schedule). Her life was so intertwined with ours it was sometimes difficult for him to distinguish between her and himself, between her and me. ... In the nightmare period when she [was] dying...John behaved, alternately, as if he was dying, and as if he was killing her off.... (*Poets in their Youth: A Memoir*, London: Faber, 1982, pp. 224–5).

43 Amiri Baraka performed a similar cross-gendered voicing in his 'Crow Jane' sequence from the 1964 *The Dead Lecturer*. But Jane there represents a symbol of the Western Muse, from his racial and cultural perspective to be more hated than loved. See Erik Reece, 'Detour to the "Alltombing Womb": Amiri Baraka's assault on Yeats's Muse' (*Learning the Trade: Essays on W.B. Yeats and Contemporary Poetry*, edited by Deborah Fleming, Connecticut: Locust Hill Press, 1993, pp. 219–22).

44 Four years after the publication of this poem, Berryman pointed up the masculine qualities of Whitman's poetic when describing his work as con-taining a 'voice...for himself and others; for others *as himself*' ('*Song of Myself*: Intention and Substance', *The Freedom of the Poet*, p. 230).

45 *Agon: Towards a Theory of Revisionism* (New York: Oxford University Press, 1983), p. 177.

46 *The Dream Songs*, p. 346.

47 Ibid., p. 334. Song 300 (p. 322) is the only poem that seems to allude directly to any of these late Yeats poems, however. 'Henry Comforted' recounts a drinking binge in Dublin bars in which, wryly, 'I recovered my spirits at once' and the couple 'at my left are giving it verbal hell', in contrast to the

humbling of the mythic hero in Yeats's Dantean 'Cuchulain Comforted', completed just over two weeks before his death.

48 Ibid., pp. 354, 343. Henry's self-association with the 'old heroes' of the Easter Rising, those 'fatuous campaigners / dewy with phantastic hope' like his own (p. 331), was shared by Berryman himself, who, in his early writing days began a play on the rebellion (Eileen Simpson, *Poets in their Youth*, p. 93).

49 Op. cit., p. 356.

50 ' "NO INTERESTING PROJECT CAN BE EMBARKED UPON WITHOUT FEAR. I SHALL BE SCARED TO DEATH HALF THE TIME." Sir Francis Chichester in Sydney'; ' "FOR MY PART I AM ALWAYS FRIGHTENED, AND VERY MUCH SO. I FEAR THE FUTURE OF ALL ENGAGEMENTS." Gordon in Khartoum'. The two epigraphs perfectly convey the precarious, ennervated and uncertain air around the project's central emotion, an air true to the instability of identification that is at the centre of the voice in the Songs. Wordsworth (' "the egotistical sublime" said Keats') is called upon in Song 380, 'From the French Hospital in New York, 901', to 'make some mere sign to me', seemingly about some possible 'fresh version of living', as Henry again lies facing death. (p. 402)

51 *We Dream of Honour*, p. 91. In his essay of 1949, 'The Poetry of Ezra Pound', Berryman had challenged the 'perverse and valuable doctrine, associated in our time with Eliot's name' of impersonality, claiming that it was a 'piercing notion' when applied to the dramatic mode of writing, but 'disfiguring' when applied to most other poetry, including Pound's. It 'hides motive, which persists' – i.e., it hides the motivating emotional force behind the writing itself (his example here is the clear contempt felt for Pope by Keats in his sonnet on Chapman's Homer). (*The Freedom of the Poet*, p. 264) His attack on a favoured doctrine of the New Criticism predicts that of de Man later in 'Form and Intent in the American New Criticism'. Berryman's early experiment with a Yeatsian mask appears in 'The Nervous Songs' sequence in his first book *The Dispossessed*; that nervousness then also underwrites much of Henry's febrile energy in the later *Dream Songs*.

52 In an interview in *The Harvard Advocate*, Berryman acknowledged that he got his three six-line stanza form from Yeats, whose songs 'don't really resemble mine, but I did get that from him. It's rather like an extended, three-part sonnet.' (John Berryman Issue, Vol. CIII, Number 1, Spring 1969, p. 8). He was presumably thinking of Yeats's 'Three Songs to the Same Tune' from *A Full Moon in March* of 1935 and their later versions, 'Three Marching Songs' from *Last Poems*. Rather than resembling Yeats's original use of the form, however, Berryman seems to take it over for an opposite purpose. Yeats's songs objectionably propound the need for a use of force by the state in order to maintain public order against those fanatics who would turn it away from its heroic past. Berryman's transposition of the form to the personal, dream-world of his undisciplined protagonist underwrites his delineation of a personal 'fate' over an impersonal history or externally-imposed order.

53 *A Map of Misreading* (New York: Oxford University Press, 1975), p. 19.

54 Op. cit., p. 407.

55 *Collected Prose*, edited and introduced by Robert Giroux (London: Faber, 1987), p. 243. That sense of the historical pressure to retain strict forms is echoed in an interview Galway Kinnell gave to Mary Jane Fortunato in 1971. In answer to Fortunato's question 'Do you think it is necessary for a poet to

go through a form and then break out of it?', Kinnell said 'That was what happened to my generation. Almost all of us began writing in strict forms. Almost all of us sooner or later turned to free verse. I doubt if this will happen in the future. I think those of my age who say you have to "learn the rules in order to break them" are wrong to generalize from their own experience. That experience was a historical quirk.' (*Walking Down the Stairs: Selections from Interviews*, p. 18).

56 Lowell's debt to Yeatsian form is evident in 'The First Sunday in Lent', 'The Quaker Graveyard in Nantucket', 'In Memory of Arthur Winslow' and 'The Drunken Fisherman'; Randall Jarrell's in 'The Bad Music', 'The Soldier', 'Mother, Said the Child', 'The Dead in Melanesia'; Delmore Schwartz's in 'For the One Who Would Take Man's Life in his Hands', 'Dogs are Shakespearean...'. Relatively often, these poets adopted (however loosely) the eight-lined stanza frequently deployed by late Yeats. Schwartz does so in 'Prothalmion', Jarrell in 'The Dead Wingman' and 'The Tower'. John Berryman's work shows a deep obsession with the form. 'The Statue', 'The Disciple', 'Letter to his Brother', 'Conversation', 'Travelling South', 'At Chinese Checkers', 'Animal Trainer', '1 September 1939', 'Farewell to Miles', 'The Enemies of the Angels', 'Boston Common', 'A Winter Piece...', and 'New Year's Eve' from *The Dispossessed* all adopt it, leading, to say the least, to a certain lack of variety there – which is to the collection's purpose. Eileen Simpson recalls Berryman telling Lowell that he felt the greatest Yeats poems were, from the early work, 'The Folly of Being Comforted' and 'That the Night Come', and from the later 'The Wild Swans at Coole' and 'In Memory of Major Robert Gregory' – although 'It changes of course' (*Poets in their Youth*, p. 130). My list of poems influenced by Yeatsian form partly echoes that in Bruce Bauer's *The Middle Generation: The Lives and Poetry of Delmore Schwartz, Randall Jarrell, John Berryman, and Robert Lowell*, Connecticut: Archon Books, 1985, pp. 100–1). Yet, in his chapter on 'Berryman & Yeats', Bauer seeks to deny the influence of Yeats on the early writing of these poets, saying that 'they took nothing from Yeats which did not belong in a poem written according to Eliot's tenets' (p. 101). But this sits oddly with the frequency with which issues of inheritance are cast in terms of family and houses in this early work. Berryman himself certainly felt that Lowell's early work is at least partly modelled on Yeats's dynastic poetry ('Robert Lowell and Others', *The Freedom of the Poet*, p. 287).

57 As he put it in his 1916 *Reveries over Childhood and Youth*, 'We should write out our own thoughts in as nearly as possible the language we thought them in, as though in a letter to an intimate friend.' (*A*, p. 102).

58 *For the Union Dead* (London: Faber, 1985 edition), pp. 70–2.

59 Faber, London, 1967, pp. 16, 21. Stephen Gould Axelrod has claimed that 'Lowell's method as a poet of social and political awareness probably owes most to Yeats', since it includes always a Yeatsian 'quarrel with [himself]' at the heart of all its readings of contemporary and earlier history ('Lowell's Living Name: An Introduction', *Robert Lowell: Essays on the Poetry*, p. 20).

60 Such an alternative present appears, sporadically at least, in the work of Robert Pinsky, for whom Yeats was 'my first hero in the art', and who feels that 'poetry must imagine a community'. 'Avenue', 'The Street', 'Local Politics' from *An Explanation of America*, and the section from *Sadness and Happi-*

ness 'The Street of Furthest Memory' all explore that possibility (*The Figured Wheel: New & Collected Poems*, Manchester: Carcanet, 1996).

61 Op. cit., pp. 15–16. Terence Diggory has claimed that 'the tradition of the self', which he sees as being shared by American poets and Yeats, both of whom were writing within a lack of tradition on their native soil, 'reaches its culmination in confessional poetry'. But, 'unlike Yeats, however, the confessional poet often discovers the self to be incapable of filling the void left by the disintegration of the public world.' (op. cit., pp. 5, 181). As poems written post *A Vision* show, however, it is not necessarily clear how Yeats felt he could 'fill the void' of apocalyptic 'Second Coming'. As I have argued throughout, the self which comes through Yeats's work throughout never seems as integrated, enduring and coherent as comments such as this by Diggory seem to make it out to be. The expressed need for the individual artist to define his nation's consciousness, which arose out of Yeats's changing feelings about the Abbey Theatre, was never invulnerable to events outside of the self, as poems like 'Easter 1916' amply prove. If anything, this seems to have intensified across the years; as 'Lapis Lazuli' confirms, 'All perform their tragic play... [but]Though Hamlet rambles and Lear rages, / And all the drop-scenes drop at once / Upon a hundred thousand stages, / [Tragedy] cannot grow by an inch or a ounce.' (*CP*, p. 294) The confessional poets seem more in line with Yeats, then, than Diggory makes out, largely because Yeats himself was not the consistent and monumentalist figure Diggory seems, in such passages of comparison and difference, to make him out to be.

62 *The Dolphin* (London: Faber, 1973), p. 47.

63 Stephen Gould Axelrod has shown that Lowell's history was always an 'existential' one, in which 'in penetrating the life of another age "one is penetrating the life of one's own"' (op. cit., p. 18).

64 Op. cit., pp. 72, 67, 74.

65 London: Faber, 1978, p. 127.

66 Op. cit., p. 301.

67 Op. cit., p. 27.

68 'Yeats', *Selected Prose of T.S. Eliot*, edited by Frank Kermode (London: Faber, 1975), p. 251.

69 Op. cit., pp. 7, 9, 12.

70 Harold Bloom's more recent acceptance of Merrill into his post-Emersonian pantheon alongside John Ashbery and A.R. Ammons depends upon his splitting of the influence of a common precursor in that tradition, Wallace Stevens. Whereas Ashbery is influenced by the 'repressed Whitmanian depths' in Stevens, Bloom claims, Merrill is most affected by Stevens as 'one of the dandies'. This dandyism he then seems to relate to the imperviousness of Merrill's poetry to 'catastrophe' and the strains of 'traditional elegiac consolation' – all losses become for Merrill in Bloom's eyes, his poetic 'Illgotten gains'. As I hope to show, however, despite his formal intricacies, Merrill's poetic is more pervious and varied – partly due to the influence of Yeats – than Bloom's superficial acceptance of his casting a cold eye on life would seem to suggest (Introduction to *James Merrill*, New York: Chelsea House, 1985, pp. 1–7).

71 *Selected Poems 1946–1985* (New York: Alfred A. Knopf, 1995), pp. 59, 88. Merrill's other poems about houses include 'The House' (*First Poems*), 'The

Broken Home' and 'From the Cupola' (*Nights and Days*), 'After the Fire', '18 West 11th Street' and 'Under Libra: Weights and Measures' (*Braving the Elements*), '164 East 72nd Street' (*A Scattering of Salts*). David Kalstone has argued that Merrill's decision to use his various houses as settings for the poetry releases his essentially Proustian sensibility (*Five Temperaments*, New York: Oxford University Press, 1977, pp. 77–128), but the reviver of the tradition of houses as poetic spaces in twentieth-century poetry was, of course, Yeats.

72 New York: Alfred A. Knopf, 1995, pp. 556–7.

73 'An Interview with J.D. McClatchy', *Recitative: Prose by James Merrill*, edited and with an introduction by J.D. McClatchy (San Francisco: North Point Press, 1986), p. 75.

74 New York: Alfred A. Knopf, 1995, p, 27.

75 'An Interview with Ashley Brown', *Recitative*, p. 43. In 'Merrill's Yeats', Leslie Brisman shows well how the later poet's aesthetic is more open, in poems like 'Willowware Cup', to the tides of experience than that of his master (*James Merrill*, pp. 189–98). Interestingly, Merrill's setting of Yeats against Rilke here is similar to that by Louise Bogan (1897–1970) of the same two figures of influence in the mid-Thirties. Bogan had from about 1917 been an avid reader of Yeats's poetry as it appeared; her 1938 appreciation of him was originally called 'The Greatest Poet Writing in English Today', and claimed that, in his late work, Yeats had achieved 'That difficult balance, almost impossible to strike, between the artist's austerity and "the reveries of the common heart"' (reprinted as 'William Butler Yeats', *Selected Criticism*, London: Peter Owen Limited, 1958, p. 99). Bogan's own poetry had from the start been preoccupied with this 'balance' and with the relation of aesthetics to life. The 1923 'Statue and Birds' envisages an image of a girl against which 'The inquietudes of the sap and of the blood are spent. / What is foresaken will rest. / But her heel is lifted, – she would flee, – the whistle of the birds / Fails on her breast' – lines curiously prophetic of 'Sailing to Byzantium' and 'Byzantium'. By 1968's 'Night', the emphasis has shifted, but the enjoinder remains the same: '– O remember / In your narrowing dark hours / That more things move / Than blood in the heart.' (*The Blue Estuaries: Poems 1923–1968* New York: Farrar, Straus & Giroux, 1968), pp. 14, 130. Yet, like Merrill, Bogan came to see in Rilke what was for her a more wide-ranging and perceptive poet (see Elizabeth Frank, *Louise Bogan: A Biography*, New York: Columbia University Press, 1986, p. 268).

76 From *Nights and Days*, *Selected Poems*, pp. 95, 99, 101–2. *The Fire Screen* of 1969 contains several poems on the Byzantium theme, most wittily 'Flying from Byzantium' in which the 'priceless metal bird' is a plane bearing a lover away from the love which he is denying. He is told by 'the man in the moon' that 'The point's to live, love, / Not shake your fist at the feast', and he returns to earth vowing to 'be born again'. Typically, that rebirth is envisaged as the beginning of a new writing as, at the end, a 'young scribe' (the Byzantine lover left behind?) 'turned a fresh / Page, hesitated, dipped his pen'. (London: Chatto & Windus with the Hogarth Press, 1970, pp. 30–1). 'Santorini: Stopping the Leak' from the 1985 *Late Settings* amiably celebrates another brush with mortality ('sporting a survivor's grin / I've come by baby jet to Santorin')

in variations on the rhyme scheme of the eight-line stanzas of the 'Byzantium' originals – variations also adopted in 'Clearing the Title' from the same collection, 'Yannina' from *Divine Comedies* and 'Tony: Ending the Life', '164 East 72nd Street' and 'Self Portrait in Tyvek (TM) Windbreaker' from Merrill's last collection, *A Scattering of Salts*, pp. 91–5.

77 'An Interview with Fred Bornhauser', *Recitative*, p. 53; *A Different Person: A Memoir* (New York: Alfred A. Knopf, 1993), p. 129 – where Merrill speaks of dressing up in fancy-dress here; 'An Interview with J.D. McClatchy', *Recitative*, p. 66. *A Different Person* contains some interesting speculation that it was in fact the 'comfort and privilege' which was the wealthy Merrill's from birth which lies behind the 'shrug and smile' attitude to catastrophe and loss which Bloom takes as the genuine strangeness of Merrill's writing (p. 22).

78 Op. cit., pp. 14, 492.

79 Ibid., pp. 529, 481, 424.

80 Jacques Derrida, *Mémoires for Paul de Man* (New York: Columbia University Press, 1986), p. 38.

81 *The Madwoman in the Attic: The Woman Writer and the Nineteenth-Century Literary Imagination* (New Haven: Yale University Press, 1979), pp. 47–9.

82 *Adrienne Rich's Poetry and Prose*, selected and edited by Barbara Charlesworth Gelpi and Albert Gelpi (New York: W.W. Norton and Company, 1993), p. 171.

83 *Writers at Work: The Paris Review Interviews Fourth Series*, edited by George Plimpton (London: Secker & Warburg, 1977), p. 417.

84 'In Yeats's House', *Coming to Light: American Women Poets in the Twentieth Century*, edited by Diane Wood Middlebrook and Marilyn Yalom (Ann Arbor: University of Michigan Press, 1985), p. 223. The chapter appears in expanded form in *No Man's Land: The Place of the Woman Writer in the Twentieth Century Volume 3 Letters from the Front*, by Sandra M. Gilbert and Susan Gubar (New Haven: Yale University Press, 1994), where Gilbert also notes verbal echoes between Plath's and Yeats's poems (on pp. 287–8 especially).

85 *The Fact of a Doorframe: Poems New and Selected 1950–1984* (New York: W.W. Norton, 1984), pp. 162–4.

86 New York: W.W. Norton, 1986, pp. 74, 33. That concern with mapping and its inadequacy continues through the title sequence of *An Atlas of the Difficult World* (New York: W.W. Norton, 1991), and the 'Then Or Now' sequence of *Dark Fields of the Republic* (New York: W.W. Norton, 1995). Strikingly, both sequences seek to resolve their uncertainties ('where do we see it from is the question', as the earlier sequence has it) through bringing the time of the poem into connection with that of the reader: 'I know you are reading this poem' in the earlier case (p. 25); 'And now as you read these poems' in the latter (p. 31). As with Yeats's more visionary 'The Fisherman', an ideal community or culture is envisaged primarily as a possible *readership*.

87 *Collected Poems*, edited with an introduction by Ted Hughes (London: Faber, 1981), p. 25.

88 Ibid., pp. 78, 91, 148.

89 *Letters Home: Correspondence 1950–1963*, selected and edited by Aurelia Schober Plath (New York: Harper and Row, 1975), pp. 223, 488.

90 Elizabeth Butler Cullingford has made a similar point about 'Daddy' and other works in 'A Father's Prayer, A Daughter's Anger: W.B. Yeats and Sylvia Plath' (*Daughters and Fathers* edited by Lynda E. Boose and Betty S. Flowers (Baltimore: Johns Hopkins University Press, 1989), pp. 241–55).

91 See for example the Preface and 'The Feminine', *The Hélène Cixous Reader*, edited by Susan Sollers (London: Routledge, 1994), pp. xxi, 60.

Select Bibliography

Bibliographical, Biographical, Critical and Theoretical Works

Ackerman, John. *A Dylan Thomas Companion: Life, Poetry and Prose*, Basingstoke: Macmillan, 1991.

Adams, Joseph. *Yeats and the Masks of Syntax*, Basingstoke: Macmillan, 1984.

Allen, Graham. *Harold Bloom: A Poetics of Conflict*, Hemel Hempstead: Harvester Wheatsheaf, 1994.

Allison, Jonathan (*editor*). *Yeats's Political Identities: Selected Essays*, Ann Arbor: University of Michigan Press, 1996.

Arac, Jonathan. *Critical Genealogies: Historical Situations for Postmodern Literary Studies*, New York: Columbia University Press, 1987.

Arac, Jonathan, Godzich, Wlad and Martin, Wallace (editors). *The Yale Critics: Deconstruction in America*, Minneapolis: University of Minnesota Press, 1983.

Axelrod, Steven Gould and Deese, Helen (editors). *Robert Lowell: Essays on the Poetry*, Cambridge: Cambridge University Press, 1986.

Bakhtin, M.M. (edited by Michael Holquist). *The Dialogic Imagination: Four Essays*, Austin, Texas: University of Texas Press, 1981.

—— (translated by Hélène Iswolsky). *Rabelais and His World*, Bloomington: Indiana University Press, 1984.

Bauer, Bruce. *The Middle Generation: The Lives and Poetry of Delmore Schwartz, Randall Jarrell, John Berryman and Robert Lowell*, Connecticut: Archon Books, 1986.

Beach, Christopher. *ABC of Influence: Ezra Pound and the Remaking of American Poetic Tradition*, Berkeley: University of California Press, 1992.

Bell, Vereen and Lerner, Laurence (*editors*). *On Modern Poetry: Essays Presented to Donald Davie*, Nashville: Vanderbilt University Press, 1988.

Benjamin, Walter. (edited by Hannah Arendt). *Illuminations*, London: Jonathan Cape, 1970.

Beum, Robert. *The Poetic Art of W.B. Yeats*, New York: Ungar, 1969.

Bhabha, Homi K. *The Location of Culture*, London: Routledge, 1994.

Bishop, Nicholas. *Re-Making Poetry: Ted Hughes and a New Critical Psychology*, Hemel Hempstead: Harvester Wheatsheaf, 1991.

Blackmur, R.P. *Language As Gesture: Essays in Poetry*, New York: Harcourt, Brace and Company, 1952.

Bloom, Harold. *Agon: Towards a Theory of Revisionism*, New York: Oxford University Press, 1983.

—— *A Map of Misreading*, New York: Oxford University Press, 1975.

—— (*et al.*) *Deconstruction and Criticism*, New York: The Seabury Press, 1979.

—— (*editor*). *James Merrill*, New York: Chelsea House, 1985.

—— *Kabbalah and Criticism*, New York: The Seabury Press, 1975.

—— (edited by John Hollander) *Poetics of Influence: New and Selected Criticism*, New Haven: Henry K. Schwab, 1988.

—— *Poetry and Repression: Revisionism from Blake to Stevens*, New Haven: Yale University Press, 1976.

—— *Ruin the Sacred Truths: Poetry and Belief from the Bible to the Present*, Cambridge Massachusetts: Harvard University Press, 1989.

—— *The Anxiety of Influence: A Theory of Poetry*, Oxford: Oxford University Press, 1973.

—— *The Breaking of the Vessels*, Chicago: University of Chicago Press, 1982.

—— *The Western Canon*, Basingstoke: Macmillan, 1995.

—— *Wallace Stevens: The Poems of Our Climate*, Ithaca: Cornell University Press, 1977.

—— *Yeats*, New York: Oxford University Press, 1970.

Boehmer, Elleke. *Colonial and Postcolonial Literature*, Oxford: Oxford University Press, 1995.

—— (*editor*). *Empire Writing*, Oxford: Oxford University Press, 1998.

Boly, John R. *Reading Auden: The Returns of Caliban*, Ithaca: Cornell University Press, 1991.

Boose, Lynda E., and Flowers, Betty S. (*editors*). *Daughters and Fathers*, Baltimore: Johns Hopkins University Press, 1989.

Bornstein, George and Finneran, Richard J. (*editors*). *Yeats: An Annual of Critical and Textual Studies*, Volume III, Ithaca: Cornell University Press, 1985.

Bové, Paul A. *Destructive Poetics: Heidegger and Modern American Poetry*, New York: Columbia University Press, 1980.

Bowers, Neal. *Theodore Roethke: The Journey From I to Otherwise*, Columbia: University of Missouri Press, 1982.

Brooks, Cleanth. *A Shaping Joy: Studies in the Writer's Craft*, London: Methuen, 1971.

—— *Modern Poetry and the Tradition*, Chapel Hill: University of North Carolina Press, 1939.

—— *The Well-wrought Urn: Studies in the Structure of Poetry*, London: Dobson Books, 1968 Revised Edition.

Brown, Merle E. *Double Lyric: Divisiveness and Communal Creativity in Recent English Poetry*, London: Routledge & Kegan Paul, 1980.

Brown, Stewart (*editor*). *The Art of Derek Walcott*, Bridgend: Seren, 1991.

Brown, Terence. *Ireland's Literature: Selected Essays*, Dublin: Lilliput Press, 1988.

—— *Louis MacNeice: Sceptical Vision*, Dublin: Gill and Macmillan, 1975.

—— *Time Was Away: The World of Louis MacNeice*, Dublin: Dolmen, 1974.

Brown, Terence and Grene, Nicholas (*editors*). *Tradition and Influence in Anglo-Irish Poetry*, Basingstoke: Macmillan, 1989.

Bruss, Elizabeth W. *Beautiful Theories: The Spectacle of Discourse in Contemporary Criticism*, Baltimore: Johns Hopkins University Press, 1982.

Cairns, David and Richards, Shaun. *Writing Ireland: Colonialism, Nationalism and Culture*, Manchester: Manchester University Press, 1988.

Callan, Edward. *W.H. Auden: A Carnival of Intellect*, New York: Oxford University Press, 1983.

Carpenter, Humphrey. *W.H. Auden: A Biography*, London: George Allen & Unwin, 1981.

Cave, Terence. *Recognitions: A Study in Poetics*, Oxford: Clarendon Press, 1990.

Cavell, Stanley. *Philosophical Passages: Wittgenstein, Emerson, Austin, Derrida*, Oxford: Blackwell, 1995.

—— *This New Yet Unapproachable America: Lectures After Emerson After Wittgenstein*, Albuquerque: Living Batch Press, 1989.

Chapman, Wayne K. *Yeats and English Renaissance Literature*, Basingstoke: Macmillan, 1991.

Cixous, Hélène. (edited by Susan Sellers) *The Hélène Cixous Reader*, London: Routledge, 1994.

Clayton, Jay and Rothstein, Eric (*editors*). *Influence and Intertextuality in Literary History*, Madison: University of Wisconsin Press, 1991.

Corcoran, Neil. *After Yeats and Joyce: Reading Modern Irish Literature*, Oxford: Oxford University Press, 1997.

——*Seamus Heaney*, London: Faber, 1986. Revised Edition, 1998.

—— *The Chosen Ground: Essays on the Contemporary Poetry of Northern Ireland*, Bridgend: Seren, 1992.

Cottom, Daniel. *Ravishing Tradition: Cultural Forces and Literary History*, Ithaca: Cornell University Press, 1996.

Coughlan, Patricia and Davis, Alex. *Modernism and Ireland: The Poetry of the 1930s*, Cork: Cork University Press, 1995.

Cowart, David. *Literary Symbiosis: The Reconfigured Text in Twentieth Century Writing*, Athens: University of Georgia Press, 1993.

Cullingford, Elizabeth. *Gender and History in Yeats's Love Poetry* Cambridge: Cambridge University Press, 1993.

—— *Yeats, Ireland and Fascism*, London: Macmillan, 1981.

Davenport-Hines, Richard. *Auden*, London: Heinemann, 1995.

Dawe, Gerald and Longley, Edna. *Across the Roaring Hill: The Protestant Imagination in Modern Ireland*, Belfast: Blackstaff Press, 1985.

Deane, Seamus. *Celtic Revivals: Essays in Modern Irish Literature*, London: Faber, 1985.

—— (*editor.*) *Nationalism, Colonialism and Literature*, Minneapolis: University of Minnesota Press, 1979.

—— *Strange Country: Modernity and Nationhood in Irish Writing Since 1790*, Oxford: Clarendon Press, 1997.

De Bolla, Peter. *Harold Bloom: Towards Historical Rhetorics*, London: Routledge, 1988.

De Man, Paul (edited by Andrzej Warminski). *Aesthetic Ideology*, Minneapolis: University of Minnesota Press, 1996.

—— *Allegories of Reading: Figural Language in Rousseau, Nietzsche, Rilke and Proust*, New Haven: Yale University Press, 1979.

—— *Blindness & Insight: Essays in the Rhetoric of Contemporary Criticism*, London: Methuen, 1983 2nd edn.

—— (edited by Lindsay Waters). *Critical Writings 1953–1978*, Minneapolis: University of Minnesota Press, 1989.

—— (edited by E.S. Burt, Kevin Newmark and Andrej Warminski). *Romanticism and Contemporary Criticism*, Baltimore: Johns Hopkins University Press, 1993.

—— *The Resistance to Theory*, Manchester: Manchester University Press, 1986.

—— *The Rhetoric of Romanticism*, New York: Columbia University Press, 1984.

Derrida, Jacques (translated by Thomas Dutoit) *Aporias*, Stanford: University of Stanford Press, 1993.

—— (translated by Barbara Johnson). *Dissemination*, London: The Athlone Press, 1993.

—— (translated by Peggy Kamuf). *Given Time: I. Counterfeit Money*, Chicago: University of Chicago Press, 1992.

—— (translated by Gayatri Chakravorty Spivak). *Of Grammatology*, Baltimore: Johns Hopkins University Press, 1976.

—— (edited by Gerald Graff). *Limited Inc.*, Evanston, Illinois: Northwestern University Press, 1988.

—— *Mémoires for Paul de Man*, New York: Columbia University Press, 1986.

—— (edited by Thomas Dutoit) *On the Name*, Stanford: Stanford University Press, 1995.

—— (translated by Alan Bass) *Positions*, Chicago: University of Chicago Press, 1981.

—— (translated by David Wills) *The Gift of Death*, Chicago: University of Chicago Press, 1995.

Devine, Kathleen and Peacock, Alan J. (*editors*). *Louis MacNeice and His Influence*, Gerrard's Cross: Colin Smythe, 1998.

Diggory, Terence. *Yeats and American Poetry: The Tradition of the Self*, Princeton: Princeton University Press, 1983.

Donoghue, Denis. *Yeats*, London: Fontana, 1971.

Doreski, William. *The Years of Our Friendship: Robert Lowell and Allen Tate*, Jackson: University Press of Mississippi, 1990.

Dunn, Douglas (*editor*). *Two Decades of Irish Writing*, Manchester: Carcanet, 1975.

Eagleton, Terry. *Criticism and Ideology*, London: Verso, 1978.

—— *Marxism and Literary Criticism*, London: Methuen, 1976.

—— *The Ideology of the Aesthetic*, Oxford: Blackwell, 1990.

Eliot, T.S. *On Poetry and Poets*, London: Faber, 1957.

—— (edited by Frank Kermode). *Selected Prose of T.S. Eliot*, London: Faber, 1975.

Ellmann, Richard. *Eminent Domain: Yeats Among Wilde, Joyce, Pound, Eliot and Auden*, New York: Oxford University Press, 1967.

—— *The Identity of Yeats*, London: Faber, 1964.

—— *Yeats: The Man and the Masks*, Harmondsworth: Penguin, 1987 edition.

Emig, Rainer. *Modernism in Poetry: Motivations, Structures and Limits*, Harlow: Longman, 1995.

Faas, Ekbert. *Ted Hughes: The Unaccommodated Universe*, Santa Barbara: Black Sparrow Press, 1980.

Finneran, Richard J. *Editing Yeats's Poems*, Basingstoke: Macmillan, 1983.

—— (*editor*). *Yeats Annual* No. 2, Basingstoke: Macmillan, 1983.

Fite, David. *Harold Bloom: The Rhetoric of Romantic Vision*, Amherst: University of Massachusetts Press, 1985.

Fleming, Deborah (*editor*). *Learning the Trade: Essays on W.B. Yeats and Contemporary Poetry*, Connecticut: Locust Hill Press, 1993.

Foster, Roy. *W.B. Yeats: A Life. I: The Apprentice Mage*, Oxford: Oxford University Press, 1997.

Foucault, Michel (translated by A.M. Sheridan Smith) *The Archeology of Knowledge*, London: Routledge, 1995 edition.

Frank, Elizabeth *Louise Bogan: A Biography*, New York: Columbia University Press, 1986.

Fuller, John. *W.H. Auden: A Commentary*, London: Faber, 1998.

Garratt, Robert F. (*editor*). *Critical Essays on Seamus Heaney*, New York, G.K. Hall & Co., 1995.

—— *Modern Irish Poetry: Tradition and Continuity from Yeats to Heaney*, Berkeley: University of California Press, 1986.

Gilbert, Sandra M. and Gubar, Susan. *No Man's Land: The Place of the Woman Writer in the Twentieth Century*, Volume 3, New Haven: Yale University Press, 1994.

—— *The Madwoman in the Attic: The Woman Writer and the Nineteenth-Century Imagination*, New Haven: Yale University Press, 1979.

Gould, Warwick (*editor*). *Yeats Annual* No. 3, Basingstoke: Macmillan, 1985.

—— *Yeats Annual* No. 4, Basingstoke: Macmillan, 1986.

Gould, Warwick and Longley, Edna (*editors*). *Yeats Annual* No. 12, Basingstoke: Macmillan, 1996.

Haffenden, John. *The Life of John Berryman*, London: Ark, 1982.

—— *Viewpoints: Poets in Conversation*, London: Faber, 1981.

Hargrove, Nancy D. *The Journey Toward 'Ariel': Sylvia Plath's Poems of 1956–1959*, Lund: Lund University Press, 1994.

Harmon, Maurice. *Austin Clarke: A Critical Introduction*, Dublin: The Wolfhound Press, 1989.

Hart, Henry. *Robert Lowell and the Sublime*, Syracuse: Syracuse University Press, 1995.

—— *The Poetry of Geoffrey Hill*, Carbondale: Southern Illinois University Press, 1986.

Hecht, Anthony. *The Hidden Law: The Poetry of W.H. Auden*, Cambridge, Massachusetts: Harvard University Press, 1993.

Hobson, Marian. *Jacques Derrida: Opening Lines*, London: Routledge, 1998.

Hoffpauir, Richard. *The Art of Restraint: English Poetry from Hardy to Larkin*, Newark: University of Delaware Press, 1991.

Howes, Marjorie. *Yeats's Nations: Gender, Class, and Irishness* Cambridge: Cambridge University Press, 1996.

Hynes, Samuel. *The Auden Generation*, London: Bodley Head, 1976.

Jarrell, Randall. *Kipling, Auden & Co.: Essays and Reviews 1935–1964*, Manchester: Carcanet, 1981.

Jeffares, A. Norman. *A New Commentary on the Poems of W.B. Yeats*, Basingstoke: Macmillan, 1984.

—— (*editor*). *W.B. Yeats: The Critical Heritage*, London: Routledge & Kegan Paul, 1977.

Jochum, K.P.S. *W.B. Yeats: A Classified Bibliography of Criticism*, Urbana: University of Illinois Press, 1990 Second Edition.

John, Brian. *Reading the Ground: The Poetry of Thomas Kinsella*, Washington: The Catholic University of America Press, 1996.

Johnston, Dillon. *Irish Poetry After Joyce*, Notre Dame, Indiana: University of Notre Dame Press, 1985.

Kavanagh, Peter (*editor*). *Patrick Kavanagh: Man and Poet*, Maine: National Poetry Foundation, 1986.

Keane, Patrick J. *Yeats's Interactions With Tradition*, Columbia: University of Missouri Press, 1987.

Kenneally, Michael (*editor*). *Poetry in Contemporary Irish Literature*, Gerrard's Cross: Colin Smythe, 1995.

Kiberd, Declan. *Inventing Ireland: The Literature of the Modern Nation*, London: Jonathan Cape, 1995.

Knottenbelt, E.M. *Passionate Intelligence: The Poetry of Geoffrey Hill*, Amsterdam: Rodopi, 1990.

Komesi, Okifumi. *The Double Perspective of Yeats's Aesthetic*, Gerrard's Cross: Colin Smythe, 1984.

Kristeva, Julia (edited by Leon S. Roudiez). *Desire in Language: A Semiotic Approach to Literature and Art*, Oxford: Blackwell, 1980.

—— (translated by Margaret Waller). *Revolution in Poetic Language*, New York: Columbia University Press, 1984.

La Belle, Jenijoy. *The Echoing Wood of Theodore Roethke*, Princeton: Princeton University Press, 1976.

Lane, Gary (*editor*). *Sylvia Plath: New Views on the Poetry*, Baltimore: Johns Hopkins University Press, 1979.

Larkin, Philip. *Required Writing: Miscellaneous Pieces 1955–1982*, London: Faber, 1983.

Larrissy, Edward. *Yeats the Poet: The Measures of Difference*, Hemel Hempstead: Harvester Wheatsheaf, 1994.

Leavis, F.R. (*editor*). *A Selection from Scrutiny*, Two Volumes, Cambridge: Cambridge University Press, 1968.

—— *New Bearings in English Poetry: A Study of the Contemporary Situation*, London: Chatto & Windus, 1932.

Lehman, David and Berger, Charles (*editors*). *James Merrill: Essays in Criticism*, Ithaca: Cornell University Press, 1983.

Lentricchia, Frank. *After the New Criticism*, London: Methuen, 1983 2nd edn.

Lloyd, David. *Anomalous States: Irish Writing and the Post-Colonial Moment*, Dublin: The Lilliput Press, 1993.

Longenbach, James. *Modernist Poetics of History: Pound, Eliot and the Sense of the Past*, Princeton: Princeton University Press, 1987.

Longley, Edna. *Louis MacNeice: A Study*, London: Faber, 1988.

—— *Poetry in the Wars*, Newcastle upon Tyne: Bloodaxe Books, 1986.

—— *The Living Stream: Literature & Revisionism in Ireland*, Newcastle upon Tyne: Bloodaxe Books, 1994.

Lynch, David. *Yeats: The Poetics of the Self*, Chicago: University of Chicago Press, 1979.

Mariani, Paul. *Dream Song: The Life of John Berryman*, New York: William Morrow and Company, 1990.

Marsack, Robyn. *The Cave of Making: The Poetry of Louis MacNeice*, Oxford: Oxford University Press, 1982.

Matthews, Steven. *Irish Poetry: Politics, History, Negotiation*, Basingstoke: Macmillan, 1997.

Mazzaro, Jerome. *Postmodern American Poetry*, Urbana: University of Illinois Press, 1980.

McDonald, Peter. *Louis MacNeice: The Poet in his Contexts*, Oxford: Clarendon Press, 1991.

—— *Mistaken Identities: Poetry and Northern Ireland*, Oxford: Clarendon Press, 1997.

McKinnon, William T. *Apollo's Blended Dream: a Study of the Poetry of Louis MacNeice*, Oxford: Oxford University Press, 1971.

McMinn, Joseph. *The Internationalism of Irish Literature and Drama*, Gerrard's Cross: Colin Smythe, 1992.

Meiners, R.K. *The Last Alternatives: A Study of the Works of Allen Tate*, New York: Haskell House Publishers, 1973.

Middlebrook, Diane Wood. *Worlds Into Words*, New York, W.W. Norton, 1980.

Mikhail, E.H. (*editor*). *W.B. Yeats: Interviews and Recollections*, Two Volumes, London: Macmillan, 1977.

Miller, J. Hillis. *The Linguistic Moment: From Wordsworth to Stevens*, Princeton: Princeton University Press, 1985.

—— *Tropes, Parables, Performatives: Essays on Twentieth Century Literature*, Hemel Hempstead: Harvester Wheatsheaf, 1990.

Moffat, Judith. *James Merrill: An Introduction to his Poetry*, New York: Columbia University Press, 1984.

Montague, John. *The Figure in the Cave and Other Essays*, Dublin: Lilliput Press, 1989.

Moore, D.B. *The Poetry of Louis MacNeice*, Leicester: Leicester University Press, 1972.

Moynihan, Robert. *A Recent Imagining: Interviews With Harold Bloom, Geoffrey Hartman, J. Hillis Miller, Paul de Man*, Connecticut: Archon Books, 1986.

North, Michael. *The Political Aesthetic of Yeats, Pound and Eliot*, Cambridge: Cambridge University Press, 1991.

O'Hara, Daniel T. *The Romance of Interpretation: Visionary Criticism from Pater to de Man*, New York: Columbia University Press, 1985.

—— *Tragic Knowledge: Yeats's 'Autobiography' and Hermeneutics*, New York: Columbia University Press, 1981.

Orr, Leonard (*editor*). *Yeats and Postmodernism*, Syracuse: Syracuse University Press, 1991.

O'Shea, Edward. *A Descriptive Catalog of W.B. Yeats's Library*, New York: Garland Publishing Inc., 1985.

Ostroff, Anthony (editor). *The Contemporary Poet as Artist and Critic*, Boston: Little, Brown and Company, 1964.

Parkinson, Thomas. *W.B. Yeats: Self Critic and The Later Poetry*, Berkeley: University of California Press, 1971.

Paulin, Tom. *Ireland & the English Crisis*, Newcastle upon Tyne: Bloodaxe Books, 1984.

—— *Minotaur: Poetry and the Nation State*, London: Faber, 1992.

Plimpton, George (*editor*). *Writers At Work: The Paris Review Interviews*, Fourth Series, London: Secker & Warburg, 1977.

Porter, Raymond J. and Brophy, James D. (*editors*). *Modern Irish Literature: Essays in Honor of William York Tindall*, New York: Iona College Press, 1972.

Press, John. *Rule and Energy: Trends in British Poetry Since the Second World War*, Oxford: Oxford University Press, 1963.

Primeau, Ronald (*editor*). *Influx: Essays on Literary Influence*, New York: Kennikat Press, 1977.

Quinn, Antoinette. *Patrick Kavanagh: Born Again Romantic*, Dublin: Gill and Macmillan, 1991.

Ramanazani, Jahan. *Poetry of Mourning: The Modern Elegy from Hardy to Heaney*, Chicago: University of Chicago Press, 1994.

—— *Yeats and the Poetry of Death: Elegy, Self-Elegy and the Sublime*, New Haven: Yale University Press, 1990.

Robinson, Peter (*editor*). *Geoffrey Hill: Essays on His Work*, Milton Keynes: Open University Press, 1985.

Sacks, Peter M. *The English Elegy: Studies in the Genre from Spenser to Yeats*, Baltimore: Johns Hopkins University Press, 1985.

Salusinszky, Imre. *Criticism in Society*, London: Methuen, 1987.

Schirmer, Gregory A. *The Poetry of Austin Clarke*, Notre Dame, Indiana: University of Notre Dame Press, 1983.

Scigaj, Leonard M. *The Poetry of Ted Hughes: Form and Imagination*, Iowa: Iowa University Press, 1986.

Sherry, Vincent. *The Uncommon Tongue: The Poetry and Criticism of Geoffrey Hill*, Ann Arbor: University of Michigan Press, 1987.

Simpson, Eileen. *Poets in their Youth: A Memoir*, London, Faber,1982.

Simpson, Lewis P. (*editor*). *The Possibilities of Order: Cleanth Brooks and His Work*, Baton Rouge: Louisiana State University Press, 1976.

Sisson, C.H. *The Avoidance of Literature: Collected Essays*, Manchester: Carcanet, 1978.

Smith, Stan. *W.B. Yeats: A Critical Introduction*, Basingstoke: Macmillan, 1990.

—— *W.H. Auden*, Oxford: Blackwell, 1985.

Spears, Monroe K. *The Poetry of W.H. Auden*, Oxford: Oxford University Press, 1963.

Spender, Stephen. *The Thirties and After: Poetry, Politics, People*, Basingstoke: Macmillan, 1978.

Stallworthy, Jon. *Between the Lines: Yeats's Poetry in the Making*, Oxford: Clarendon Press, 1963 2nd edn.

—— *Louis MacNeice*, London: Faber, 1995.

—— *Vision and Revision in Yeats's 'Last Poems'*, Oxford: Clarendon Press, 1969.

Stead, C.K. *The New Poetic: Yeats to Eliot*, London: Hutchinson, 1964.

Steiner, George. *After Babel: Aspects of Language and Translation*, Oxford: Oxford University Press, 1975.

—— *Antigones*, Oxford: Clarendon Press, 1986.

—— *Language and Silence*, Harmondsworth: Penguin, 1979 edition.

Stevenson, Anne. *Bitter Fame: A Life of Sylvia Plath*, London: Viking, 1989.

Sullivan, Rosemary. *Theodore Roethke: The Garden Master*, Seattle: University of Washington Press, 1975.

Tapping, G. Craig. *Austin Clarke: A Study of his Writings*, Dublin: The Academy Press, 1981.

Thomas, Harry (*editor*). *Berryman's Understanding*, Boston: Northwestern University Press, 1988.

Tolley, A.T. *The Poetry of the Forties*, Manchester: Manchester University Press, 1985.

Wade, Allen. *A Bibliography of the Writings of W.B. Yeats*, 3rd edn, Revised and Edited by Russell K. Alspach, London: Rupert Hart-Davis, 1968.

Wallingford, Katherine. *Robert Lowell's Language of the Self*, Chapel Hill: University of North Carolina Press, 1988.

Whitaker, Thomas R. *Swan and Shadow: Yeats's Dialogue with History*, Chapel Hill: University of North Carolina Press, 1964.

Williams, Keith and Matthews, Steven (*editors*). *Rewriting the Thirties: Modernism and After*, Harlow: Longman, 1997.

Wills, Clair. *Improprieties: Politics and Sexuality in Northern Irish Poetry*, Oxford: Clarendon Press, 1993.

—— *Reading Paul Muldoon*, Newcastle upon Tyne: Bloodaxe Books, 1998.

Wilson, Francis. *W.B. Yeats and Tradition*, London: Methuen, 1968.

Witek, Terri. *Robert Lowell and 'Life Studies': Revising the Self*, Columbia: University of Missouri Press, 1993.

Worton, Michael and Still, Judith (*editors*). *Intertextuality: Theories and Practices*, Manchester: Manchester University Press, 1990.

Yenser, Stephen. *The Consuming Myth: The Work of James Merrill*, Cambridge, Massachusetts: Harvard University Press, 1987.

Index